DRUGFREE

DRUGFREE

A Unique, Positive
Approach to *Staying*
Off Alcohol and
Other Drugs

RICHARD B. SEYMOUR
& DAVID E. SMITH, M.D.

The Haight Ashbury
Free Medical Clinic

Sarah Lazin Books

Facts On File Publications

New York, New York ● Oxford, England

Drugfree
A Unique, Positive Approach to *Staying* Off Alcohol and Other Drugs

Library of Congress Cataloging-in-Publication Data

Seymour, Richard B.
   Drugfree: a unique, positive approach to staying off alcohol and other drugs.

   Bibliography: p.
   Includes index.
   1. Drug abuse. 2. Drug abuse—Prevention.
3. Alcoholism. 4. Alcoholism—Prevention. I. Smith,
David E. (David Elvin), 1939-   . II. Title.
HV5801.S44 1987   613.8   87-455
ISBN 0-8160-1363-2

British Library CIP Data available

Printed in the United States of America

10 9 8 7 6 5 4 3 2 1

Contents

Acknowledgments

"What Is Co-Dependency?", Kathryn Snell, St. John's Hospital Chemical Dependency Treatment Center, Salina, Kansas, published in 1984.

"Dear Abby" column by Abigail Van Buren. Reprinted with permission of Universal Press Syndicate. All rights reserved.

End of the Line: Quitting Cocaine, by Kathleen R. O'Connell. Copyright © 1985 Kathleen R. O'Connell. Reprinted and used by permission of The Westminster Press, Philadelphia, Pennsylvania.

East Right! by Dr. Donald Land. Copyright © 1935 by Hazelden Foundation, Center City, MN. Reprinted by permission.

The Twelve Steps reprinted with permission of Alcoholics Anonymous World Services, Inc.

An Introduction to Zen Buddhism by D. T. Suzuki. Copyright © 1964 by D. T. Suzuki. Published by Grove Press.

The Three Pillars of Zen by Philip Kapleau. Copyright © 1966 by Philip Kapleau. Published by Harper & Row, Publishers, Inc. Reprinted by permission of the author.

Zen Flesh, Zen Bones: A Collection of Zen and Pre-Zen Writings by Paul Reps. Published by the Charles E. Tuttle Co., Inc., of Tokyo, Japan.

"A Proposed Mechanism for the Visions of Dream Sleep" by J. C. Callaway, 1986. Reprinted with permission from the author.

"Alcoholism, Other Attachments and Spirituality" by C. L. Whitfield, M.D. The Resource Group, 7402 York Road, #101, Baltimore, MD, 21204, 1985. Reprinted with permission from the author.

The Complete Poems of Robert Frost edited by Edward Connery Lathem. Copyright © 1923, 1969 by Holt, Rinehart & Winston, Inc. Copyright © 1951 by Robert Frost.

Counseling for Relapse Preventions by Terence T. Gorski and Merlene Miller, Herald House-Independence Press, Independence, MO, 1982. Reprinted with permission from the authors.

Preface

This is not a book on how to *get* off alcohol and other drugs; this is a book on how to *stay* off alcohol and other drugs.

Many books have been published recently on the nature of abuse, addiction and addictive drugs. Among them is our own *The Little Black Pill Book*, a comprehensive consumer's reference and guide to psychoactive pharmaceutical drugs, and our *Physicians Guide to Psychoactive Drugs*. Other books on how to get off alcohol and other drugs—and newspaper and magazine articles and television spots and specials—have covered everything from the dangers of teenage drug experimentation to the evils of adult cocaine addiction and drunk driving. Most of these emphasize the great difficulty users experience when trying to get off drugs.

Drugfree is the first book to take the next step. It tackles the crucial question that follows from these earlier works: "What do you do now that you're off drugs?" It has been our experience in the treatment field that even at its most difficult, getting off drugs and alcohol is infinitely easier than *staying* off. And yet, properly prepared, anyone is capable of doing just that and leading a happy, fulfilling, and productive life that doesn't include the use of psychoactive substances.

This book is for all of you who want to try. We understand that you may feel you have very good reasons for using drugs. At the same time, we know that few of us would continue abusing drugs if we believed that we could live without them and still cope with our problems. Use becomes abuse as soon as it's perceived as a problem. In fact, we've found that most of the time the actual problem an abuser is trying to cope with is that of abuse itself. In this book, therefore, we're talking to anyone who has developed a substance abuse pattern, regardless of how the pattern was initiated or why.

I am personally very excited about this book because the writing of it has caused some major positive changes in my own life. I hope reading it will do the same for you.

When Dr. David Smith and I started working on this book in the spring of 1982, one of the first items I found to include was a story about the Indian holy man Mohandas Gandhi. Little did I realize at the time that the Mahatma was reaching across space and time to profoundly affect my life.

In the story, Gandhi was leaving a gathering one day when a young woman asked for a word with him.

"Mahatmaji," she said. "I have a son who must not eat sugar. I have told him. His father has told him. The doctor has told him, but he will not stop eating sugar. He will not listen to them, but you he reveres. He will do what you say. If you told him to stop eating sugar, he would. Will you please tell him to stop eating sugar?"

Gandhi looked into her eyes and nodded.

"I will do as you wish for the good of the boy. Please return here with him in three months' time."

The young mother was puzzled by this, but she followed his instructions to the letter. In three months she returned with her son. No words of introduction were needed. Gandhi looked compassionately at the boy whose hands were joined in worshipful Namaste and said to him, "My boy, you must stop eating sugar."

The boy bowed his head in reverence.

"Yes, Gandhiji," he said. "I will obey you."

The mother was overjoyed but puzzled still.

"Mahatmaji," she asked, "I thank you with all my heart, but tell me, why could you not have done this three months ago?"

"Madam," replied Gandhi, "three months ago, I had not stopped eating sugar."

A great little story about Gandhi and intervention, I thought, without really reflecting on its meaning as I filed it with other materials to review in developing this book. But the story wouldn't stay filed. It kept drifting into my mind, demanding my attention.

In the years that I had worked at the Haight Ashbury Free Medical Clinic, several of my other bad habits slid away of their own accord. Still, movement toward general abstention had been a haphazard affair. I was successfully navigating corporate waters, but my keel still had barnacles trailing from it. As long as I was efficiently running major projects, designing continuing medical education for health professionals, and writing effective articles on substance-abuse treatment, my own use of legal or at least "recreational" drugs didn't seem all that important.

I knew a lot about abstention and recovery as an observer and health professional. But somehow that wasn't enough, and it was difficult for me to start work on this book. Something was missing. Finally, Gandhi provided the missing piece to the puzzle. In all my own ways, I was still eating sugar!

In the fall of 1983, I realized that I could not write this book and continue to use any psychoactive substances. I could not tell all of you that there were alternatives to the alcohol and other drugs that were still a part of my own life. A few days before Thanksgiving, after a long night of deliberation, I stopped using any chemical substance for its psychoactive qualities.

In some ways this was harder than I thought it would be. For instance, caffeine in coffee proved especially difficult. In other ways, it was easier. Over these past three years, I've used many of the alternatives that you find in this book, and I am happy to report that they do work. One immediate activity that I reengaged in was recording my dreams. Looking back at my nocturnal notes on those first few days of complete abstinence, I'm surprised at the degree of collaboration from my unconscious that they show.

As a consequence of my decision, I have been able to write this book with the courage of conviction that abstinence truly is an opening of doors, the beginning of a great adventure. Today, at the threshold of my second half-century, I feel healthier, saner, and more ready for whatever life has to offer than ever before. I'm traveling light, and the best is yet to come.

Namaste

Thank you, Gandhiji!

Rick Seymour
San Rafael, California

Introduction|

THE SCOPE OF THE PROBLEM

Substance abuse, the abuse of alcohol and other drugs, is one of the major public health problems of our time and will no doubt continue to be into the foreseeable future. Alcohol abuse now ranks as the third leading cause of death in North America. Only heart disease and cancer kill more people here. When you add in drug abuse and consider that such factors as cigarette smoking are major contributors to both heart disease and cancer, it's clear that substance abuse is the greatest killer known.

We have become a drug-abusing culture. Not only do we take an astonishing quantity of prescription and over-the-counter medications, we now lead the world in the use of illegal drugs as well. In 1962 the National Institute on Drug Abuse estimated that less than 4 percent of the population had ever used an illegal drug. By 1982, they estimated that at least 33 percent of Americans over the age of twelve had experimented with marijuana, hallucinogenics such as LSD (lysergic acid diethylamide), MDA, MDMA (also known as Ecstasy) and mescaline, cocaine and heroin. Included on the list were prescription drugs such as Valium, amphetamines and barbiturates used for nonmedical purposes. The crime-related costs of drug abuse have been estimated at between $10

1

billion and $20 billion a year in the United States alone. Actual costs in lost work time, ruined careers, shattered families, accidents, sickness and death soar far, far beyond a mere $20 billion.

Statistics on the spectacular economic and personal costs of substance abuse grab our attention and may galvanize efforts for treatment and prevention, but they don't represent the whole story. In the real world, the personal consequences of alcohol and other drugs lie along a human spectrum. At one end of that spectrum are those whose lives have been destroyed by alcohol and other drugs. At the other are those who, for medical, religious, cultural or personal reasons, have never indulged. The rest of us are somewhere in between. Moreover, many of us are not very happy about where we find ourselves.

DENIAL

Often, we may find ourselves feeling defensive and apologetic about our drug use and yet grasping for reasons to continue. "I'd quit smoking now if only I didn't have so many crises in my life." "Sure, I drank too much Chardonnay at the party, but I do need to unwind." "I could quit heroin any time I want, but why should I?"

We may think that we are in control, but often that is an illusion. All these substances, including alcohol and nicotine (tobacco), are *psychoactive drugs*. They all directly affect our minds. One way psychoactive drugs do this is by clouding our ability to see or to believe that their use is against our own best interests. In the substance-abuse treatment field, this is called "denial." *Denial* is a word you will see often in this book, and its definition will be expanded as we go along.

As we learn about psychoactive drugs, one thing becomes more and more obvious. Aside from their occasional medical facility in our lives, none of them really does us any good. Although many of us have realized that truth, for one reason or another we cling to obsolete and unnecessary habits. Often we are able to abstain for a period of time, only to fall back into use during a moment of stress or craving for the drug we're trying to avoid. When this happens, we tend to give in to the habit, thinking, "I'm hooked, so why fight it?" Unfortunately, such thinking is often reinforced by our culture. The problems engendered by this reinforcement are especially acute when the drug problem actually involves abuse.

We at the Haight Ashbury Free Medical Clinic believe that people who are trying to stop using alcohol and other drugs and the people around them who are trying to cope with another's use or abuse are often not getting the right information. We have discovered that, contrary to popular belief, getting off drugs, including alcohol—which *is* a drug—is not the hardest part of an abuser's struggle to live a drugfree life. It is life *after* drugs that's the real hurdle. Society's and the abuser's uninformed attitudes and expectations about what that life should be often push would-be recoveries back to drugs. The results of these failures in treatment are obvious: mental and physical harm to the abuser and psychological and social damage to his or her friends, family and other loved ones.

THE HAIGHT ASHBURY FREE MEDICAL CLINIC

Since its opening in the summer of 1967, the Haight Ashbury Free Medical Clinic has had over 700,000 patient visits. Many of these patients were experiencing drug problems that ranged from acute reactions to onetime use all the way to addiction. As clinicians, we believe that there are countless others across the country who may or may not be addicts or alcoholics, but who are caught up in abuse patterns that they neither need nor want. We estimate that in the next five years, approximately 20 million people will try to quit their drug of abuse. Of those, only about 2.8 million will still be clean one year later. The majority—over 17 million people, or roughly the population of New York City and Chicago combined—will lapse back into their harmful abuse patterns. In many cases, these relapses will occur because people—both abusers and those around them—simply don't know how to deal with abstinence. We have written this book in an attempt to even those odds.

Since its founding on June 7, 1967, the Haight Ashbury Free Medical Clinic has treated clients in all the configurations of drug abuse. The Haight Ashbury district of San Francisco, where the Clinic is located, has been and continues to be one of the nation's most critical drug-using areas. Situated on the front lines, the Clinic attracted and retained many of the foremost practitioners and scientists in the substance-abuse field. Here they encountered succeeding waves of abuse patterns and worked to analyze the problems, develop treatment modalities and treat the victims. Often Clinic units, such as the Emergency/Rock Medicine Section (E/RM), provide drug crisis intervention and front-line treatment in the streets and at rock concerts while operating as combination aid stations and M.A.S.H. units. The abusers of exotic drug combinations may be identified by E/RM, or they may come in off the streets to the Drug Detoxification, Rehabilitation and Aftercare Section. The Clinic has expanded far beyond its countercultural beginnings to serve a clientele that ranges from street addicts and the working poor (now classified as MIAs, or Medically Indigent Adults) to middle-class and upwardly mobile professionals, not necessarily young, and a demographic range that can include every racial and cultural minority. The Clinic's research, as well as its professional training and education in the field of substance abuse, is national—often international—in scope.

The one thing that hasn't changed in the past two decades is our basic philosophy. The Haight Ashbury Free Medical Clinic was founded on the principle that health care is a right, not a privilege, and should therefore be free at the point of delivery. Everyone at the Clinic follows a working belief that health care should also be humane, demystified and nonjudgmental. The Clinic doesn't advertise or take diversionary cases (clients placed in drug treatment rather than sent to jail) at random from the criminal justice system. It doesn't have to. Its reputation is such that there is a continuous overload of patients coming in voluntarily for treatment.

The Clinic's reputation is based not only on its philosophy but also on local and national recognition of its expertise and respect for the needs, trust and humanity of each and every patient who walks through its doors. However, there is more. While the Clinic's services are still free at the point of delivery, the *free* in the name means much more than "without cost." It also describes a freedom to work beyond the confines of traditional medicine in finding its answers and a freedom of close interaction between treater and treated in developing a humane and understandable approach to health and the pursuit of happiness.

This book is meant to be an example of that philosophy and dynamic. This book is our attempt to change the future by coming directly to you, the public, with our knowledge and beliefs on long-term solutions to substance-abuse problems. Its publication is a step toward reducing the toll that substance-abuse takes on its victims and their loved ones—spouses, children, friends and coworkers. We now know that the presence of a drug or alcohol abuser in a home has a profound effect on other members of the household—particularly the children. It's clear that when we speak of the problems of drug abuse, we are talking about problems that continue in time, potentially affecting future generations.

MYTHS ABOUT SUBSTANCE ABUSE

There is much work to be done. In an age when we know more about drugs and their effects on us at a clinical level, the general public is still surprisingly ignorant of the facts about drug abuse, treatment and recovery. Drugs and drug abusers are the subjects of powerful myths that are destructive to all of us. The myths surrounding addiction are one example.

Many people in our culture still view addiction as a moral or criminal issue and see addicts as morally corrupt individuals who need to be punished. Others consider addiction synonymous with chemical dependency and don't understand why treatment programs based solely on drug or alcohol detoxification don't work.

Addiction is not a simple matter of substance immersion or criminal behavior; its cure is not withdrawal or a jail term. Addiction is a disease that is progressive and may be fatal if not treated. Our society has come to accept the idea that alcoholism is a disease that requires a lifetime of treatment. Now we know that other drugs may create problems that require long-term, even lifetime, care. Current evidence strongly suggests that approximately 10 percent of all people who try *any* psychoactive substance will become addicted. This percentage may be higher for the more compelling substances such as nicotine and cocaine. For these addicts, substance abuse is more than a habit, it's a disease. As with such diseases as diabetes, the prognosis is long-term. There is no *cure* for addiction. Also like diabetes, however, there is a means by which the addict or the addiction-prone individual can keep his or her disease in remission. That means is very distasteful to the disease sufferer, in that it involves complete abstinence from all substances that have a profound effect on human consciousness.

One of the strongest and most persistent myths about drugs in our culture is that once you become dependent on a substance, be it tobacco, alcohol or heroin, that dependency is all but impossible to break. Movies, television programs, books, magazine articles and the media play a role not only in encouraging experimentation with substances in the first place by glamorizing substance abuse, but they also help foster the feelings of helplessness and inadequacy many abusers harbor that can ultimately defeat them in their struggle to live drugfree lives. The "man with the golden arm" who rushes back to heroin every time that he returns to his old friends after he's taken the cure, the coughing smoker who can't give up the three-pack-a-day habit even after emphysema or lung cancer has been diagnosed, the "wine-and-roses" alcoholic who stays on the bottle until he dies of galloping DTs—all these represent what most people believe are typical attempts at recovery from substance abuse: temporary success followed by inevitable failure. The message is clear: Life without drugs is hell! It's no wonder that the average user/abuser looks at his or her own habit and says, "If those folks can't buck it, nobody can. What chance do I have?" They give up before they've given themselves a chance. Worse yet, other people who are close to abusers, those on whom they must depend for help and support believe the same myths. Overdepicting and exaggerating the tyranny of drugs does both the abuser and his or her loved ones a real disservice. These images, pervasive and unquestioned in our society, tell the abuser who is attempting to recover things he or she does not need to hear: "You are a helpless victim." "Your life is beyond any control." We are here to say that those are lies.

The truth is that more and more people are experiencing long-term recovery from drug abuse and addiction that involves a self-satisfying, rewarding and productive life without the use of psychoactive drugs. The field of drug treatment and prevention is in its infancy, but we are learning and are changing our approaches as we learn. When the Haight Ashbury Free Medical Clinic first began treating people with drug problems, we concentrated on the acute problems of bad trips and overdoses and on detoxification for the chemically dependent. Today, when clients are undergoing detoxification or supervised withdrawal, we discuss the nature of addiction and try to steer them toward aftercare, abstinence and recovery. We interact with a network of inpatient and outpatient programs whose staffs have trained at our Clinic and practice these long-term approaches. We also maintain close ties with the recovering community and use its twelve-step support programs, such as Alcoholics Anonymous, Narcotics Anonymous, Cocaine Anonymous, Al-Anon, Nar-Anon, Alateen and Adult Children of Alcoholics. We have developed and maintain our own specialized support groups that respond to a wide range of recovery needs.

There are an increasing number of resources available to the recovering, abstinent individual, and we explore them in the opening chapters of this book. The resources that concern us most, however, are the inner ones, and it is to these that the focus of this book is devoted. We are here to blast the stereotype of recovery and abstinence as a negative, hopeless experience and to show instead how it can be the most positive step in anyone's life. To do that, as the old song goes, "you have to accentuate the positive, eliminate the negative, latch on to the affirmative, and don't mess with Mr. Inbetween."

WHITE-KNUCKLE SOBRIETY

Of course, there are always problems, and none of this is a piece of cake. It's ironic that the people who *must* abstain usually find the prospect a shattering experience. Many addicts and dependent people never recover from abstention. They go through life feeling that they are "crippled," that they are missing out on everything that they enjoy, that they have socially lobotomized themselves in order to stay sober. *You've heard the story of the man who gave up women and booze and cigarettes so he could live forever? Well, he didn't, but it sure felt like it.* In the recovering community, this condition is known as "white-knuckle sobriety," a state of unsupported abstention that is a far cry from real recovery.

White-knuckle sobriety takes a variety of forms. It can be a spiritual and emotional gridlock; a state of rigidity in the face of compelling drug or alcohol hunger; the internalizing and denial of unresolved family, community and personal conflicts; an ongoing state of rage, or self-pity, or righteous indignation. Often, the born-again teetotaler's heavy proselytizing is an expression of white-knuckle sobriety. The world, according to diehard white-knucklers, is made of extremes: stark black or white. The rules are rigid. Although knucklers are technically drugfree, one could argue that their lives are just as out of control as those of addicts.

White-knuckle sobriety is more than just uncomfortable. It can be dangerous and debilitating. It can become a source of constant negative stress, eroding the immune system and theoretically could make the knuckler especially vulnerable to dangerous, even terminal illness. Fortunately, white-knuckle sobriety isn't the only alternative to the instant gratification that drugs seem to offer. Not only is it not a viable alternative, knuckling is probably one of the leading causes of recovery failure. And finally, the greatest tragedy is that such a seemingly restricted life is totally unnecessary.

POSITIVE ALTERNATIVES TO ALCOHOL AND OTHER DRUGS

We believe that there are positive alternatives, ways of living a life of pleasurable and rewarding recovery. In the following chapters, we review the realities of substance dependency and addictive disease and then share these alternatives, gathered and developed in our years of work in the treatment and prevention of drug abuse and addiction. We share these alternatives to alcohol and other drugs in the firm belief that abstinence is not the closing of a door but the opening of our lives to all the experience and joy that has been withheld from us by the disabling effects of drugs.

In the conclusion, we talk about primary prevention and the role it can play in helping people, especially our children, avoid abuse and addiction. These comprehensive approaches are the best we have, so far, in fighting drug abuse and addiction before they begin. However, even though some aspects of these approaches are positive, such as improving self-concept and developing decision-making and coping skills, in their overall context they still represent attempts at "preventing" undesirable behavior. What we propose is taking a bold step beyond the whole concept of prevention.

In primary prevention, no matter what methods are being used, the focus remains on eliminating the abuse of drugs. In the scope of human development, however, the abuse of alcohol and other drugs is one among several wrong paths that people have followed in attempting to deal with some pretty basic human problems. It is our contention that these wrong paths often are followed because training in positive solutions to individual human problems is not readily available in our culture. Instead of teaching positive ways in which to enhance our lives at an early age, we are busy establishing taboos and trying to prevent negative behavior.

There is a passage in the *I Ching* that says you cannot fight the devil directly. When you do, you tend to become the devil that you are fighting. Instead, the Chinese oracle recommends that you fight the devil by emphasizing what is good and allowing that to replace the darkness. In that sense, we dislike the very phrase "prevention." We dislike it because the core of what needs to be done is misrepresented by the term. Prevention sounds like a limiting, the creating of taboos in order to circumscribe behavior. What is needed by young people—by everyone, for that matter—is not limiting but expanding, not curtailing freedom but increasing it by providing opportunities for growth and development that make the use of drugs superfluous.

We feel that a better term than prevention is "life enhancement," a process whereby people work together for mutual growth. People are ideally called upon to help themselves and one another by developing their own potential to the highest degree, practicing the principles they have learned in all their affairs and carrying their own physical and spiritual awakening to others.

Our children are growing up under a cloud. The world that they learn about is most often one of violence, crime, abuse, injustice, environmental destruction and potential nuclear annihilation. We try to teach them, and ourselves, that drugs are not a viable means of escaping this reality. What we fail to teach our children, and ourselves, is that the most viable means of escaping such a woebegone reality is by changing it.

In attempting to cope with adversity, we lose sight of the fact that most of the current and potential disasters facing humanity are manmade. We forget that, short of Armageddon, anything made by man can be changed by humanity. The alternatives to alcohol and other drugs that we will present in this book are also alternatives to the continuing juggernaut of egoistic self-destruction that our culture at its worst seems bent on acting out. They tell us what we need to tell our children: that it is not only right but important to be high, but that there are positive, constructive ways of being high.

When Lama Anagarika Govinda was asked what individual human beings could do to turn things around, he answered, "Sit down, cross the legs, breathe easily and clear the mind." He also said, "The future of humanity lies in the synthesis of Eastern psychology and Western technology." The spiritual pathways that are a product of this synthesis teach us that the more we develop our higher consciousness the more we are cocreators in our own lives.

In identifying with creation, people belong in the realm of causes, not the realm of effects. It is therefore incumbent on us as individuals to dedicate ourselves to bringing forth the best instead of the worst that is in us, and thus "escaping" from reality by *changing* it. We can do this by educating our children in ways of wisdom, compassion and equanimity. And we can do that by learning these ways ourselves and making them part of our homes, our schools and our communities.

Why Me? | 1

ANITA

Anita is seventeen years old. Her comfortably middle-class family lives in upstate New York, near Lake Champlain. Her father works for the state government, and her mother is active in their church and in the local women's club. When Anita was younger, her mother developed a dependency on Valium, which the family doctor prescribed to treat the "nervous condition" brought on by her husband's "drinking problem." Fortunately, the dependency was detected in its early stages and Anita's father managed to clean up his act, so her mother's withdrawal from Valium was without incident.

A shy girl, Anita concentrated on her studies. In the summer after her sophomore year of high school, she tried marijuana, but she didn't care for it and couldn't understand what her friends saw in it. Alcohol was a different matter entirely. The first time she drank a few beers at a party she didn't particularly like the taste, but the effects seemed very positive. Her shyness disappeared, and she discovered a new and unsuspected personality. When she drank, she became forward, she sparkled, she was the life of the party. Her life, so lackluster before, now seemed bright with promise. It did, that is, until the night in her senior year, after some heavy partying, when she wrapped the family car around a tree on the way home from a football game.

No one was injured, but an officer smelled beer on her breath, and a police test showed a high blood alcohol level. The authorities diverted her to the county drunk-driving clinic. Her parents were understanding and secretly grateful that Anita had been "only drinking" and not using what they considered "drugs."

During the clinic's thorough intake interview Anita was candid and open about her experience. She talked about her reactions to her father's drinking and her mother's bout with Valium. She was also truthful about her own involvement with alcohol. Anita described starting to drink at fifteen, occasionally, usually on weekends. She said that her drinking had increased some, but that she had always been able to control it.

The clinic director's face tightened into a knowing look of frustration when Anita mentioned that she didn't remember leaving the football game, much less hitting the tree. Had she ever had these lapses in memory before?

"Yes. A few times when I had too much to drink. But I never had any problems with it before. At least *I* don't get silly or throw up and pass out like some of the other kids do."

The director shook her head and made some notes on the intake form. "Do you ever drink during the day? Or by yourself?"

"In the morning sometimes, if I'm feeling shaky from the night before. Sometimes to get my courage up. But *everybody* does that."

More questions and answers confirmed the clinic director's diagnosis. She looked across her desk at the pretty teenager and knew that the girl wasn't going to like what she had to say. The girl would be outraged and bitter; her parents would be incredulous. But she had to do it.

"Anita," she said, "you have a drinking problem. If we let it go, you could become an alcoholic."

Anita's eyes widened, and her lips tightened into a narrow white line. Her hand shook and her voice trembled as she exclaimed, "That can't be! Alcoholics are dirty old men who sleep in doorways. I've seen them in the city and on TV. I'm only seventeen, and I come from a good home. There's nothing *wrong* with me. God! I've never gotten drunk, or thrown up, or passed out. I'm a nice girl!"

The director explained to Anita that it's not a question of how old you are or how long you've been drinking. What matters is how the drug alcohol affects you. She pointed out that such symptoms and behavior as blackouts, morning shakes and solitary drinking are all pathological responses to alcohol that indicate a predisposition to alcoholism. She added that Anita's mother's problem with Valium and her father's alcoholism could be an indication of genetic vulnerability and explained that the children of people who have a history of drug or alcohol problems are more at risk of becoming substance abusers or addicts than others. Anita shook her head in confused disbelief.

"Are you telling me that I should stop drinking completely? Forever?"

"It would be best to do that and start some regular counseling and support work to get you through this."

Tears ran down Anita's young cheeks as she buried her face in her hands.

"Why me?" she cried. "Everybody else does it. Why me?"

ALAN

Alan had turned on to LSD, tuned in with marijuana and dropped out in the psychedelic sixties. In the mid-seventies he traded in his buckskin jacket for a master's in business administration and by 1980, at age thirty-eight, he was a more or less successful junior partner in a Montgomery Street, San Francisco, brokerage firm.

Al knew what cocaine was. Even though he had avoided all drugs in recent years except the occasional social cocktail and weekend joint, he was an ex-hippie. When the host passed around a mirror with thin lines of white powder and a glass tube at a party that fall, Alan sniffed up two lines without hesitation. His younger colleagues had talked about the lift they got from cocaine and how harmless it was. One lawyer he knew even predicted that it would be legalized before marijuana because so many important and influential people were using it.

He tried it and nothing happened. So what was the big deal? And why was the stuff so expensive? The lack of effect didn't keep him from trying it again a few weeks later, and again, until he did indeed start getting a lift from the drug. When the bond market got crazy and work intensified that winter, he even bought a gram to keep him on his toes and improve his concentration. Then he bought another.

"Why not?" he asked himself. After all, he reasoned, no one at work or at home could tell that he was snorting. Cocaine was a great drug! It helped in those demanding business situations, where he was now brilliant, and also kept him in shape for a very busy social life. A great drug.

By the time Al went to see a doctor in 1984, most of his personal assets had been converted to powder and gone up his nose. His partners were ready to throw him in the street, and he hadn't slept with his wife, much less anyone else, in months.

"But cocaine is a safe drug. Everybody says it's nonaddictive. How could I get in trouble with it?" he asked his doctor.

"Looks like everything everybody says about it is wrong."

"Guess you're right, Doc. No more coke breaks for me." Al grinned his winning never-say-die grin. "I guess it's back to the two-martini lunch instead of the four-liner."

The doctor shook his head.

"You are headed for treatment, Alan. And the last thing you want to do is go back to any kind of martini lunch."

"What are you telling me?"

"I'm telling you that once your use of cocaine became compulsive and uncontrollable, you crossed the line into addictive disease. *Any* use of *any* mind-affecting drug—and that includes alcohol—could catapult you back into cocaine addiction."

"But Doctor, that'll ruin me. If I can't drink, how am I supposed to conduct business?"

"A heck of a lot better than you're doing it now, Al," he answered, But Al was no longer listening. He stared blankly out the window of the doctor's Sutter Street office down to where the lights of San Francisco's nightlife were shining, where in the old days he and his wife and colleagues would be getting ready for a night on the town. He looked down at the vinyl floor, thinking about the beige future he saw ahead. No more parties, no more brilliance, no more euphoria.

"Why me?" he asked. "It just isn't fair."

ADDICTION IS A DISEASE

No. It's not fair. But then neither is cancer, MS, diabetes or any other disease. And addiction *is* a disease. Addictionologists, those physicians and other health professionals who have made a specialty of treating addictive disease, see addiction as "a primary disease entity" that can be manifested through the compulsive use of any psychoactive substance. The symptoms of addiction are compulsion, loss of control and continued use in spite of adverse consequences.

The disease of addiction appears to have both genetic and sociocultural origins. Children whose parents have had problems with drugs, including alcohol, have a statistically higher vulnerability to the disease than children whose parents have not had this problem. However, there is as yet no way of knowing for sure who else is predisposed to addictive disease. With Anita, we have the indication that both her parents may have been vulnerable. This is said to raise her own probable vulnerability by about 400 percent. With Al, we don't know.

Whether one has a genetic vulnerability or not, some sociocultural factors are absolutely necessary for addiction to occur. These factors include social attitudes toward drugs, peer activities, and drug availability, in its permutations. Put simply, one can have all the vulnerability in the world, but if one is never exposed to any psychoactive substance, addiction cannot take place. Of course, in our own culture such limits on exposure are virtually impossible. The basic equation reads: **Genetic Predisposition + Sociocultural Factors = Addictive Disease**.

Health professionals working in the drug treatment field see addiction as a pernicious disease that carries its own psychopathology, often manifested by the addict's conviction that there really is no problem. Further, it is a progressive disease that can be fatal if it is not diagnosed and treated. At present, there is no cure for drug addiction. However, as with such diseases as diabetes, there can be remission. In addictive disease, remission is called *recovery*. Recovery involves both supportive treatment and abstinence from *all* psychoactive substances. In effective recovery, the addict can lead a fully satisfying, productive and happy life, but he or she can never indulge in controlled use of the drug he or she was addicted to or of any other psychoactive drug. For many addicts, this blanket abstention may at first seem very, very difficult, if not impossible, to maintain.

It's one of life's classic ironies that those very people who seem to gain the most pleasure and support from drugs are precisely the people who shouldn't be using them, while those who can pretty much take them or leave them are usually able to do just that. The role that drugs play in our lives may be part of the answer. The one thing that Anita and Al have in common is that they both found something in their drug use that was otherwise missing from their lives. They both nurtured the illusion that the drugs they used had somehow magically made their lives better.

In the beginning, the drugs may have seemed to help. No one, with the possible exception of a handful of people bent on slow suicide, sets out to make him- or herself ill. Drugs have been with us for a long time, and the *intention* in their development has almost always been good: to provide greater insights, to relieve suffering, to bring one closer to God, to help one pass the physiology exam or drive the big rig all the way from Chi-town to L.A.

DEFINING LEVELS OF ABUSE

Let's start by answering the questions, "What is drug use?" "What is drug abuse?" and "Just what is addiction?"

In 1973, the National Commission on Marihuana and Drug Abuse, set up by President Nixon to explore the nature of abuse, defined what are still considered the levels of nonmedical drug use. Their classifications can be helpful in understanding one's position on the spectrum:

EXPERIMENTAL USE: A short-term, nonpatterned trial of one or more drugs, motivated primarily by curiosity or a desire to experience an altered mood state. Experimental use generally begins socially among close friends.

RECREATIONAL USE: Occurs in a social setting among friends or acquaintances who desire to share an experience that they define as both acceptable and pleasurable. Generally, recreational use is both voluntary and patterned and tends not to escalate to more frequent or intense use patterns.

CIRCUMSTANTIAL USE: Generally motivated by the user's perceived need or desire to achieve a new and anticipated effect in order to cope with a specific problem, situation or condition of a personal or vocational nature. This classification would include students who utilize stimulants during preparation for exams, long-distance truckers who rely on similar substances to provide extended endurance and alertness, military personnel who use drugs to cope with boredom or stress in combat situations, athletes who attempt to improve their performance and housewives who seek to relieve tension, anxiety, boredom or other stresses through the use of sedatives or stimulants.

INTENSIFIED USE: Drug use that occurs at least daily and is motivated by an individual's perceived need to achieve relief from a persistent problem or stressful situation or by his or her desire to maintain a certain self-prescribed level of performance. . . . A very different group of intensified users are those youths who have turned to drugs as sources of excitement or meaning in what they perceive as otherwise unsatisfying existences.

COMPULSIVE USE: A patterned behavior of high frequency and high level of intensity, characterized by a high degree of psychological dependence and perhaps physical dependence as well. The distinguishing feature of this behavior is that drug use dominates the individual's existence, and preoccupation with drug taking precludes other social functioning.

DEFINING ADDICTION

You'll notice that addiction is not included among the stages of drug use described above. That's because addiction really isn't a stage of drug use. Like the Fool in a deck of tarot cards, addiction transcends all stages of use and abuse. Also like a fool, the concept of addiction has cavorted about in a motley coat of definitions and paradigms that have alternately helped and hindered attempts to make sense out of the problems engendered by drugs.

According to the *Oxford English Dictionary*, addiction was originally a term in Roman law meaning "a formal giving over or delivery by sentence of court. A surrender, or dedication, of anyone to a master." In the mid-seventeenth century another definition was added: "The state of being addicted or given to a habit or pursuit: devotion." At first, this definition held only positive connotations, such as addiction to books, to the freedom of speech and to other positive things, but in 1779 the first drug reference appeared, when Samuel Johnson wrote of an "addiction to tobacco." In 1859, John Stuart Mill referred to "a man who causes grief to his family by addiction to bad habits." However, in 1597, William Shakespeare scooped them all with a close approximation of modern usage in *Henry IV, Part II* by having Falstaff urge his merry men ". . . to forsweare thinne Potations and to addict themselves to Sack:" [as sherry was then called].

Contemporary dictionaries define the noun *addict* as "a person addicted to some habit, as to the use of drugs."

Many recent technical definitions of addiction have tended to use the term as synonymous with chemical dependency, making both the development of tolerance and physical withdrawal symptoms, such as those found in the abrupt termination of alcohol or heroin, prerequisites for addiction. This use of the term can mislead. It can even generate dangerous attitudes toward certain drugs, such as the belief that cocaine is a safe drug because it doesn't cause physical withdrawal and is therefore not "addictive."

Equating addiction with physical dependency is a result of looking at the physiochemical effects of the drug as the defining characteristic. Actually, what is important is how the specific person *reacts* to the drug. Physical dependency may be a characteristic of compulsive use, but addiction is more than that. Let's look at the evolutionary changes in the concept of drug use and addiction in recent years.

As we have seen, definitions can influence our attitudes toward drug abuse, the way we treat substance abusers and the ways in which we regulate the availability of psychoactive drugs. Two decades ago narcotics users—popularly called junkies—were all considered to be criminals. In those days, treatment for morphine or heroin addiction consisted of what amounted to cold turkey withdrawal during incarceration in federal prison. When their terms were up and they were no longer using drugs, these "criminals" were released back into society, usually back into a subculture where their need for narcotics was quickly satisfied and their narcotic dependence reestablished. Such treatment was acceptable to most observers. After all, they reasoned, addicts were moral degenerates who willingly engaged in the criminal activity of using narcotic drugs. Even the articulate who found themselves dependent on narcotics, such as *Life* magazine editor and author of *Mine Enemy Grows Older* Alexander King, and William Burroughs, business machine heir and author of *Junky* and *The Naked Lunch*, while trying to humanize narcotics addiction, still bought the "moral degeneracy" stereotype for themselves.

At this same time, therapists working with alcoholics were beginning to define alcoholism as a progressive disease which, if left untreated, could lead to increasing biological, psychological or social dysfunction and probably death. E. M. Jellinek gave voice to this view in 1960 in his book, *The Disease Concept of Alcoholism*. The concept gained rapid acceptance and was promoted by Alcoholics Anonymous, the National Council on Alcoholism, the National Institute on Alcohol Abuse and Alcoholism and the American Medical Association. The fact that so many people know and love alcoholics has probably made it easier for alcoholism to be fully accepted as a disease.

In the sixties, when illicit drugs spread from ethnic and economic minorities to the middle-class young throughout America and Western Europe, our culture was forced to consider the possibility that, like alcoholism, drug addiction might be a medical as well as a moral dilemma. The federal government set up a President's Special Action Office for Drug Abuse Prevention and followed this with the establishment of a National Institute on Drug Abuse, empowered to award grants for research on and treatment of drug abuse. As part of its so-called War on Drugs, the federal government also increased penalties for a wide range of illicit drug use and beefed up its enforcement efforts. Drug abusers were still criminals, but maybe they were "sick" criminals.

Since the 1960s, the use of drugs has proliferated and has extended across all social and economic strata. We no longer have a drug-using subculture. We are a culture that uses drugs. Yet the basic dichotomy between enforcement definitions and clinical definitions of substance abuse and addiction continues.

These differing views have caused their own problems in understanding. For example, the enforcement view that any and all use of illicit drugs is abuse has led many people to conclude that any use of licit or legal psychoactive drugs cannot be abuse and can't lead to addiction. In the same vein, the view that only drugs that cause physical or chemical dependency can cause addiction has led many to ignore the dangers of those drugs that don't cause the so-called classic withdrawal symptoms, including anxiety, nervousness, sleep disorders, tremors, gastrointestinal distress, headaches, delirium and seizures. In fact, it was the dramatic rise in what we now call cocaine addiction (which we'll discuss in greater detail later) that led many in the treatment field to rethink our working definitions of dependency and addiction.

The most current definition describes addiction as a disease entity with its own psychopathology characterized by compulsion, loss of control and continued use in spite of adverse consequences. Addiction is progressive, potentially fatal if untreated, and incurable but remissable through abstinence and recovery.

When we left Alan, he was staring at the floor of his doctor's office. As the shock of what he had been told played Ping-Pong with his denial system, various thoughts came to him. "What do doctors know?" he thought. "Look at all the dumb stuff they recommend on television. I wouldn't trust the whole pack of them if they were all in a room together. Addicted!"

Nevertheless, civilized man that he was, Alan thanked the doctor and accepted the referrals to a cocaine support group and Cocaine Anonymous that the doctor wrote out for him. He stuck these in the outside pocket of his jacket, the same pocket that contained ticket stubs from a Forty-Niners' home football game that he and some friends had gone to two seasons earlier. On his way home, he felt the flood tide of his anger subside.

"Oh, what the hell," he thought. "He's only doing his job, and I guess he is right. My cocaine use did get a little out of hand. What did he call it? Compulsive. That's it. Well, compulsive behavior is what leads us to success—good old Type A personality and a coronary around the corner. Guess I should cool it on the coke. But that doesn't mean I have to stop drinking. What's one got to do with the other? That's ridiculous!"

Alan made a great show of calling the hospital-based outpatient counseling program to which he had been referred to make an intake appointment. His wife smiled for the first time in ages and hugged him after he hung up. Then he postponed the appointment twice because of emergencies at work.

The week after, a client from out of town invited him to discuss some portfolio changes up at the Carnelian Room bar atop the BankAmerica Building. Promising himself he would "watch it," and also to actually keep the counseling appointment set for the next day, Alan accepted. Two Irish coffees later a colleague down the bar suggested that he and Alan go to the men's loo and "powder their noses."

"What the hell," he thought. "One toot's not going to hurt me."

Meanwhile, back in upstate New York, Anita's parents were outraged. When she tried to explain what the drug and alcohol program director had told her about genetic vulnerability, her mother swore that her father had never had a drinking problem. The very idea! And Father, for his part, impatiently explained that Mother's "allergic reaction" to Valium was a medical matter that only a doctor could understand. There were no drug or alcohol problems in *their* family—with the possible exception of Great-aunt Sarah, who always did act a little funny. Obviously, the real problem was that Anita hung out with the wrong kids at school.

She had shamed them, and they weren't going to let it go any further. There was, of course, no question of her attending Alcoholics Anonymous meetings or getting any other sort of treatment. They had a position to maintain in the community, and this whole shameful matter had to be kept quiet. Instead, her father grounded her for the rest of the semester and applied her allowance to the car repair bill, and her mother announced that she would search Anita's room and monitor her behavior regularly. The next day her father put a lock on the cabinet where the alcohol was kept.

Anita was a "good" girl. She vowed to herself that she would never drink again. She would keep a tight hold on herself. She studied hard and even after the grounding was lifted, never dated or went to parties or even engaged in extracurricular activities at school. She stopped using makeup and took to wearing clothes even the Puritans would have considered unbecoming.

At first her parents were relieved. She wasn't going to cause any more trouble. They then became alarmed as her life-style became increasingly ascetic. The beginnings of the compulsion that she had exhibited around alcohol went out of control over abstention. She was in mourning for the life she couldn't have, the part of herself alcohol had brought out, and she was taking it out on herself and everyone around her.

Anita was suffering from what the recovering community calls white-knuckle sobriety. Cut off from any meaningful support system, she kept herself in a state of social lobotomy and emotional gridlock. The eventual consequences of this exercise can be dire. Her compulsive behavior could be focused in a variety of self-destructive directions. She could become suicidal. She could lapse into eating disorders such as bulimia, which is binge eating and forced regurgitation, or anorexia nervosa, the little-understood disease that involves fasting and extreme weight loss. She could become a hateful and acerbic woman, old before her time. Or she could even bottle up the stress of white knuckling, keeping it all suppressed, keeping the lid on until it exploded into some mortal disease.

Fortunately, Anita did none of these things. Besides being a "good" girl, she was also a sensible young woman. In time she realized what she was doing to herself and went for help.

There's a saying in the recovery community that "denial is not just a river in Egypt." In fact, denial tends to be one of the major roadblocks in trying to deal with drug dependency and addiction. While mostly seen as a strongly motivated refusal to face the fact of one's loss of control in addiction, denial can take many forms. In Anita's case, denial appears strongly on two fronts. Her own denial of addiction, manifested by overreaction and "martyr" behavior, is complicated by her parents' refusal to look honestly at their own drug problems. Even the victims accept the moral judgments society makes about drug users.

Obviously, part of the motivation is social. Position in the community and reputation are at stake. If the family admits that it has problems, or if Anita enters treatment for alcoholism, the family loses face, or so they believe. However, such concerns are often the window dressing, the surface manifestation of much deeper concerns—concerns of which the individuals involved are probably not consciously aware.

Behind standing in the community is one's self-image, the way we really see ourselves, and within self-image is the very crucial issue of maintaining control. The fear of losing control is so strong that the last thing an addict ever wants to do is admit that he or she has lost control. And yet the admission that one has lost control and is incapable of avoiding continued use without help is necessary for the initiation of effective treatment of and successful recovery from addiction. Many in the recovery community have long believed that an addict has to "hit bottom"—get into a totally desperate situation—before he or she will honestly seek or accept help. In recent years, however, new techniques of "intervention"—strategies for breaking through addiction denial—have begun to show some success in getting people into treatment and recovery before they destroy their lives.

In San Francisco, Alan had his two drinks and two toots in the men's room and then went home with a smile on his face. "I can do it," he thought proudly. "I've proved that I can go back to controlled use."

Alan was on the crest of a wave. He even went to his first counseling session the next day and listened smugly to the counselor explain the impossibility of any return to controlled use. "Ah, but I know better," he thought. Actually, it took Alan about three weeks to get back to the level of cocaine abuse he had attained before seeing the doctor.

His wife had heard about a program director, a woman in the East Bay who specialized in organizing and facilitating interventions. The first night that Alan holed up in his office with a gram of cocaine and called home to say he "had to work late and might work straight through the night," she called and made an appointment.

The intervention was thorough. It included Alan's wife, their long-time best friends the Jacksons and the Wangs, and Alan's partners at the brokerage office. Had his parents been alive, they would have been included, too. He was "set up." Madeline, his wife, told him that she was getting some stress counseling and that the counselor wanted to speak to him, too. He was reluctant to go, especially across the Bay Bridge and through all that traffic. But if it would help Madeline cope with the real world and get off his back, fine, he'd go along.

"What the hell is going on here?" he asked as he walked into the room.

The counselor got up and led him to a chair.

"Sit down, Alan," she said. "Your friends and loved ones have some important things to say to you."

They did. In a very matter-of-fact and loving and supportive way they cited incident after specific incident detailing his abuse. It took time and effort, and to Alan it seemed like a very nasty surprise party, but they broke through his denial and resistance. By the end of the afternoon it was down to the nuts and bolts. No fooling around with counseling referrals and canceled appointments. Alan was to go immediately to an inpatient chemical dependency program in southern California that his company health insurance would pay for. After three weeks of treatment, Madeline would join him for a week of codependency treatment. Joe and Frank would take on his brokerage client load and administrative duties until he was well enough to go back to work. When they got back, he and Madeline would be enrolled in an aftercare program at the director's center. Madeline would also attend Al-Anon meetings. Alan would go to a weekly cocaine support group for professional people in San Francisco and otherwise attend nightly Cocaine Anonymous meetings.

He took one last shot at resistance. "Good God! That's an awful lot of time to tie up in recovery."

"A lifetime's an awful lot of time to tie up in addiction, Alan," responded Madeline as she guided him to the door.

In New York, Anita went back to the program director who had made the original diagnosis. Her motivation, as she rationalized it to herself, was to confront that diagnosis with her *easy* state of sobriety and abstinence and get the woman to withdraw the original pronouncement, and so get the onus of being diagnosed "addiction prone" off Anita's back. Once in the director's office, however, Anita's reserve broke, and, sobbing, she related all that had happened to her since the accident. The director came around her desk and held the girl, who continued to cry against her shoulder.

"You *have* had a hard time of it!"

"It's terrible! There's nobody I can turn to or talk to, not my parents, none of my friends. What can I do?"

"First of all, you need to learn that you're not a bad person. You don't need to punish yourself, or anyone else, for that matter. What you need to do is pick up your life and get back to being the happy, productive person that you really are. To do that, though, you're going to need some help."

"I'll do anything. I just can't stand it any longer."

"Then come and talk to me as long as it helps. And there are some meetings you can go to."

Anita didn't tell her parents about the meetings at first. After all, the organizations were anonymous. She was surprised to see familiar faces there, some of the local solid citizens and even a few family friends. They smiled in recognition when they saw her at the meetings but never mentioned this association if they saw her elsewhere. Some were even her own age. One boy was a star on the football team, and there was a girl who had won scholastic honors and a scholarship to Smith. Could all these people be sick? she wondered.

These meetings filled her with questions, and each week she saw the director, who was also a substance-abuse counselor, and asked for answers. What is self-help? What do the twelve steps mean? What else can I do to help myself? And finally, How can I talk to my parents about what's happening to me?

Anita and Al have several things going for them. They're both intelligent. They're members of the established middle class. They are both young. They both have entered a treatment network.

On the other hand, both of them are devastated by the discovery that they are addicts. We hope they'll both respond to treatment and be on their way to recovery. They do have a lot to work out, though. Anita, for example, has accepted the notion that addiction equates with moral degeneracy and has reacted accordingly to the seeming paradox of her condition by crying, "But I'm a good girl!" Al, more a part of the social ambiguity surrounding substance use, asks, "But how am I going to conduct business?" Both ask the most common question of confrontation and realization, "Why me?"

It's too early in this book to talk about happy endings, but we can look at a few happy beginnings.

At first Anita sat at the back of the AA meetings and listened. Slowly she moved toward the front. As the weeks passed, changes were coming over her. Resentment, denial and martyred behavior were melting away to be replaced by a sense of purpose and a new sense of self. Finally, one night there was a pause between speakers. Anita was now sitting in the front row, and it was as if she had received a cue. She walked to the podium, looked out at the group of old and new friends and smiled. "My name is Anita," she said, "and I'm an alcoholic."

On the other coast, at a Cocaine Anonymous meeting in San Francisco, a young man got up and said, "My name is Alan, and I am a cocaine addict."

Getting High
and Its Effects | 2

NOTHING NEW

We tend to approach drug abuse and addiction as a new problem—the product of contemporary pressures and conflicts. In this view, users are deviates. But history shows us that human beings have probably always sought the means of altering consciousness.

Primitive humanity probably first encountered drugs when a caveman got tipsy after eating fermented fruit from the base of a tree, or the spirit from a particularly spirited herb got into an ancient shaman. The natural world abounds in psychoactive substances. Psychoactive is the name we give to these drugs because their effect is on consciousness, the psyche. They're also called central nervous system, or CNS, drugs because they act on the brain and affect mood and consciousness. It was no great feat for our ancestors to try these substances and become aware of their effects. Getting high on chemical substances isn't even a human invention. Ornithologists will testify that cedar waxwings, for example, will fly great distances in order to get loaded on pyracanthas berries, and larger birds get the staggers and are easily captured after eating the fruit of the nutmeg tree.

Andrew Weil, M.D., author of *The Natural Mind: A New Way of Looking at Drugs and the Higher Consciousness*, and a notable figure in the science of ethnobotany (in part the study of primitive plant use), believes that the desire to alter consciousness is a basic human drive. He cites the actions of young children spinning around in order to get dizzy and holding their breath as early manifestations of this drive. Dr. Weil holds the belief that where we went wrong was in developing destructive synthetics and highly purified forms of naturally occurring consciousness-effective substances. While an interesting theory overall, Dr. Weil's thesis regarding the relative dangers of refined as opposed to naturally occurring drugs does have one shortcoming: People are often as vulnerable to addiction to natural substances as they are to refined or synthetic ones.

As soon as humanity developed social organization, use of the powerful psychoactive substances was limited to a privileged few. In primitive tribal groups their use became the exclusive province of the shaman, or witch doctor. As more complex cultural units developed shamanism metamorphosed into state religions wherein psychoactives were regulated by the priesthood. In studying these ancient cultures, anthropologists and ethnobotanists have discovered repeated direct and symbolic references to a wide variety of naturally occurring psychoactive substances.

Although some psychoactives, such as cannabis and the opium poppy, became mainstays of primitive and classical medicine, others were used primarily to incite prophetic visions in members of the priesthood or to instill a sense of holy awe and wonder in the populace at large. During the classical Greek civilization, which traces its beginnings to Minoan Crete and pre-Homeric Mycenae four thousand years ago and which continued as Hellenism in the eastern Mediterranean long past the fall of Rome, there were several major mystery religions that involved the use of psychoactive drugs in their worship.

One of these religions involved the goddess Persephone, or Kore, the daughter of Zeus and Demeter, the goddess of the earth and fertility, who spent part of each year in the underworld of Hades, Zeus's brother who had kidnapped her. When Persephone is underground, Demeter grieves and the world is in winter. The "Rites of Spring" took place at the town of Eleusis, near Athens, where a temple was built over the hole in the rocks where Persephone allegedly emerges from Hades's realm for eight months to console her mother, who, in gratitude, brings the earth back into flower and allows crops to grow. For the classical Greek citizen, Eleusis functioned as Mecca does for the modern Moslem. One made a once-in-a-lifetime pilgrimage there to "see the Goddess." Thousands came before dawn on the first day of spring and were given a concoction that included ergotamine, a rye grain mold that is the primary ingredient in the hallucinogenic drug LSD. The psychedelic potion was said to give one visions of holy wonder.

The ergotamine potion may have given rise to one of the first recorded incidents of drug abuse. About 420 B.C., Alcibiades, a renegade Athenian noble who had been a friend and disciple of the philosopher Socrates, didn't think this libation should be controlled by the priesthood and used only for religious purposes. Just before leaving for a military expedition to Sicily, he and a group of young followers stole some of the potion from the temple. Under its influence they rampaged through Athens, mutilating the phallic statues of Hermes, the messenger of the gods and guide of travelers, that stood outside each household. Alcibiades turned out to be a thoroughly bad chap. He eventually sold out Athens to both Sparta and the Persians. It's not known what other drugs Alcibiades may have indulged in, but he is remembered in the *Oxford Companion to Classical Literature* as having been "a man of remarkable beauty and talent, but arrogant, unscrupulous, and dissolute."

In the Middle Ages, outbreaks of ergotamine poisoning and other encounters with hallucinogenic drugs were determined to be the result of "demonic possession." Then as now, the most popular drug of abuse was alcohol. Its use was widespread, and public drunkenness common. In the Near East, the use of opium and cannabis for medicinal purposes was salvaged from the ruins of the Roman Empire, while their nonmedical use was encouraged by the Moslem strictures against alcohol. We now know that nearly all cultures throughout the world have had naturally occurring psychoactive drugs since early times. Many of them have also had abuse problems with these drugs.

Treatment of drug abuse, humane and inhumane, has taken a variety of forms. A means of detoxifying opium addicts in ancient India presupposed the modern method of calculated withdrawal. The addict was given a piece of chalk that weighed the same as the opium used in a day and told that each morning he must write the holy world *om* on a slate with the chalk. He could then weigh out a day's worth of opium using the chalk as a counterweight. As the chalk wore away writing oms the daily ration of opium decreased slowly to nothing. Apparently, it was hoped that by writing the holy symbols the addict's attention would shift from drugs to God as well.

In medieval Europe and colonial America, alcohol consumption and abuse were tolerated, but drug use could incur drastic penalties, including burning at the stake for witchcraft. The Inquisition, which came to the Americas with the Spanish conquistadors, vigorously suppressed the use of psychoactive drugs by the Native Americans. This suppression was so thorough that the existence of such native hallucinogenics as psilocybin or "magic mushrooms" and yage was considered myth until their rediscovery in this century. The United States government tried to do the same with the hallucinogenic peyote cactus in the American Southwest in the nineteenth century, but the Indians involved in its use took legal measures to preserve the use of peyote as a religious sacrament.

The penalties for use of drugs and attitudes toward their abuse have varied greatly from culture to culture and from era to era. Often, these penalties and attitudes have been greatly influenced by the fears and stereotypes of the culture involved. When tobacco was first introduced into Europe in the late 1500s, it was preached against from the pulpit and condemned from the palace and the parliament. Although its users were vaguely aware that its use was compulsive and probably unhealthy, tobacco smoking subsequently gained worldwide support, and eventually most of the world stopped considering tobacco a drug. It's only in our own time that overwhelming physical evidence of tobacco's role in lung cancer, emphysema, heart disease and other ailments has begun to turn the tide against tobacco; yet despite that our government continues to subsidize the industry. Alcohol, the sale of which was illegal in the United States between 1920 and 1933, is once more a major industry here, and in fact was continuously produced and consumed, albeit illegally, even during Prohibition. Heroin, which was used initially as a remedy for sore throats and a possible cure for morphine addiction, is hated and feared in most Western nations. The United States has banned it completely. Conversely, in many Moslem countries the word for heroin is "medicine," while the use of alcohol is forbidden on pain of death.

Cultural attitudes toward a drug and those who use it influence that culture's legislation and regulation of the drug. One of the first statutes against drug use in the United States, for example, was an 1875 San Francisco city ordinance, reflecting both our Puritan heritage and whites' prejudice against orientals, that forbade the smoking of opium by Chinese. Subsequent laws were aimed at controlling the use of heroin and cocaine by blacks and the smoking of marijuana by Mexican-Americans. Like the attempted regulation of peyote, these laws came not from the desire to deal with the drugs' possible medical dangers but rather from the dominant culture's fears that these drugs would enhance the strength of the minority populations who used them and undermine the dominant culture.

Treatment approaches to the abuse of drugs have often been influenced by the emotions surrounding cultural acceptance or taboo. Drug use and abuse can inspire powerful emotions that obscure medical reality and make use a moral and emotional issue. There is still a great deal of controversy in our culture over whether drug abuse and addiction are medical, moral or legal problems.

DRUGS BY CATEGORY

Now, we may well wonder, just what are these substances that seem capable of exerting so much power over us? A glance through the *Physicians' Desk Reference*, with over 3,000 pages describing prescription drugs alone, is enough to make our heads spin—and it doesn't even mention illegal drugs or over-the-counter drugs. The drugs we are concerned with here are called "psychoactive" because their effect is on the psyche. Instead of fighting disease entities in the body, these drugs work by making temporary changes in the way our central nervous system operates. At present there are hundreds of psychoactive drugs on the market, and many more are synthesized, by either pharmaceutical companies or underground chemists, every year.

Fortunately, there is a relatively clear means of sorting out this bewildering blizzard of pills, powders and potions. All of these psychoactive drugs can be grouped into four general categories: uppers, downers, psychedelics and a handful of drugs that have qualities of more than one of these. The drugs in each of these categories have similar properties and effects. In this chapter, we'll start by looking at the nature of these drug categories.

UPPERS

These are the drugs we also call stimulants. This category contains our culture's most common psychoactive substance. Some of these drugs have become so much a part of our lives that we have long ceased to think of them as drugs. I doubt that many of us say to ourselves, "Wow! Think I'll get stoned on a piece of chocolate!" or hear sweet old Auntie Em say, "Let's all have a cup of tea and get high!" Yet both chocolate and tea contain psychoactive stimulants, as do cigarettes, coffee, sugar and many soft drinks. Most cultures, worldwide, make use of naturally occurring stimulants. These include yerba mate in much of South America, betel nuts in the Far East, ginseng and ephedra in China, yohimbe and khat in Africa and the coca leaf that is chewed with lime in the South American highlands. Tea is actually a variety of different shrub leaves and herbs most of which have stimulant effects.

Curiously, the stimulants most commonly used in North America and Western Europe all came from other cultures. Tea came from India and the Far East, coffee from the Near East, and chocolate and tobacco from Native Americans. What did the medieval European do for chemical stimulation?

The more potent stimulants—the ones we do indeed consider drugs—are either purified active ingredients from plants, stimulants, such as cocaine, or purely synthetic drugs, such as amphetamines.

Cocaine

At this point we will take a more detailed look at the history of cocaine. Not only has this drug presented one of the most serious medical and social crises in history, but its early acceptance and widespread use have offered professionals an almost unprecedented opportunity to reexamine and redefine earlier concepts of addiction.

Ever since its isolation from the South American coca leaf by Albert Niemann in the 1880s, cocaine has been a very controversial drug. Some doctors have seen it as a great breakthrough in the practice of medicine. Others have considered it a "scourge of mankind." A few, including Sigmund Freud, have held both views at different times in their life and practice.

Since ancient times, Indians in the South American uplands have chewed the coca leaf for its stimulant effects and as a dietary supplement. Used in this way, it represents one of the many comparatively mild regional stimulants that have been identified and used by specific cultures throughout the world. Other substances in this category include tea, coffee, yerba mate, khat and chocolate.

Cocaine, the coca leaf's most active alkaloid, was put to a number of medical and quasi-medical uses when it was first isolated and purified into cocaine hydrochloride. One of these uses was as a cure for morphine dependence. One of Sigmund Freud's colleagues, a doctor named Ernst von Fleischl-Marxow, had become morphine dependent by using that drug to treat postoperative pain after the amputation of an infected thumb. Freud had experimented with cocaine on himself and, when he became aware of his friend and colleague's plight, introduced him to it. At the time, Freud described Fleischl's reaction to cocaine therapy to his future wife, saying the doctor had clutched at the drug "like a drowning man." Today, such a reaction would be seen for what it is, but those were pioneering times. In fact, as noted by S. Bernfeld in his commentary on Freud's *Cocaine Papers*, Ernst von Fleischl-Marxow rapidly transformed himself from the first morphine addict in Europe to be cured by cocaine to the first cocaine addict in Europe.

Although cocaine dependence was recognized in many circles, its medical usefulness continued to be lauded by a number of respected health professionals, not to mention world leaders, including at least one president of the United States, William McKinley, and a pope. This was an era of patent medicines, tonics and formulas, and cocaine found its way into many of these remedies. Vin Mariani, an elixir sold worldwide, was the second most famous of these. First-place honors, however, go to Coca-Cola. The original Coke was first marketed in 1886 as a patent medicine and advertised as "a valuable Brain tonic and cure for all nervous affections—sick headache, neuralgia, hysteria, melancholy, etc." Let's see our modern-day Madison Avenue adpersons top that! Coca-Cola abandoned the use of cocaine in its syrup in 1903 and since then has used a flavoring derived from decocainized coca leaves. Because the actual formula for Coca-Cola is an industrial secret, we don't know when the stimulant caffeine was added.

The availability of cocaine in the United States was first regulated by the Harrison Narcotics Act of 1914. Since that time a succession of laws has restricted its use but, unlike heroin, marijuana and LSD, has not banned it. Cocaine is still commonly used as a topical or local anesthetic for eye and nose operations.

The street use of cocaine has had its ups and downs. After being legitimized by Freud, used by Sir Arthur Conan Doyle's fictional detective Sherlock Holmes to fight boredom between cases and adopted by younger elements in the British and American upper crust, cocaine underwent a major drubbing in the mass media between 1900 and 1920, after its use was adopted by urban blacks. It then disappeared from all but the seediest of scenes and was considered a drug of great depravity. In the late 1960s, along with other "drugs of depravity" such as heroin, cocaine reemerged from the ghettos, and by the mid-1970s it had reattained a degree of respectability in certain circles. Alan's lawyer friend was probably right: At that time cocaine probably did have a better chance of being legalized than marijuana.

Up until the late 1970s, many health professionals who were dealing with substance-abuse issues and treatment were sending mixed messages about cocaine to the general public. Cocaine was not generally seen as all that threatening. Its use didn't seem to promote tolerance to any great degree, and the withdrawal symptoms seen with dangerous drugs like heroin and alcohol didn't seem to occur. Street cocaine was both weak and expensive—many called it "the Cadillac" or "the champagne" of drugs. Finally, the route of administration involved what appeared to be self-limiting factors. Although a few people injected cocaine, these were clearly in the minority. Most users inhaled the crystalline powder into their nostrils, from where it was carried to the bloodstream by the tiny blood vessels in the nose's mucous membrane. In that cocaine shrinks blood vessels, the drug itself was thought to rapidly render these capillaries incapable of transporting it.

Several things happened that drastically altered professional opinions that cocaine was a benign drug. The practice of freebasing, which involves inhaling the vapor of a highly concentrated form of cocaine directly into the lungs, was developed. Cocaine became not only a "safe" drug but a prestige drug, prized for its lack of detectability, effects on various types of performance, and elite reputation. With a rapidly increasing market, cocaine became cheaper, easier to find, and much, much stronger. Finally, there was an alarming escalation in cocaine-related medical emergencies and fatalities. Recognizing the growing trend, Mark S. Gold, M.D., started the National Cocaine Hotline, 800-COCAINE, to provide advice and referral to those with cocaine problems. Gathering data from the program, Gold reported in 1984 that one out of every ten—or about twenty-two million—Americans had tried cocaine, and that every day around five thousand more teenagers and adults try it for the first time. The casualties were beginning to mount.

Crack

In 1985, a new form of freebase cocaine called "crack" appeared on the East Coast and began spreading across the country. This underground product is processed from cocaine hydrochloride into a base, smokeable form by mixing it with ammonia (with or without sodium bicarbonate) and water, then heating the mixture to remove the hydrochloride. Unlike the more volatile freebase procedure that uses ether, this method doesn't remove the impurities usually found in street cocaine. It is believed that the name, crack, comes from a crackling sound when it is smoked that's caused by residual sodium bicarbonate.

Once the conversion process is completed, the resulting powder is processed into crystals, known as "rocks," and either sold in transparent vials that resemble large vitamin capsules or packaged in foil or heavy paper. The individual crystals are white and about the size of a pencil eraser. The National Institute on Drug Abuse reports that crack is usually sold in ready-to-smoke form, about 300 milligrams per piece, for $5 to $10.

Smoking freebase in general is much different from snorting cocaine, both qualitatively and quantitatively. Smoking freebase allows for more rapid drug absorption. Contrary to popular myth, when cocaine is snorted it doesn't go directly to the brain. It passes through the bloodstream to the lungs and heart and then to the brain. This process can slow down the drug's toxicity to some extent. When freebase vapors are smoked, however, the drug is absorbed directly into the pulmonary circulation and reportedly can cross the blood-brain barrier in massive dosages within six seconds.

Although crack is not a new drug, its extreme potency and ease of use make it especially dangerous. In the past, dedicated freebase users had to get a freebase kit, score a lot of relatively pure cocaine hydrochloride and go through an expensive and complex do-it-yourself conversion to get their freebase. With crack, the drug is ready to use, readily available and sold at prices that the youth market can afford. Further, smoking crack is perceived by many young people as being as acceptable as snorting.

In any form, cocaine can disturb the electrical rhythm between the brain and heart and cause potentially fatal seizures. Although some people are more vulnerable than others to cocaine-caused heart attacks or brain seizures, the healthiest person in the world can die of cocaine overdose. Perhaps the recent tragic deaths of several nationally known sports stars will help turn young people away from this new and particularly deadly form of cocaine. We can only hope and do our best to educate.

Amphetamines

Amphetamines, first developed in Germany during the 1930s, bear a strong resemblance to our own internal stimulants. Their effects are like those of cocaine but tend to be much longer lasting. A single dose of cocaine will last about forty minutes, while the stimulant effects of one oral dose of amphetamine may continue for over four hours.

During World War II, both sides made extensive use of amphetamines to increase the "war effort." Bell and Trithowan (1961) reported that "more than seventy-two million energy tablets were supplied to service personnel in Great Britain and much the same quantity to the United States Armed Forces." We can be sure that Germany and Japan also supplied great numbers of these pills to their forces. Then it was generally believed that amphetamines would make combat troops march longer and fight better, as well as increase the alertness and concentration of pilots and bomber crews. In several countries these stimulants were also issued to factory workers in hopes of increasing production. It should be noted that while such practices may have shown some very short-term increases in productivity, long-term results were always negative.

After the war, amphetamines were described in various science magazines as "miracle drugs" that vastly improved both performance and stamina. Some researchers even claimed that these drugs increased intelligence. Is it any wonder that these drugs were popular? Physicians liberally prescribed and dispensed amphetamines for a variety of complaints, including obesity, depression, fatigue and anxiety. Amphetamines were easily available on college campuses, where their use in cramming for exams was widespread; on the nation's highways, where cross-country truck drivers, often running from coast to coast with no sleep, took them to stay awake; and in locker rooms, where amateur and professional athletes took them to increase stamina and develop a "fighting edge."

The first major indications that amphetamines could be dangerous and cause a drug problem of national proportions came from postwar Japan, where supplies were plentiful and amphetamine pills were available on a nonprescription basis. By 1954, the Japanese government estimated that it had over 200,000 active amphetamine addicts, and it placed controls on the drug. Although epidemic-size outbreaks occurred elsewhere, manufacturers in the United States continued to produce large quantities of amphetamines throughout the 1950s and 1960s. Ads in medical magazines urged their readers to prescribe them for the depressed and the overweight.

National awareness of amphetamine abuse came in 1969, not from the chronic abuse patterns of those who swallowed pep pills, but from a bizarre form of abuse that may have originated in the Haight Ashbury District of San Francisco in 1967, during the Summer of Love. It was there that a coterie of drug users, generally referred to as "speed freaks," initiated the practice of injecting extremely high dosages of methedrine and other stimulants directly into their veins. These speed freaks explained that this method of use gave them an incredible rush that they described as being like an intense orgasm over the entire body. The high-dosage intravenous use of amphetamines spread rapidly throughout the United States, but its appeal quickly faded. For one thing, speed freaks looked terrible. The drug took a heavy toll, both physically and mentally, reducing its users to wasted and incoherent specimens. The massive use of amphetamines also hastened a form of amphetamine psychosis, a drug-induced paranoia that led to violent and destructive behavior. Given the fact that violent speed freaks were their own worst advertisement and created a climate of fear wherever they went, prevention and education were highly effective in dealing with the epidemic. There are still a few speed freaks around, mostly in the nation's "skid rows," but this form of substance abuse no longer constitutes a growing national drug problem.

Amphetamines in general played a major role in the spreading, youth-oriented, "subterranean" drug culture that had at least its media origins in the Haight Ashbury. Under the collective name "speed," amphetamines were used both as intoxicants in their own right and as a chemical method of mediating the less desirable long-term effects of downers and psychedelics. Nor was their use limited to the "hippie" counterculture.

By the early 1970s, health professionals working with the National Institute on Drug Abuse had identified an extensive middle-class "polydrug problem." Much of the polydrug abuse that they cited involved either the compulsive use of oral amphetamines and amphetaminelike drugs, or their use in upper/downer drug patterns similar to those seen earlier in the counterculture but utilizing prescription rather than street drugs. At the same time, the extensive use of stimulants in the treatment of so-called hyperkinetic, or hyperactive, children came under public scrutiny. These drugs have a paradoxical effect on true hyperkinetics: They appear to calm them down. With children who merely have behavior or attention problems, however, the drugs have a worsening effect. Increasingly, highway accidents were traced to pep-pill-popping truck drivers. The last straw may have been the scandal surrounding use of amphetamines for performance by athletes in two successive Olympic Games.

Public outrage forced manufacturers, enforcement organizations, drug administration, and the medical community into collective action. Medical indications—the reasons a doctor can prescribe a stimulant—were reduced to four:

1.   The short-term management of weight reduction.

2.   The treatment of sleep disorders (such as narcolepsy, when one is apt to spontaneously fall asleep at inappropriate times, such as while driving a car or operating machinery).
3.   Hyperactivity in children.
4.   Depression.

The pharmaceutical manufacturers worked with the administration to set realistic manufacturing quotas for amphetamines. These drastically reduced the available quantity of legally made amphetamines in this country, keeping them more or less in line with estimates of prescription needs. Law enforcement agencies, armed with new laws regulating the prescribing of stimulants, were enabled to proceed against doctors who appeared to be prescribing excessive amounts of these and other drugs.

All of this had an effect on the middle-class abuse of prescription stimulants and decreased the tremendous diversion of pharmaceutical amphetamines into underground markets. What it could not do, however, was eliminate the public market for nonprescription stimulants. One attempt to supply at least a part of that market was the production and sale of what are known as "lookalike stimulants."

Lookalike Stimulants

Lookalikes were made from legal stimulant substances, such as caffeine, the common drug found in coffee, tea, soft drinks and over-the-counter medications; ephedrine, found in allergy medicines; and phenylpropanolamine (PPN), used in many cold medicines, antihistamine preparations and over-the-counter appetite suppressants. Often manufactured to look like prescription stimulants (hence the name), lookalikes are marketed as "legal speed" or pep pills, et cetera. Many of their users are the young and drug-naive, who think they are getting a real amphetamine.

Similar ingredients are found in cocaine lookalike drugs. These, however, usually add a topical anesthetic such as lidocaine to approximate the numbing effect of cocaine on teeth and gums. When sold by dealers as the real thing, these cocaine lookalikes are often hard to tell from cocaine, even by habitual users. Although both amphetamine and cocaine lookalikes are resold as counterfeits of the drugs they are made to resemble, they have also come to be used as what they are for their own sake.

All stimulants create the illusion of increasing a person's energy and stamina by using up internal energy reserves. Stimulants may be used for any of several desired effects. First there is the desire for increased energy and performance facilitation. This may involve maintaining wakefulness and alertness over long periods, increasing the ability to concentrate on detailed work or play. Appetite suppression is another desired effect that gains importance in our fashion-conscious times, when thinness is held at a premium. Euphoria and just plain feeling good are other reasons cited for using stimulants. Cocaine and amphetamines produce a rush that combines sexual and euphoric feelings and is highly prized by users. Compulsive cocaine users who come in for treatment often talk about the overpowering rush they felt the first time they ever used the drug and refer to it as a feeling that they have tried to reexperience ever since.

What happens, though, is that the stimulant effect of these drugs decreases each time they are used. This decrease is due in part to the development of tolerance, in part to the depletion of internal energy supplies. The user needs more and more of the drug just to "stay even," or feel the drug's effects as intensely as the time before, and after a while, when the internal energy stores are used up, the system just shuts down. This is what happens at the end of an amphetamine or cocaine run, when the user collapses into total inactivity for a period.

"Amping out," or overdosing on a stimulant, can be dangerous. The body's "shutting down" may involve respiratory or cardiac arrest or the cessation of breathing and can be fatal. Emergency-room crises resulting from the use of cocaine have increased dramatically in the last few years.

Long-term use of stimulants, especially when coupled with chronic lack of sleep, can result in stimulant psychosis. This condition is characterized by extreme paranoia, for example, feelings that one is in danger or being hunted by the law or by criminals, as well as auditory and visual hallucinations. Among cocaine dealers and others involved in the underworld of drugs, this paranoia is often not without some basis in fact. The psychosis is usually related directly to the drug use, however, and disappears as the drug is withdrawn and the patient returns to normal, often with a sense of abashed wonder at "how could I have been so crazy?" Drug-related or not, though, an armed speed freak in the grip of stimulant psychosis is a danger to himself and others.

We have not talked about tobacco, which Dr. Andrew Weil has called on occasion "the most addictive drug on earth." In the last few years, nicotine has been under fire for its role in cancer, heart disease and other diseases. Recently, the fact that, as a psychoactive drug, it causes addiction just as surely as cocaine, heroin or alcohol has again come under scrutiny.

For a long time there was confusion as to whether or not stimulants did indeed cause addiction. In fact, that question as applied to cocaine has in part resulted in a general rethinking of just what we mean by addiction and what that means in terms of treatment. Our own conclusion is that all stimulants can be agents of addictive disease. Besides being abusable drugs in their own right, stimulants also figure in multiple-drug abuse with our second category of psychoactive drugs, the downers.

DOWNERS

The drugs we refer to as downers are also known as depressants. Just as stimulants stimulate the central nervous system, elevating its energy level, depressants lower the central nervous system's energy level. Depressant drugs are usually clustered in three subgroups. These are the *narcotic analgesics*, the *general anesthetics* and the *sedative hypnotics*.

Narcotic Analgesics

Narcotic analgesics are also called opiates or opioids. Opiates are derived from the opium poppy, a white-flowered variety of poppy that develops large seed pods behind the blossom, while opioids are fully synthetic drugs with similar effects. All the narcotic drugs are used for the management of pain. The word "narcotic" itself comes from Greek and means "stupor," a state of diminished sensibility in which brain function is reduced. Law enforcement has muddied the clear understanding of the nature of these drugs by labeling all illegal drugs as "narcotics." In this book, however, we will refer only to painkilling drugs as narcotics and not apply the term to stimulants and other drug categories.

Opiates

Opium is one of the oldest medical drugs. There are records of its use for pain management in the clay tablets of early civilizations. The Egyptians depicted opium pods in their wall paintings, and opium was in the pharmacopeia of classic Hippocratic Greek medicine. In early preparations, the opium poppy pods were ground up and eaten or steeped into a liquid, which was drunk like tea. Later the opium, a milky substance drained from cuts in the mature pods, was dried into a dark, sticky substance and eaten. Smoking was unknown in the Eastern world until after the discovery of America, and the smoking of opium wasn't initiated until much later. Contrary to popular stereotypes, opium originated in Southern Europe and the Middle East and was unknown in China until it was introduced there from India by the British in the nineteenth century.

Among the common medical preparations that included opium were a diluted tincture mixed with camphor (now called paregoric) and laudanum, which was opium dissolved in alcohol. These preparations, like opium itself, produced a sense of euphoria or well-being but didn't provide sufficient pain management for severe physical trauma patients.

In 1803 Frederick Sertüner, a German chemist, isolated the primary active ingredient in opium. He called this substance morphine, after Morpheus, identified by Ovid as a son of Somnus, the Roman god of sleep, who appeared in dreams in human form. Morphine was the most important of about twenty different ingredients in opium. Its discovery marked the first time a scientist had isolated the active principle of a drug plant and, as we shall see, foreshadowed the discovery of cocaine in coca and mescaline in the peyote cactus.

Development of the hypodermic syringe in 1853 made it possible to deliver the purified drug morphine quickly into the body for the rapid relief of pain—or for the rapid onset of euphoria. There followed an era of "morphinism," or addiction to the drug morphine. This addiction was most pronounced as an aftermath of America's brutal Civil War, for many wounded veterans were unable to kick the painkiller habit they had developed in hospitals.

In 1874, C. R. Wright, working for Bayer Pharmaceutical Products of Elberfeld, Germany, synthesized a combination of refined morphine and acetic anhydride that was marketed by Bayer in 1898 as a cough suppressant and a possible cure for morphinism. The trade name for the new drug was Heroin.

While it was known that all the narcotics could cause chemical dependency, attitudes toward these drugs were not what they are today. Dr. John P. Morgan of the Sophie Davis School of Medicine in New York points out in lectures that the turn-of-the-century opiate addict in the United States was a white, middle-aged, middle-class housewife with two or more children. She usually used her drug of choice in a tonic or tincture. A possible example would be the two pixilated sisters on the television show "The Waltons." The restorative formula that they trotted out on special occasions would in real life have been a tincture of morphine or heroin dissolved in alcohol, with a little cocaine added to provide an "uplifting" quality.

As the twentieth century progressed, however, heroin became increasingly notorious as a street drug used by poor and minority populations. Its medical use was restricted, and with the passage of the Harrison Narcotics Act of 1914 its very importation and sale in the United States became illegal.

Paradoxically, morphine continues to be a workhorse painkiller in the practice of medicine. One other natural derivative of opium is used extensively in pain management, and that is codeine, a drug used for minor postoperative and dental pain. Opiates are also capable of controlling diarrhea, and mild tinctures such as paregoric are used even for small children.

Opioids

In recent years, a number of synthetic painkillers have been developed that resemble opiates in their structure and effects but vary greatly in strength and duration of effects. Methadone was synthesized in Nazi Germany during World War II when the Germans' supply of opiates was cut off. An extremely long-acting painkiller, methadone is used in the United States for the maintenance and withdrawal of heroin addicts. Other relatively well known synthetic opiatelike drugs are the extremely powerful and fast-acting drug fentanyl, used often during childbirth; meperidine (brand name Demerol), pentazocine (brand name Talwin), and propoxyphene (brand name Darvon). Fentanyl is the base for a series of "designer drugs," substances in which the psychoactive properties have been retained or enhanced while the molecular structure has been altered in order to avoid criminal prosecution for their possession and use. Several of these fentanyl analogues are hundreds of times stronger than morphine—so strong, in fact, that their dosages are measured in millionths of grams, micrograms, rather than the usual milligrams. These dosages are so minute that they cannot be detected by the chemical means usually used to detect opiates in the system. These infinitesimal dosages also make overdoses much more probable with these drugs, and many deaths have occurred from their use. Meperidine, or Demerol, also has a designer analogue that has been responsible, through an impurity in the underground synthesis process, for producing paralysis among some of its users by actively destroying brain cells.

Any narcotic can produce a life-threatening overdose. These drugs act in part by slowing down the system. Too much of any narcotic slows down the body below the level at which it can function. The result can be coma and death. Fortunately, there are chemicals that can reverse the effects of an overdose if it is caught in time. These are known as narcotic antagonists and include naltrexone and naloxone.

Long-term use of narcotics can result in physical dependency and addiction. Withdrawal from these drugs can be very uncomfortable and usually involves a variety of physical symptoms such as sleeplessness, anxiety, pain and gastrointestinal distress, but it is not usually life-threatening.

Most of these drugs are either injected or swallowed, although heroin may also be snorted through the nose or smoked. Narcotics are often used in an upper/downer pattern with stimulants. In fact, one way of taking both is called a speedball. Originally this meant the simultaneous injection of heroin and cocaine, but today it can be any combination of a narcotic and a stimulant.

General Anesthetics

General anesthetics are a group of powerful depressants that are used in surgery to negate pain. These drugs come in the form of gases or volatile, highly vaporous liquids, and they are inhaled or injected rather than swallowed. When they are breathed, general anesthetics enter the bloodstream very quickly and depress brain functions within seconds. The stronger ones induce complete unconsciousness. In the operating room, they are administered by trained anesthesiologists who monitor the patient's vital signs and administer the drug in order to maintain a state of unconsciousness as long as is needed. Too much anesthetic can be fatal or cause permanent damage to the brain and nervous system. One of the oldest drugs in this group is chloroform, but it is very toxic and hard to regulate dosage. Its use has been discontinued.

With the exception of nitrous oxide (also known as laughing gas), few of these drugs are used outside the operating room. Ether was used initially as a recreational drug, but is rarely abused by choice. Nitrous is still popular, especially at parties. It produces a short but intense high.

In general, these anesthetics are not considered to be a major drug threat. In their book *Chocolate to Morphine: Understanding Mind-Active Drugs*, Andrew Weil, M.D., and Winifred Rosen point out, "Some people like nitrous oxide a great deal and may breathe it off and on over months and years. Many of them eventually come to feel that such activity is a waste of time."

Sedative-Hypnotics

Sedative-hypnotics as a group include drugs that produce sedation, or relaxation and restfulness, or induce sleep. This group is similar to narcotics. The sedative-hypnotic group includes the most ancient and widespread drug of all, alcohol.

Alcohol

Like the more popular stimulants, alcohol is rarely thought of as a drug. Yet it has been used medicinally since early times. Prior to the availability of general anesthetics and in such areas as the American frontier, a bottle of "Old Red-eye" was often the only painkiller available. Throughout history, it has been used for a wide range of medical indications. Today it has only one medical use, and that is for the emergency treatment of acute alcohol poisoning. Such a use may seem paradoxical, but it will make sense when we talk about the effects of alcohol and other drugs on the brain.

Barbiturates

Although there are many similarities between the three subgroups of downer drugs—enough to make them a cohesive group—sedative-hypnotics have long filled medical needs that are not served by either narcotic analgesics or general anesthetics. Anxiety and insomnia may seem byproducts of our hypertechnological society, but both have been part of the human condition for a long time. Treatment of these, of convulsions and of certain forms of epilepsy are the special medical tasks of sedative-hypnotic drugs.

In the nineteenth century these afflictions were treated with opiates, bromide salts, chloral hydrate (developed in 1869), paraldehyde (developed in 1882) and alcohol. Each of these substances had its problems as a depressant. The opiates simply weren't depressants. The bromides could cause chronic bromide poisoning; many patients refused to take alcohol; and chloral hydrate and paraldehyde had objectionable taste and smell.

In 1864, Dr. Adolf von Baeyer synthesized barbituric acid (some say he named it after a cocktail waitress of his acquaintance), and the era of barbiturates began. These drugs were hailed as the saving of humanity, until their problems became apparent between the 1920s and 1940s as their abuse escalated.

Under pressure to find a "safe" substitute for barbiturates, which had been developed as a "safe" substitute for bromides, the pharmaceutical industry devised glutethimide, ethchlorvynol, and methyprylon. These appeared on the market as nonbarbiturate sedative-hypnotics in 1954 and 1955 but were found to have the same potential for abuse as the barbiturates that they were meant to replace.

Ever since alcohol, the history of sedative-hypnotic drugs has involved the search for a substance or family of substances that would make us feel good and control anxiety, depression and sleeplessness without the risk of dependence, debilitating side effects and life-threatening overdoses. Time and again, a new drug or group of drugs has been discovered and marketed as "safe and effective," only to fall out of favor as reports of abuse, overdose and death come to light.

Methaqualone

A prime example of the rise and fall of a sedative-hypnotic can be seen in the history of methaqualone. Sold in the United States as Quaalude and overseas as Mandrax, methaqualone was a synthetic organic chemical unrelated structurally to the barbiturates. Originally developed to fight malaria, it was remarketed as a sedative after its barbituratelike effects became known. Sold as a safe, effective and nonaddicting substitute for barbiturates, it rapidly became America's sixth best-selling sedative. It did even better as a street recreational drug after picking up an undeserved reputation as an aphrodisiac. Within fifteen years of its introduction, methaqualone had become number three on the federal government's most-abused drug list. In 1984, the sole manufacturer of this drug in the United States ceased production.

Sedative-hypnotics are a medical necessity and have been for a long time. We need them to treat certain physical and psychological disorders, such as anxiety and depression. Yet we also need to recognize that the development of "safe and effective" sedative-hypnotic drugs has been a cycle of tragic repetitions. We need to be aware that any chemical substance that effectively makes us feel good and curbs anxiety, depression and insomnia will cause intoxication and will create dependency and abuse in certain people.

Benzodiazepines

The most recent addition to the sedative-hypnotic pharmacopeia is the benzodiazepine family of drugs. There are a number of these, but the best known are chlordiazepoxide (brand name Librium) and diazepam (brand name Valium). Over the past twenty years, these benzodiazepines have become the backbone of sedative-hypnotic therapy. Valium, in fact, has perennially been one of the most frequently prescribed medications in the United States.

Sedative-Hypnotics in General

Although the benzodiazepines are considered to be safer than barbiturates when they are taken as directed, even at prescribed dosages they can cause addiction and physical dependence particularly in individuals with a history of alcoholism. Sedative-hypnotic drugs in general are known to be more physically destructive than the narcotic analgesics and have been known to cause extensive tissue damage to the brain at doses that greatly exceed therapeutic levels. By the same token, withdrawal from any of the sedative-hypnotic drugs, including alcohol, can be a life-threatening procedure. Patients withdrawing from these drugs are usually kept in hospitals throughout this period so that their vital signs can be regularly monitored and sedative medication used to eliminate withdrawal seizures.

Intoxication with these drugs tends to resemble drunkenness on alcohol. The exact effects of sedative-hypnotic intoxication will vary depending on the individual and a number of other factors. Outward signs of intoxication include unsteady gait, slurred speech and eye wiggle. There is impaired motor coordination and a reduction in the ability to make accurate judgments.

The desired recreational effect from these drugs is clinically referred to as "disinhibition euphoria." In this state, mood is elevated; self-criticism, anxiety and guilt are reduced; the user feels an increase in energy and self-confidence. Although a mood of euphoria can occur with these drugs, it is often fleeting, giving way to sadness, rapidly fluctuating mood changes, irritability, imagined illness, anxiety, agitation and increasing states of intoxication.

Aside from the obvious problems that can result from accidents or making a fool of oneself, the greatest danger from sedative-hypnotic intoxication is overdose. Too much drug can cause loss of consciousness, coma and even death when the respiratory system or other vital organs cease to function.

Although tolerance to these drugs develops over time, giving the user a false sense that he or she is more in control of the intoxicated state, the danger of overdose becomes greater. While the amount of the drug needed to achieve the desired effects keeps rising, the amount of the drug that can be fatal remains essentially the same. As use of a sedative-hypnotic drug becomes habitual the difference in dosage between becoming high and becoming dead becomes minuscule.

Increasing tolerance leading toward a fatal dose isn't the only danger. Because all sedative-hypnotics are similar, they are cross-tolerant. This means that as an individual is developing tolerance for alcohol, let's say, he or she is also developing tolerance for barbiturates, benzodiazepines and all other drugs in this group, whether he or she has taken them or not.

To further complicate matters, these drugs have an additive effect when more than one of them are in the system at the same time. All drugs are digested or metabolized by the liver, and the liver can only handle so much drug at a time. For a better idea of what happens when there's a lot of drug in the system, imagine six lanes of bumper-to-bumper rush hour traffic on the freeway, all trying to take the same off-ramp at the same time. Inside the body, the situation is further complicated by the fact that the liver is selective about what it digests, taking the least toxic or least dangerous chemicals first. Picture someone directing this traffic mess by being equally selective. "Okay! Volkswagens and Toyotas into the exit lane. You big double-rig diesels to the left and come around again!" If this goes on long enough, gridlock develops. So let's say someone is mixing two prescription drugs, or alcohol and Valium, a sedative that's usually safe enough by itself because it has a high fatality threshold compared to its clinical dose. Whatever can't get through the liver just keeps circulating through the bloodstream. If you take successive dosages while a steady flow of alcohol is still coming through, it can keep building up and assaulting the central nervous system until an overdose occurs.

Once tolerance and physical dependence develop, withdrawal from sedative-hypnotics can be a complex and serious process. As we pointed out above, withdrawal from these drugs can be life-threatening. In this it differs from narcotic withdrawal, which can be painful and disquieting but is not, in and of itself, physically dangerous, and which can often be accomplished on an outpatient basis with symptomatic nonnarcotic medication or even "cold turkey."

Although seizures don't always occur, each sedative-hypnotic has its own danger period for the onset of seizures once the user has quit. If the patient has been using more than one of these drugs—for example, alcohol, pentobarbital and Valium—predicting the onset and duration of possible seizures can be dicey. Generally, a patient withdrawing from sedative-hypnotics is kept in the hospital during the withdrawal process.

Instead of abruptly stopping the use of these drugs, which can be extremely dangerous, a long-acting sedative-hypnotic, usually phenobarbital, is substituted for the drug or drugs the patient has been using; then this drug is gradually withdrawn over a period of days or weeks.

PSYCHEDELICS

Psychedelic drugs are also known as hallucinogenic, psychotomimetic, or consciousness-altering drugs. Virtually all psychedelic drugs have some hallucinogenic effects; that is, they distort sensory input in some way. However, the psychedelic family of drugs is known primarily for its effects on consciousness and the way we deal with incoming data, and that is why they are designated as a separate class of psychoactive drugs.

Because these drugs burst upon the national consciousness during the countercultural mid-1960s, we tend to think of psychedelics as something new in the history of psychoactive drugs. In fact, they're every bit as old and well established as our other drug categories. Cannabis, or marijuana, has been in use just about as long as both opium and alcohol. In Chapter 1 we talked about the use of ergotamine, the rye grain mold from which LSD was later derived, in classical Greek mystery religions. A number of other consciousness-effective drugs were in use in the ancient world as well.

We have seen that the use of consciousness-effective drugs was lost to the Western world during the Middle Ages, when the accidental intoxication by such substances was attributed to witchcraft and demonic possession. In the Western Hemisphere, native use of psychedelics was vigorously suppressed, first by the priests of the Spanish Inquisition who accompanied the conquistadors and later by the various governments of the Americas. While the native stimulants tobacco, chocolate and coca leaves were adopted by Europeans and passed into general use, most of the psychedelic drugs either disappeared outright or went far underground, their use shrouded in myth until their rediscovery. An exception was the bud of the peyote cactus.

Peyote and Mescaline

Peyote had been used ceremonially by Indians in Northern Mexico and the Southwestern United States since ancient times. Neither the Inquisition nor a succession of American governments were able to eradicate its use as a stimulant, general medicine and ceremonial psychedelic. In fact, in the mid-nineteenth century its use spread even further, throughout Southwestern tribes that had previously been drug-free, as an antidote to the despair caused by the white man's encroachment on their lands and destruction of their culture.

Churches and government agencies characterized peyote as evoking a variety of gruesome Indian practices, none of which appears to have had any foundation in fact. It was claimed, for example, that Indian women tore off their clothes in states of sexual frenzy and that braves intoxicated with the drug hacked helpless victims to death. In actuality, physical activity during peyote use seems to have been limited to prescribed ritual behavior punctuated by bouts of nausea and vomiting. The drug has a purgative effect that the Indians who used it accepted as part of a purification process. It also has a bitter taste that no one who has taken it will ever forget.

Some nineteenth-century anthropologists, intrigued by the reported effects of the drug, took part in peyote ceremonies. Most were put off by the nausea, vomiting and bitter taste but wanted to learn more about drugs that could give people visions. In the late 1890s the active ingredient of peyote was isolated and named mescaline, for the Mescalero Apaches of Northern Mexico. By the turn of the century, mescaline was readily available for research purposes. Physiologists discovered that there was a clear structural relationship between mescaline and the recently discovered adrenal hormone epinephrine, which occurs naturally in the human brain, while psychologists including Sigmund Freud, William James, and Havelock Ellis wrote about the drug's subjective effects.

Popular interest in mescaline was sparked by the English philosopher and novelist Aldous Huxley and the French artist Henri Michaux. Both men wrote graphically of their personal experiences with the drug in a style that the general public could understand. At a time when the psychological theories of Sigmund Freud and C. G. Jung, with their glimpses of libido and mass unconscious, were coming into vogue, mescaline provided a means of directly experiencing altered perceptions.

LSD-25

The pharmacology of consciousness-effective drugs took a quantum leap in 1943 when Dr. Albert Hofmann, working for Sandoz Pharmaceuticals in Basel, Switzerland, discovered the awesome psychedelic properties of a drug he called lysergic acid diethylamide-25. Dr. Hofmann had actually synthesized LSD-25 from the rye mold ergotamine in 1938 but was looking for other effects at the time and put the compound aside. Various mythological theories have been put forth to explain the five-year hiatus before the drug's effects became known. One popular story is that the substance was actually psychically inactive when first discovered but that God breathed life into it after the Americans threatened His Creation by exploding a nuclear device earlier in 1943.

Be that as it may, on a fateful afternoon in 1943, Dr. Hofmann accidentally ingested a small quantity of the drug. The vial had leaked around the cork, and he absently licked his finger while tidying up his work space. As he tried to bicycle home he realized that he had discovered the most potent psychoactive drug then in existence.

Psilocybin, or "Magic Mushrooms"

Since the discovery of LSD-25, a number of other psychedelic substances have come to light. We know about mescaline and peyote and the rediscovery of psilocybin mushrooms. As recently as the late 1950s the existence of "magic mushrooms" was first considered mythical; later these were identified as a rare breed of fungus that grew only at a few specific locations in Mexico. Now it is known that various types of psilocybin mushroom grow virtually everywhere in the world, and many varieties have been classified by mycologists, or mushroom specialists. Another mushroom, the *amanita muscaria* has been associated with a variety of early religions.

Psychedelics from the Spice Cabinet

The intoxicating qualities of nutmeg and mace, spices found in most household cabinets, were well known to ornithologists, but side effects, including intense kidney pain, abdominal cramps and nausea, limited their use among humans. Nutmeg and the oil of sassafrass provided the basis, along with amphetamines, for a whole subclass of drugs that spanned both the psychedelic and stimulant groups and had similar psychedelic properties and structure to mescaline. These include the "alphabet soup" methoxylated amphetamines such as MDA, DOM (STP), MMDA, MDMA and MDME and number over a thousand different but related chemical substances. The letters that identify these drugs are acronyms for their chemical names. For example, MDA stands for 3,4,methylenedioxyamphetamine. The one exception is "STP," which is an acronym for the drug's street name. Most of the basic ones were synthesized in Germany before World War I, but their psychedelic effects were unknown until the 1950s.

Psychedelics in the Garden

Chemicals in the seeds of morning glory and Hawaiian woodrose vines, ornamental plants that grow in gardens throughout the Western world, were found to closely resemble LSD. This "poor man's acid" was used sporadically throughout the 1960s, but was much less potent than LSD and had gastrointestinal side effects that gave rise to the belief that seed wholesalers soaked these seeds in poisons to discourage their ingestion.

And Around the World

While fewer than a dozen psychedelic plants were known in the Eastern Hemisphere, over ninety species were known and used in the Western Hemisphere, not counting synthesized compounds. Besides the substances we have already named, there are the harmala alkaloids, found in the seeds of the Near Eastern shrub *Peganum harmala* or Syrian rue, in the bark of a variety of vines in the South American Amazon River basin; ibogaine, which comes to us from the root of the West African plant *Tabernanthe iboga*; DMT or N,N-dimethyltryptamine, from South American vines; muscimole from the *Amanita muscaria* mushroom; and a group called the anticholinergic deliriants that includes deadly nightshade, mandrake, black henbane, jimson weed, and over twenty other species of henbane and datura. Without a doubt, there are many other consciousness-effective substances in the natural world. Ethnobotanists and ethnopharmacologists maintain that with the exception of the Arctic and Antarctic circles there are probably one or more species of psychedelic-bearing flora in or near every inhabited point in the world.

The Effects of Psychedelics

Over the next two decades, research on LSD and other consciousness-effective drugs proliferated. This search underwent a three-stage evolution, as reflected in the collective names given to this group of drugs. At first they were called *psychotomimetic*, because they were perceived by the research scientists as mimicking the symptoms of psychoses and were used in attempts to understand the mechanisms of mental illness. In the second stage they came to be called *hallucinogenic*, when the focus was on the mechanisms of perception. The third stage characterized the drugs as *psychedelic*; here the experience, under proper conditions, was seen as one of enlightenment and productive consciousness expansion. In the psychedelic model, these drugs were seen as potential cures of the very mental illnesses that the psychotomimetic school saw them as imitating.

It would be a mistake to view these models as succeeding one another. All three terms are still used, often interchangeably, and research on these drugs continued on all three paths. It was as psychedelics, however, that these drugs came into public use and subsequent abuse.

With the psychedelic model, LSD, peyote, mescaline, the recently rediscovered psilocybin mushrooms and even marijuana, which had been smoked by ethnic and bohemian minorities before its burst of middle-class popularity, all took on a religious, mystical cast. The occult nature of the psychedelic drugs preoccupied a number of researchers, most notably a group of psychologists at Harvard University in the late 1950s and early 1960s headed by Dr. Timothy Leary and including Dr. Richard Alpert and Dr. Ralph Metzner. Under their supervision a number of artists, writers and musicians underwent the "Psychedelic Experience," wrote of their experiences in books and articles and discussed them on radio and television. A similar program on the West Coast involved Ken Kesey, author of *One Flew over the Cuckoo's Nest*.

From this point, not everyone agrees on exactly what inspired the vast popularity of psychedelics. What is certain is that their nonmedical use was widespread among young people in Europe and North America during the late 1960s and early 1970s. These drugs had a profound effect on an entire generation, shaping art, music and writing and attitudes about life, war and politics. Unfortunately, they also caused many problems, including a conviction among many young people that all drugs had consciousness-expanding qualities and were perfectly okay.

Although they were relatively rare in controlled research environments, adverse reactions to psychedelics became widespread when the drugs were used indiscriminately. The most common bad reaction was acute psychedelic toxicity, known on the street as a "bad acid trip" or a "bummer." The subjective experience in this state can be similar to that of becoming self-conscious in the midst of a frightening dream and being unable to wake up. The user is aware of having taken a drug but is incapable of controlling the powerful psychedelic effect and wants to be taken out of the state of intoxication *immediately*.

Experience has taught us that the best method of dealing with bad trips is through a reassuring and nonthreatening talkdown. This can take many forms, but usually involves the redirecting of attention away from whatever the subject sees as frightening. Restraint of any kind, bullying or treating the subject as a "sick" person only compounds the problem. Use of other psychoactive substances, such as alcohol, speed or narcotics, to counter the drug's psychedelic effects can be dangerous. An experienced physician may use a controlled amount of a minor tranquilizer, such as Valium, in extreme cases, but this should not be done ordinarily. The effects of a bad trip will ease with talkdown and as the psychedelic drug is metabolized in the body.

Longer-term effects of psychedelics include flashbacks. These are times when the consciousness effects of the drug may recur spontaneously, sometimes long after the drug has been used. No one is sure just what causes flashbacks. In and of themselves, they seem to be neither good nor bad. What's important is the subjective reaction of the experiencer. Some treat flashbacks as a free ride, a psychedelic experience without the drug. Others are frightened by the experience and take it as a sign that they are losing their minds. Again, the best treatment is reassurance that the experience of flashbacks is not dangerous and is not a harbinger of mental illness. Contrary to popular belief, flashbacks don't happen to everyone, and when they do, their occurrences fade with time. We know of no cases from personal experience or from the literature where flashbacks have taken place more than a year after the last use of a psychedelic drug.

Psychedelics rarely cause chemical dependency or addiction, but there are several long-term adverse reactions to their use. Besides flashbacks, three other chronic reactions have been recognized. These are:

1. Prolonged psychotic reactions.
2. Depression sufficiently severe as to be life-threatening.
3. Exacerbation of preexisting psychiatric illness.

All three of these reactions usually require hospitalization and psychiatric treatment. The most common complaint we have encountered, though, is a less severe form of depression that is usually characterized by what clients describe variously as "an emotional flatness," "inability to relate to the world around me," "a sense of isolation," or "feeling cut off." The symptoms described to us by these clients greatly resemble those that appear with white-knuckle sobriety in "clean" addicts. This leads us to believe that sufferers from chronic psychedelic toxicity are in need of the care and support that represent effective recovery, even though their actual drug use was incidental and not marked by compulsion, loss of control and continued use in spite of adverse consequences. Indeed, one of the clear dangers in psychedelic depression is that of self-medication with other psychoactive substances, such as marijuana, alcohol or other sedative-hypnotics or narcotics or stimulants. This only exacerbates the problem and may well lead to a full-blown addiction.

PHENCYCLIDINE, KETAMINE

Finally, there are the dissociative anesthetics, phencyclidine (PCP) (also known as krystal, angel dust etc.), ketamine and their many analogues. These drugs cross over our categories and according to dosage can have the effects of a stimulant, a depressant or a psychedelic. Their dissociative qualities make them especially dangerous in that at high dosages the user is cut off from bodily input. They are literally "feeling no pain" and are consequently at the mercy of their delusions and hallucinations. Further, these drugs stay active in the body and brain for long periods of time and can accumulate. A user may think he or she is taking reasonable dosages over time and may then go into crisis with a phencyclidine toxic psychosis. PCP users may spend weeks, even months, under the influence of the drug and suffering in a state of psychological overdose before they return to normal thinking. Often an important factor in early therapy with these people is the reassurance that they have not gone permanently crazy, that the drug simply is still in their bodies and affecting their minds.

DRUGS AND THE BRAIN

All the drugs in these four categories work through the central nervous system. The central nervous system is basically the brain and that part of the spinal cord that serves as the brain's communications center. It's here that we find the neurotransmitters, a group of chemicals that act as the brain's messengers, transmitting electrochemical impulses between nerve fibers in our brain and delivering all the messages that affect our lives and the way we do things, both consciously and unconsciously, from moment to moment. They carry information about all of our sensations—heat, cold; roughness, smoothness; brightness, darkness; pain and pleasure—to the parts of the brain that interpret these signals and act on them. The flow of these neurotransmitters control sensory input, and such reactions to it as heartbeat, temperature, blood pressure and bowel action can be triggered by an internal or external cause.

Let's look at one cluster of external causation, fear. Now, fear is fear, whether it's set off by a saber-toothed tiger at the mouth of your cave or a surprise call from an IRS auditor. A message travels from your sense organs to the central nervous system, where the appropriate neurotransmitters swing into action to produce a proper response. The response to fear includes body changes that contribute to a metabolic "operational readiness." In the case of fear, this is readiness for either "fight" or "flight." You may decide to stand your ground and duke it out with whatever menace confronts you, or you may just want to run away. In either event, pretty much the same things happen. Heartbeat quickens; pulse rate and blood pressure increase; blood vessels contract, forcing more blood to the vital organs; breathing gets more rapid; energy reserves are readied for rapid consumption. The neurotransmitters that make all this happen are called catecholamines (pronounced cat-e-ko-la-means). These catecholamines include epinephrine (adrenaline), and norepinephrine. Curiously enough, amphetamines and other amphetaminelike stimulants closely resemble these natural catecholamines, and they achieve their stimulant effect by mimicking or releasing catecholamines in the brain. This is called a sympathomimetic effect.

Fear is not the only sensation that naturally releases catecholamines. Any stimulation that calls for action on our part will do so to a greater or lesser extent. These include excitement, elation, sexual arousal, the referee's whistle or the starting pistol. These are all occasions when we speak of "adrenaline coursing through our bodies." Actually, what we're feeling are the effects of catecholamines in the brain.

Amphetamines and other stimulants mimic the natural stimulation that usually precedes physical action, and the result is interpreted as pleasurable. However, the result is also artificial. The stimulation produced by these drugs is qualitatively similar to, but far in excess of, what we normally experience in "energized" states. Also, repeated dosages of these drugs extend the state long beyond its usual duration. The compulsive use of cocaine, for example, prevents the reabsorption of the catecholamines thus increasing their brain levels and producing more stimulation. Instead of these chemicals turning off and resting once their message has been delivered, they continue zinging around the brain, setting off alarms and expending energy stores until the messengers and the energy stores are both exhausted and the entire system has no choice but to shut down.

The whole mechanism, the interaction between stimulant drugs and the central nervous system, is only now beginning to be understood. The study of drugs and consciousness—for that matter, the whole study of consciousness from a biochemical viewpoint—is a very new direction in science. This doesn't mean that what is happening is new, just that our understanding of it is becoming more refined. It has been said that more has been learned about human consciousness in the past ten years than in all of previous human history. It should be added, however, that such a statement is merely from the standpoint of Western science, and that perhaps the operative word should be "understood" rather than "learned." A little story about our own experience at the Haight Ashbury Free Medical Clinic may help illustrate the difference.

One day in the early 1970s, William Pone, a doctor from China, came to the Clinic's Drug Detoxification, Rehabilitation and Aftercare Section. As a boy in Malaysia, Pone had been instructed in the use of acupuncture, an ancient medical practice passed from generation to generation, from father to son. He became a merchant as well as a physician and in the 1930s had gone into business in China. In those days, before World War II and the Communist revolution, business was often transacted over the opium pipe. As a consequence, many of Dr. Pone's fellow businessmen became chemically dependent on opium and discovered that they were unable to stop using it on a regular basis without falling prey to the withdrawal symptoms that we encountered in detoxifying heroin addicts. Knowing that he was a doctor of the "old school," they came to him and asked for help in getting off opium. Dr. Pone used acupuncture on his colleagues, reportedly with remarkable results.

"I used a method that I had been taught for the treatment of anxiety and problems of the spirit. It involves using two needles in each ear, one in the lung point and one in the gate of heaven point, as needed. That was the only treatment I used, except for prescribing teas with restorative herbs—the way you would use vitamins. The men I treated were able to stop using opium without ill effects."

Bill Pone had read about the Clinic and about our work with heroin addicts and reasoned that we were trying to do basically the same thing he had in China years before. "Give me a small space," he asked, "and send me heroin users who are motivated to try acupuncture for their addiction. Let's see what happens."

In that most progress in the field of drug abuse treatment and most of the Haight Ashbury Free Medical Clinic's growth have come from individuals following up on an idea, we found space for Bill Pone's Acupuncture Treatment Component on the third floor of our Detoxification Unit. Intake personnel suggested acupuncture, along with counseling by our staff counseling teams, as an alternative to the "symptomatic, nonnarcotic medication" that we usually offered to help ease the pains of withdrawal from heroin.

Acupuncture didn't work with everyone, but many of the clients who opted for the experimental treatment and stayed with the program reported that pain during withdrawal was reduced at least as much as it would have been with the usual medication. We saw that acupuncture was getting results, but how did it work?

At that time, Western medical observers could explain acupuncture's success only as a result of the "placebo" effect. In other words, they assumed that acupuncture worked because the people who were treated with acupuncture believed that it would.

Every time we asked Bill to explain what acupuncture does, he would wave his hands vaguely in the air and talk to us in incomprehensible terms like "yin" and "yang," "polarity" and "energy blockages." That got us nowhere. But obviously acupuncture did work. How?

The answers were not all that long in coming. Others were asking similar questions about acupuncture and its effects on pain in general. At the University of California Medical School, San Francisco, dental researchers discovered that they could deaden pain from an exposed tooth nerve with acupuncture. Then they found that if they gave the pain-free subjects a shot of a narcotic antagonist, Narcan, ordinarily used to reverse narcotic overdose, the nerve pain would return in full force. What was going on?

At Stanford University, Dr. Avram Goldstein and a team of scientists were working on similar problems. Around the medical world, questions were being asked: "What is the relation between opiates and shock?" and "How is it that the body deals with pain?"

It was discovered that opiates, or narcotic painkillers, interact with the central nervous system through specialized sites called "opiate receptor sites." The opiate molecules attach to these sites like keys fitting into a lock. But what were we doing with specialized sites in our brains for the utilization of a drug from a plant that grows in the Middle East? In 1975, shortly after the discovery of opiate receptor sites, Dr. John Hughes and his associates announced that they had isolated naturally occurring opiatelike substances in the brains of pigs. Dr. Goldstein and his associates proceeded to do animal and human research, working out the pharmacological implications of what they called "endogenous opioid peptides," or internal, naturally produced painkillers and euphoriants.

The theoretical model that has developed from this research is as follows. In our brains we have specialized sites designed to receive internally produced substances called peptides that include endorphins and enkephalins, two types that have similar functions. Because their chemical compositions are similar, opium products and synthetic opioid painkillers use these same receptor sites. Narcotic antagonists, such as Narcan, will also occupy these receptor sites, but they have no psychoactive effect on the central nervous system. These antagonists reverse the effects of a narcotic overdose by kicking the narcotics out of the receptor sites and blocking their reattachment.

The internal peptides perform several important functions, among them regulating our pain centers by cutting off pain messages once they've been received and acted upon. This is why when you cut a finger or bash your thumb with a hammer it hurts like the dickens for a while, but later the pain is either forgotten or at least manageable, and you can go on with your activities. The peptides have rushed over and sent out neurotransmitters that tune down the pain. If pain is too much for us to handle—say we've been in a serious accident and sustained a major injury—a massive amount of internal opioid peptides are produced, and they put us into shock. Essentially a protection against traumatic pain, extreme shock involves loss of consciousness as well as depression of both breathing and heartbeat. Even with the similarities, scientists were surprised to realize that shock is the internally produced equivalent of a narcotic overdose. Yes, the scientists have determined that Narcan, which will reverse a narcotics overdose, will also reverse the symptoms of shock.

If narcotics are used on a regular basis, the body gets the message that its task of producing these peptides has been taken over, and it shuts down operation. This is one reason withdrawal symptoms occur when an opiate addict tries to quit. There are neither opiates nor endorphins there to protect the cleaning-up addict from all the pain of regaining a systemic balance. This is also why acupuncture works in decreasing the pain of opiate withdrawal. One of the things Dr. Goldstein and his colleagues, especially Dr. Li, discovered about internal opioid peptides is that their production is stimulated by acupuncture.

Discoveries about the workings of stimulants and narcotics in the brain have been echoed by discoveries concerning the other psychoactive drug groups as well. Recently the receptor sites for benzodiazepines were identified, and scientists have developed a benzodiazepine antagonist that is reported to occupy the appropriate receptor sites and reverse seda-tive-hypnotic overdoses much the way Narcan does with opiate overdose. Many of the psychoactive drugs may have internally produced counterparts, whether we are presently aware of them or not.

It is now known that most, possibly all, psychoactive substances act by enhancing or interfering with the communication between nerve cells in the brain, or neurons, by modifying the chemical signals carried by neu-rotransmitters that are passed at the synapse, or junction, between two nerve cells. We have looked at a couple of these interactions, but there are many systems involved, and they are highly complex. Each cell may have many synapses connecting a number of nerve message systems, and these may vary depending on what part of the brain is involved. Also, a single drug may affect several neurotransmitter systems at different dos-ages and in different parts of the brain. This may in part account for the dose-dependent variable reactions to PCP we discussed earlier. It may block transmission completely or replace the neurotransmitter with its own material.

Psychedelics are known to inhibit the effects of the neurotransmitter serotonin, which acts as an electrochemical messenger, regulating our perceptions in some parts of the brain, while in other parts of the brain they may mimic it or intensify its transmission. They also affect two other neurotransmitters, dopamine, which mainly affects motor coordination, and norepinephrine, both of which are among the catecholamines that we encountered earlier in connection with stimulant drugs.

One psychedelic, dimethyltryptamine, is considered by Dr. Andrew Weil to be an endogenous human psychedelic that also occurs in nature. We'll be discussing this interesting substance later when we talk about dreams. One could infer that all these relationships are analogous to those between the opiates and endogenous opioid peptides, or between amphetamines and the stimulant neurotransmitters. At the very least, one could speculate that, in terms of brain chemistry, psychoactive drugs do have internally produced counterparts.

DRUGS AND SOCIETY

OUR MATERIAL WORLD

As the pop singer Madonna keeps telling us, "We are living in a material world!" One consequence of that location is that we tend to look for material solutions to all our problems, needs and desires. If you want to go somewhere in the world, get a car! If you feel bad, take a pill! If that doesn't work, take two pills!

In our society, we are bombarded by advice on how to beat the blues, get the red out, suppress that cough all day and night, avoid the heartbreak of psoriasis and the embarrassment of hemorrhoids, get rid of nagging headaches, backaches, neuritis, neuralgia and the pain of arthritis, put spring in your step, get the lead out and take years off your life. One evening of television-watching will identify all the salves, pills, capsules, suppositories and elixirs you need to accomplish all these things and more. Almost everything you need—or can be convinced you need—is available at the local drug store or pharmacy. If you can't find it there, just go up the street to the bar or liquor store. If that won't satisfy, call up your dealer and order a lid, or a gram, or whatever measure your drug of choice comes in.

When confronted with their role in all of this, doctors complain that their patients are disappointed when they don't prescribe something at the end of a visit. Some doctors do overprescribe, but look at the spot *they* are in. If you think the general population is bombarded by drug advertising, look at a medical journal some time. Every facing page brings the solution to the physicians' most pressing cases in full color and in hype that would make the advertising director of a beer company blush. Behind every ad is a pharmaceutical company detail man or woman with a case full of free samples and other persuaders as to the efficacy of their latest product. And how do most health professionals respond to this kind of pressure? Like any other red-blooded citizens of the material world. It's an old joke in the field that a few years ago physicians seemed to be treating us for a widespread Valium deficiency.

What is true for prescription and over-the-counter drugs is equally true for the so-called recreational drugs, both legal and illegal. The legal ones are obvious. Advertising agencies employed by the tobacco and liquor industries use every positive icon they can think of, from sex, manhood and womanhood (you've come a long way, baby!) to the unachievable "good life" in order to sell their product. As with any successful campaign, it's not just the product sold, but the whole way of life that supposedly goes along with it.

In recent years, attempts have been made to limit, or at least modify, the runaway advertising of recreational drugs. Ads for hard liquor are banned from television, and no one can be shown actually drinking beer or wine on the tube unless you're watching *My Dinner with André* or a rerun of *The Days of Wine and Roses*. Cigarette packages now carry various health warnings from the Surgeon General of the United States. The industry has adopted some social consciousness. At least we are some way from the days when the likes of Humphrey Bogart and Edward R. Murrow chain-smoked on movie and TV screens, when levels of sophistication were measured by the number of champagne cocktails Mrs. North could down in one scene. It's a beginning, but we still have a long way to go.

The promotion of illegal drugs, of course, has no restrictions whatsoever. Apologists for heroin, cocaine or marijuana can say anything they want about these drugs without fear of censure by some underground surgeon general, control by an illegal food and drug administration or recourse to the Better Clandestine Business Bureau. Users of illegal drugs are truly at the mercy of an unregulated industry. Unless they have access to sophisticated testing laboratories such as those used by the Drug Enforcement Administration they have to trust dealers who say they're getting super-duper weed from the Emerald Triangle and not Indiana brown that's been laced with PCP, or Colombian cocaine, not baking soda mixed with a decongestant and the stuff your dentist shoots into your jaw to numb your teeth.

In some extreme situations, word-of-mouth counteradvertising has helped to limit some acutely dangerous drug threats. We saw this happen in the late 1960s when the street rallied around attempts to curb the high-dose intravenous injection of amphetamines. It's happening now with MPPP, an underground form of meperidine that has an impurity, MPTP, that causes Parkinsonianlike paralysis. Most of the time, though, the underground chemists and dealers have free rein, and the motto is, "Let the buyer beware!" But for all the danger and uncertainty involved, the buyer keeps buying and using. Why?

PEER PRESSURE

Peer pressure is often cited as a major incitement to drug experimentation and continued use. Among teenagers, in particular, there can be a lot of pressure to "go along with the group" and to do something because "everybody else is doing it." Anita probably drank her first beer at a party because had she not done so she would have gone against the group and been considered "out of it." Nancy Reagan and others have spearheaded a major drug prevention effort against juvenile and adolescent peer pressure in drug experimentation and use. Their recommendation is a simple one: just say no. Don't bow to pressure from your mates. Be your own person and avoid drugs.

Although we usually think only younger people succumb to peer pressure, a more subtle form of that probably led Alan to take his first snort of cocaine. He was surrounded by colleagues who were obviously using the drug. Further, his exposure to cocaine "advertising" had prepared him so that when the drug was in front of him, he was ready to try it. His friends, the media and general word of mouth had told him that cocaine would give him a lift, be an enjoyable experience and not have adverse consequences.

MEDICALLY PRESCRIBED DRUGS

As important as peer pressure is in the initiating of experimental use and the sustaining of recreational use of drugs, it doesn't fully explain the compulsive use that we associate with addiction. Other very powerful forces are at work. To those who are vulnerable to addictive disease, for instance, drugs seem at first to deliver just what they have promised.

Just as the rich are different, victims of addiction are different. They react differently to drugs than do other people. Take, for example, two people in a hospital, recovering from surgery. They are put on the same narcotic painkiller. The drug is effective with both. One, however, experiences general discomfort. The drug kills the pain, but the patient finds the side effects distinctly uncomfortable. This patient may ask for more of the drug, but only because of pain. The patient can't sleep right, feels dopey, can't eat, feels out of touch with his surroundings. Patient One develops chemical dependency and experiences mild withdrawal symptoms before leaving the hospital. Although he may experience some residual pain from the operation, he prefers the discomfort to the drugged feeling he gets from the medication. The patient says good riddance to the medication.

The second patient also experiences nausea and some discomfort the first few times the drug is administered. Soon, though, the patient looks forward to each injection. He feels all his cares and pains float away while under the drug. This patient complains that the injections are not given often enough and are not strong enough. He may go into withdrawal when the drug is stopped, but he continues to complain of postoperative pain and insists on a prescription for painkiller when released from the hospital. Every attempt to stop the prescription results in a return of "postoperative pain." The ex-patient has become drug-wise enough not to mention withdrawal symptoms to the doctor, or doctors, because more than one may be providing him with prescription narcotics, and now he is a full-fledged addict.

It is important to note in terms of this last example that when dealing with pain, overprescribing may be one problem, leading to chemical dependency, but *under*prescribing is just as great a problem. All too often doctors will not prescribe or administer enough of a drug to deal with the patient's pain level, because the doctor is afraid that the patient may become addicted. Less than 10 percent of all people exposed to narcotic drugs will fall into compulsive use of these drugs, and those who do develop chemical dependency can usually be detected and detoxified before leaving the hospital. Where chronic pain is a factor, there are alternative means of dealing with it. These are discussed later in this book. The fear that patients in general may become dependent on a drug is no excuse for underprescribing to the point where people are left in pain.

Overcoming Obstacles and Finding Help | 3

PRIMARY PREVENTION

Because drugs can be such compelling advertisements for themselves, much of drug-use prevention is aimed at keeping people from trying drugs that are considered dangerous in the first place. Many of the laws regulating drug use are established to make it difficult for people, especially children, to have access to drugs. Most potent medical drugs are available only by prescription; prescription of drugs with high abuse potential is carefully monitored by the federal government and, in many states, by medical peer boards working with the government. Legal recreational drugs, such as nicotine (tobacco) and alcohol, are available only to people above certain age limits. Legislation is pending in many states to make age twenty-one the national limit for buying alcohol. These legal drugs are also heavily taxed. This is done not only because it provides a great deal of revenue, but also in an attempt to make prices on these drugs too high for young people to afford.

The same theory is the backbone of drug enforcement in this country. The various enforcement agencies know that they cannot intercept all drugs made by underground chemists, cultivated in this country or brought in from other countries. Their stated aim, however, is to make the process of placing drugs on the market a costly proposition, thus pricing dangerous drugs out of the buying capacity of most young people. By now it's common knowledge that once someone is hooked on a drug, he will find a way to pay the price. Enforcement is like the two-dollar lock on a military footlocker. It may keep an honest person honest, but it won't stop a criminal.

What we call primary prevention is the effort, beyond enforcement, of countering the propaganda in favor of drug use. One way of doing this is to paint vividly the dark side of drugs and their consequences.

Drug prevention efforts of this type have often been so heavy-handed that they have backfired. A well-known example is the "reefer madness" propaganda perpetrated after marijuana was made illegal in 1937. Outrageous claims were made concerning the "moral and physical degradation" caused by even one use of the drug. Lurid films and articles depicted immediate addiction and corresponding corruption in one's values and actions brought on by the "devil's weed." So ludicrous were these claims that the 1935 film *Reefer Madness* became and remains a cult classic.

Long-term, regular marijuana smoking does, indeed, have long-term adverse effects. But these were not immediately apparent to its users when the practice began to proliferate in North American and Western European middle-class youth in the 1950s and 1960s.

Early experimenters in this group had grown up with the "reefer madness" propaganda of the 1930s and 1940s and were hypersensitive to any signs of danger from their own smoking. One of these experimenters "turned on" for the first time at a party in San Francisco's North Beach area with a middle-aged jazz musician friend when he was a college freshman in 1955. The young man carefully monitored himself for several days, watching for any signs of an irresistible urge to smoke more marijuana, hit a policeman, find a heroin pusher or do any of the other things marijuana "addicts" were supposed to do. All that surfaced was the recollection of some possibly pleasant sensations at the time he had smoked, but no recognizable aftereffects. Finally, he ran into the musician with whom he had gotten high and asked him point-blank, "Ted, you've been around a long time and, I imagine, smoked a lot of the stuff we smoked the other night. Do you think that it could be addictive?"

The musician shook his head and looked scornfully at our friend. "I've been smoking marijuana just about every day for the last fifteen years, and I've never seen any sign of addiction."

The young man is now in his forties and stopped smoking marijuana himself about two years ago, after using it "sometimes sporadically, sometimes regularly" for about twenty-eight years.

"And in those twenty-eight years did *you* see any sign of addiction?"

"Not as we understood addiction back then," he answered. "Grass is insidious, because as long as you're using it you don't see anything wrong with it. You match it up against all the claims made against it and say, That's bullshit! It's really a benign substance, especially compared to any of the alternatives. I became a real spokesperson for grass and defended it against its enemies.

"Since I stopped using it, though, I've realized that I'll never go back. For one thing, I don't miss it. I used to put a lot of energy into getting high, and I don't have to do that anymore. Mainly, though, its the colossal waste of time. Nobody talks about that. Here I am, forty-eight, and I'm doing things for myself I should have done in my late twenties and early thirties. I didn't because I was busy being high instead."

The dangers from such drugs as marijuana are subtle and were not immediately apparent to the users. Also, until after the late sixties, there wasn't a large pool of drug users/abusers to study. In the sixties the realization that marijuana was *not* causing the dire and immediate adverse consequences of which the "reefer madness" prevention propaganda had warned led many young people to decide that they were probably being lied to about amphetamines, barbiturates and heroin as well. This backfire of prevention efforts had disastrous results. One of the greatest disasters has been the impact of marijuana and other drugs on the very young, kids starting use at ten, eleven and twelve years of age. The result is often a loss of maturing experience that deprives young people of growth and leads to emotional flatness and loss of any motivation other than that of regaining the chemically induced euphoria they find in the drugged state.

In the seventies the emphasis in prevention shifted to clear descriptions of psychoactive drug pharmacology. In reaction to the scare tactics used earlier, many prevention speakers leaned over backward to give an objective and nonjudgmental picture of drugs, often creating an overly permissive atmosphere for indulgence and experimentation by young people. The consequences of that approach can be seen today in the need to reestablish the actual dangers of such drugs as marijuana and cocaine that were all but given a clean bill of health a decade ago.

That need has become acute with the introduction of cocaine freebasing and its facilitation through the availability of "crack." Cocaine snorting has proved to be a potentially fatal activity, but many users, even those engaged in the even more dangerous freebasing, continue to see what they are doing through the attitudes of a decade ago until they face a personal medical emergency.

Today, a variety of prevention methods are being tried, each one based on a different interpretation of the relationship between psychoactive drugs and humanity. Many well-intentioned people have returned to a modified reefer madness approach, using hasty research and speculation to back up a rigid, moralistic, selective and paternalistic approach to drug use and abuse. The main problem with this approach is that it obscures the really hopeful strides that are being made in understanding abuse and addiction as not a moral corruption but as a disease that can be treated and that, with treatment, has every indication of a successful remission.

REASONS SUBSTANCE ABUSERS DON'T GET HELP

THE MYTH OF HELPLESSNESS

There is a myth in our culture that says once you are chemically dependent—once you are addicted to alcohol or other drugs—your situation is hopeless. In part, the myth originates in the view held by many in our culture that addicts are "sick" in the sense of being morally depraved. Puritanical strains in our background often lead us to think of addicts themselves as somehow evil. This attitude works against our acceptance of addiction as a disease, not an irreversible character weakness.

This destructive fiction is fed by stories of alcoholics dying by inches under the volcano of their addiction and by films about characters like Johnny Machine, in the 1956 film *The Man with the Golden Arm*, who returns to heroin every time he gets out of jail and goes back to the old neighborhood. The myth is compounded by television and newspaper stories of prominent people who appear to be helpless in the grip of their drug habits and the sight of folks next door who can't control their compulsive smoking, coffee drinking or martini swilling. The equally effective reverse of this is seen in the glamorization of rock stars, sports figures and others whose drug use is flaunted as part of their "star" identity. Faced with this overwhelming "evidence," we are forced to accept the so-called fact, "Once an addict, always an addict."

Even well-meaning antidrug groups push this myth by overstating the case against drugs and citing "irreversible brain damage" and other dire forms of permanent deterioration as consequences of drug use and abuse in their otherwise noble efforts to keep young people from ever trying drugs in the first place. Their pronouncements may appear to be based on scientific findings, but often they are based on conjecture and negative wishful thinking. Unfortunately, their dire prognoses can dull the promise of remission and recovery from addiction, giving addicts, abusers and their friends and loved ones the message that it's already too late to do anything about their problem. "Why should I try to quit," they think, "if I have already damaged myself for life?"

Among others who don't think of themselves as being addicted but who are strongly habituated to such accepted drugs as tobacco or caffeine in coffee, there's a tendency to think, "This is the only bad thing I do." They fail to see that *any* dependence on psychoactive drugs works to their disadvantage and that there is no reason to continue a dependency.

Even the alcohol- and drug-abuse treatment communities have strengthened the myth by using faulty or incomplete treatment methods that have resulted in massive relapses among their patients.

Though the "facts" are false, the myth is powerful enough to keep many people from seeking help for the very real afflictions of chemical dependency and addiction. Against all reason, it even keeps people from attempting to rid themselves of habits that have overstayed their welcome, like smoking or drinking too much coffee. "Why should I try," they think, "when so many others have tried and failed?"

But as powerful as this myth certainly is, it has one major flaw: It's a lie. As we learn more about chemical dependency, as we understand more of the mechanisms of addiction, we realize just how great and dangerous a lie it is.

Every year more and more people enter into or continue in successful abstention and recovery from substance-abuse and addiction. Every year the examination of people in long-term recovery reveals that what was once considered irreversible physical and psychological damage from drugs and alcohol disappears with a year or more of abstinence. The long-held theory that addiction is a result of some underlying psychopathology is giving way to the realization that in most cases the psychopathology linked to substance-abuse is a result, rather than a cause, of that abuse, and with healthy, supported recovery it, too, fades with time.

Addiction, whether you call it alcoholism, chemical dependency or any other name, is a disease. Addictive disease is characterized by compulsion, loss of control and continued use in spite of adverse consequences. In other words, when the disease is active, the victim is out of control and needs help. Addictive disease can result in a number of adverse consequences. These include loss of everything in life that one values: health, ability to perform both physically and mentally, loved ones, relationships with friends and coworkers, job, property, self-respect and even life itself. The addict's process of loss has been compared to peeling an onion: It involves a lot of discomfort and grief, and in the end, nothing is left. Addiction has also been described as the building of walls that trap the builder on the inside, cut off from everything he or she holds dear. Addiction is a progressive disease that, left untreated, can result in death.

The Reality

There is good news. With treatment, the disease can be brought into remission. It can't be cured. If it could, the victim could go back to recreational use of drugs or alcohol. We know the addict can't do that. By definition, addiction involves loss of control over use, and the addict cannot regain that control. The addict can, however, lead a happy, productive, and self-fulfilling life in recovery without the use of drugs or alcohol.

The first step is getting help. That's not always easy. One symptom of the disease is that the victims often hide the unpleasant fact of their addiction from themselves or others. This is called "denial." We saw denial in action in Chapter One with both Anita and Alan.

DENIAL

In the most common form of denial, the addicts are not consciously aware of their addiction. They may realize that their lives are filled with problems, but they will perceive their drinking or other drug use as a means of coping with their troubles, rather than as the root of them. Instead, they will blame other people or circumstances for all the things that are wrong in their lives.

One reason that has been cited for this form of denial is that addiction is a misdirected dependency on the self. Someone who is totally self-dependent tends to be very concerned with self-control. To admit to addiction would be to acknowledge that the self is out of control, and this is the last thing addicts want to acknowledge, even to themselves. Instead, they will lash out at family, friends, coworkers, the other guy on the highway, the coach, anyone they can blame for their misfortunes. At the same time, they will manipulate these people into becoming "coalcoholics" who support the addicts' distorted view of reality and "enable" them to continue on the destructive path of addiction.

Anyone who comes into contact with an addict can fall into the role of being an enabler. It can be the secretary who covers for his or her boss, explaining time and again that "Mr. Bullard is in an important meeting and can't be disturbed," or, conversely, the boss who excuses a secretary's chronic Monday absenteeism. The wife who calls the office to say her husband is "running a fever and too sick to go to work" and the husband who explains to the kids that "Mommy is very tired and is upstairs taking a nap" also fall into the category of coalcoholics, or "co's."

Denial is intrinsic to the disease of addiction. We have seen it with both Anita and Al in the first chapter of this book and we will encounter it again and again in the chapters to come, especially when we discuss the "three-headed dragon" and explore the nature of twelve-step programs and the self-help movement. Denial and its effect of blocking both the primary and secondary victims of addiction from recognizing the true nature and extent of their affliction is what led many self-help adherents to insist that an addict must "hit bottom," i.e., have nothing left in life and nowhere to turn, nowhere to hide, before he will seek or accept help in dealing with his addiction. Until that takes place, it was reasoned, the addict will only seek and accept help in *maintaining* the addiction. In other words, denial will cause the addict to surround himself with enablers and do his best to shut out anyone who tries to bring him a shred of truth. Unfortunately, those who often bear most of the pain and grief in these situations are not the addicts themselves but rather those who are close to the addicts.

We tend to characterize drug abuse and addiction as "victimless crimes," but they are neither crimes nor victimless. Families and friends of abusers often suffer a great deal from their roles in the drama. Fortunately, this suffering, which includes a range of feelings from powerlessness to rage and fear that are engendered by a loved one's addictive behavior, are an increasing concern. There are a number of organizations and fellowships dedicated to helping the families and friends of the drug-afflicted. Al-Anon provides fellowship and help for the families and friends of alcoholics on the Alcoholics Anonymous twelve-step model. Alateen is associated with Al-Anon and is a voluntary program for persons age twelve to twenty who have alcoholic relatives or friends. It provides friendship, information and help with alcohol-related problems. A relatively new but rapidly growing organization is Adult Children of Alcoholics. Many chapters of these organizations are not limited to alcohol and will help those close to abusers of other drugs as well.

A primary concern of the families and friends of the drug-afflicted is how can they stop "helping" and begin to help. How can they get the addict to see the problem for what it is? How can they help the addict break through denial?

Intervention

It used to be a truism that an alcoholic or addict had to *hit bottom*, arrive at a point of total desperation, before he or she would accept the reality of the problem and seek help. That's changing now. Professionals in the substance-abuse field are learning that denial can be broken before the addict hits bottom. The most promising technique for accomplishing this is called "intervention." Intervention is a means of forcing the addict or alcoholic to look at his or her behavior without the mask of denial. There are an increasing number of experts in the practice of intervention.

The aim of intervention is to convince an addict that he or she needs help before he or she hits bottom. This is done by bringing together family, coworkers and other significant individuals in the addict's life. They are rehearsed in their roles by the intervention counselor. The idea is that they are to speak truthfully, out of love, and stick with the facts and specifics, things that the addict can't argue with. They don't recriminate, they don't judge. They confront the addict with concrete and specific instances of the disease. "On Christmas Eve, you passed out under the tree." "You missed a crucial meeting because you couldn't stop snorting coke until you were incapable of going to work." We saw intervention in action with Alan in Chapter 1. It has been said that addicts are often lured into intervention sessions under false pretenses. This is true. However, when one is in heavy denial, subterfuge may be the only way of luring the addict to the intervention site. In such a case, the ends may, indeed, justify the means. Intervention shows the addict that the game is up and that those around him will support him in trying to live life drugfree. The desired outcome of a successful intervention is that, overwhelmed by such undeniable facts, the addict admits to him- or herself that help is needed and voluntarily enters treatment.

OTHER WAYS TO GUIDE ABUSERS TO TREATMENT

TESTING FOR ABUSE AND ADDICTION

Sometimes addicts are aware of their addiction and are afraid exposure will ruin their reputation or career. This is often the case in professions where the individual is in the public eye or is held to rigid professional standards. Viewing addiction as a "moral" or "criminal" problem, where the victims must be punished, instead of as a disease requiring medical treatment, feeds this kind of denial. Such entities as the military and amateur and professional sports that have followed a program of exposing and "taking action against" members with drug problems may be doing themselves, their participants and their following a real disservice.

One recent outgrowth of our society's eagerness to "take action" against our drug problems is the demand for drug testing, which has gotten a lot of press lately. School systems seem eager to institute mandatory urine tests for all their students. Spokespersons for both amateur and professional sports leagues see periodic testing for drugs as a solution to drug problems. The military has been discharging service personnel on the basis of drug testing for a while now, and many Fortune 500 companies are eager to do the same. Many questions have been raised as to whether the mass urine screening of sports teams, high school students, employees or military units is a realistic approach to dealing with denial and uncovering drug use in schools and in the workplace. Setting the complex and difficult moral considerations and the questions of civil liberties aside, there are clinical issues that need to be fully explored. First and foremost of these is the question, "Is urine screening for drug use 100 percent accurate?" The answer is absolutely no. False positive readings on these tests have been reported to be as high as 60 percent. That means over half the results stating that people have used drugs could be incorrect. Results are often nonspecific. That means, for example, that the same reading could indicate use of an illegal stimulant drug or an over-the-counter cold remedy. Then there is the potential for human error. Even when a test is accurate, quality control in the field by technicians who are unfamiliar with the processes or who are dealing with hundreds or thousands of tests may be called into question. In view of all these facts, we would consider mass urine screening for drugs to be both counterproductive and deceptive in its results. Punitive actions should never be taken solely on the results of such screening.

We use urine screening at the Haight Ashbury Free Medical Clinic, but as a diagnostic aid or a nonpunitive additional indicator when a client is already suspected of having relapsed into use. A counselor might say, "We have a lot of things to talk about. Your actions here at the Clinic indicate that you might be using again. Among other things, your urine test came back dirty." We would never use it as a sole "proof" of use or base any action on its results.

EMPLOYEE ASSISTANCE PROGRAMS—HELP IN THE WORKPLACE

Many businesses have found a viable alternative to the "punitive" approach in adopting employee assistance programs (EAPs). These were spearheaded by the medical profession, which decided that doctors were too valuable to throw away when they developed drug or alcohol problems. Instead they set up a nationwide system for diverting doctors into treatment for addiction so that their careers would be intact and waiting for them when they were again drugfree and able to resume work.

Doctors are especially vulnerable to having their careers shattered by personal substance abuse and addiction. More important, though, is the fact that people in the health care professions are responsible for the care of others and for making life-and-death decisions every day. Abuse and its denial by physicians constitutes a public threat and cannot be tolerated. Owing to a variety of factors, including sustained stress and access to drugs, health professionals are at the highest risk for abuse and addiction of any professional group, and doctors head that list. Doctors who were placing their patients at risk by their own drug and alcohol problems had to be identified. Further, their training and experience represented a national asset that it would be tragic to lose. The State of California came up with a solution, and although it is far from perfect, it is working. The California plan has formed a point of departure for other states and other health professions, including nurses, pharmacists and dentists. This is how it works.

Legislation enacted in 1979 directed the State of California Division of Medical Quality Assurance to "seek ways to identify and rehabilitate physicians with impairment due to abuse of dangerous drugs or alcohol, or due to mental illness or physical illness affecting competency so that physicians so afflicted may be treated and returned to the practice of medicine in a manner that will not endanger the public health and safety." This legislation set in place the three major supports of physician diversion: It allowed physicians on diversion to keep their licenses intact, even though they might have violated the law; it established confidentiality for physicians in the program; and it directed that appointments to the Diversion Evaluation Committee be made strictly on the basis of expertise.

The Diversion Evaluation Committee is the body that decides whether or not a physician is treatable on the basis of data and the physician's attitude. This committee looks pragmatically for an attitude that says, "I have a problem with addiction. I can overcome this problem with medical help, but I always have to work at it, keep at top priority abstinence from drugs or alcohol and do what people tell me to do to maintain sobriety." If the physician has that sort of mental determination, then he or she has a chance to benefit from treatment and to succeed. That ability, implicit at the outset, is the prime requirement for admission into the diversion program. As is true of anyone seeking help, denial must be overcome before the prognosis is favorable.

Once a candidate is accepted, treatment elements and a monitoring schedule are combined to form an itemized treatment contract. The treatment contract is an actual contract drawn up between the Committee and the patient and signed by both parties. Elements brought together to form a comprehensive treatment contract could include:

1. Follow directions of the assigned treating physician.
2. Abstain from alcohol or other drug use.
3. Consent to body fluid testing on a random basis at specified intervals.
4. Participate in peer support group meetings and/or AA meetings with a specified frequency and verified attendance.
5. Participate in individual psychotherapy.
6. Take Antabuse (for recovering alcohol addicts).
7. Take naltrexone HCL (for recovering narcotics addicts).
8. Practice in a supervised work setting; get the approval of the committee before changing the work setting.

9. Voluntarily relinquish DEA number (this is a permit doctors receive from the Drug Enforcement Administration for prescribing controlled medications).
10. Live in a specified treatment facility.
11. Participate in a certain number of hours (up to twenty-five) of continuing medical education related to appropriate prescribing practices. (These hours are in addition to those required for renewal of license in California.)
12. Cooperate with periodic examinations by a psychiatrist who will report findings to the Diversion Evaluation Committee.

The contract is completed by a general statement that reads: "I agree to adhere to the following terms and conditions of my treatment program and agree to accept supervision to assure my compliance with these terms and conditions. The Diversion Evaluation Committee will accommodate me with written verification of my participation in this treatment program if I so request."

Treatment, rehabilitation and monitoring in the diversion program may last from three to five years. That may seem like a long time, but as Alan's wife, Madeline, said, "A lifetime's an awful lot of time to tie up in addiction." This is especially true when you throw in a lost medical education and career. Once the physician has achieved rehabilitation in the program and can safely return to unsupervised practice, the diversion program is concluded and the physician's file is purged. No records of participation in the diversion program remain.

Most employee assistance programs that are actually designed to help the employee also maintain a system of confidentiality. At most, the addict, his or her supervisor, and the consultant who refers the employee into treatment are the only people in the workplace who know what has taken place. Appropriate treatment is entered into, and when it is completed and the patient is judged to be in a sufficient state of recovery, he or she returns to work with no blot on his or her record.

Many companies now describe their EAP procedures in their employee handbooks or equivalent information sources. If a written source of information is unavailable, you can ask whoever is in charge of personnel about EAP procedures, company health insurance coverage and other pertinent details on an informational level. In situations where work performance has come into question, an employer may request that an employee see the company's EAP representative. In other cases, the employee can go directly to the representative on his own and be protected by full confidentiality.

Employee assistance program representatives are not usually direct employees of the company that they serve nor do they, themselves provide treatment. They are under contract to serve as an impartial conduit for services. They will evaluate an employee and if they consider it necessary recommend treatment and make a treatment referral. In most cases, the only thing they will report back to an employer is whether or not a deliquent employee who that employer has told to see the representative has actually done so. Information on evaluation and referral is strictly confidential.

In general, criteria for treatment referrals should include the following:

- Demonstrable knowledge of substance abuse and mental health treatment procedures and philosophy as well as a grasp of the client's clinical needs.
- A philosophic basis of no drug use during treatment.
- Directed to the special problems of the client.
- Involve the family.
- Actively help the client overcome dependence and encourage change.
- Treatment free of harangues and judgmental lectures.
- Maintain an emphasis on the present and the client's responsibility for his own recovery.
- Include adequate initial and post-detoxification evaluation to identify concomitant medical and psychiatric conditions and either provide treatment or refer for necessary treatment of these.

It should be the responsibility of both the EAP representative and the client that the treatment referent meets these requirements and is appropriate to the clients overall wellbeing.

HELPING YOURSELF

Not all drug problems require professional help or supervised treatment and detoxification. There are times when we find it easier to slide along, aware that what we are doing is probably not good for us, uncomfortable with our use, and yet unwilling to take the time or unable to spend the money that professional help requires. Yet if one had a splinter in our hand, he or she would want to get it out before it festers.

Oddly enough, we are provided with the means for dealing with splinters. In most households one can find a magnifying glass, a needle, alcohol to sterilize the needle. The basic medical lore of splinter removal is passed on, usually in the demonstration, from generation to generation. Still, we are totally unprepared for and untrained in the removal of psychic splinters. If anything, our social myth concerning the unbeatable nature of psychoactive drug habits tells us that their removal is next to impossible, even with professional help. The major drug and alcohol problems either get dealt with or lead to disaster, but what of the so-called minor ones? For want of incentive and wherewithal to deal with them, they usually fester.

One may well ask, "If it's minor, why mess with it?" Why indeed? A lot of reasons come to mind. Peace of mind and self-respect are among them. Major and minor are relative concepts. What may appear a molehill from the outside *is* a mountain if the person who is dealing with it can't climb it. Is the chronic smoker who may contract lung cancer, emphysema or another disease in any less jeopardy than the alcoholic with a deteriorating brain and liver? How about the caffeine-sensitive person who drinks four cups of coffee a day and experiences acute chest and shoulder pain?

Contrary to the old "bromide" (a form of sedative-hypnotic used before the discovery of barbiturates), neglect is rarely benign. To bring it back to our original example, the German romantic poet Rainer Maria Rilke died from blood poisoning that developed when he ignored an infection caused by a thorn that broke off in his finger when he paused in a garden to smell a rose. Doubtless this was a romantic way to die, but totally and tragically unnecessary.

The big myth is wrong. Thousands of people are getting rid of their long-term alcohol and other drug habits. We know this statistically: The consumption of cigarettes is down in certain populations; the per capita use of recreational drugs is generally decreasing. We also know this from personal experience. One colleague said about the changing consumption patterns in his own social circle:

> I really noticed the change this year during the holiday season. My wife teaches English as a second language for the community college district, and I work in community social services. As a result, we have three circles of friends that intermix to a greater or lesser extent. During December, we always attend a number of parties. These used to create a lot of wear and tear on all of us. It still takes stamina to keep up with it all, but something has changed.
>
> The change has been subtle and over time. Ten years ago, everybody drank. I remember the main concern at any party was, is there enough to drink? If the booze supplies showed any sign of diminishing, collections were taken and volunteers dispatched to the nearest liquor store. Often, the host or hostess would bring out a rolling box in the course of the evening and joints would be passed around. Even at the stuffiest parties, there would be a room or some part of the garden where reefer was being smoked. At the hipper gatherings, there were mirrors of cocaine lines being passed around. I remember parties where

the host just dumped an ounce or so on a glass coffee table along with a pile of spoons, and the guests just dug in. Some of the more clinically oriented parties scored tanks of nitrous oxide or passed out amyl nitrate poppers. A party just wasn't a party unless you got loaded in one or more ways. Everyone was busy all evening, seeing how much they could drink, smoke, inhale, or snort.

This year it's different, and it's been getting different for a few years now. In the kitchen, there's lots of Perrier or Calistoga, at the hipper parties it's designer grape juices from the Napa Valley. There's usually several bottles of red and white wine, but the people who drink them take one or two glasses and nurse them through the evening. Cocaine may be happening in the bathroom, but I haven't smelt marijuana at a party in a long time.

I don't think its a question of age or economics, or even ethnicity. The people we see represent a wide spectrum of all three. I think the health kick a lot of us are on is involved, but it may be another result, rather than a cause. It's as though a lot of people decided that there are better things in life than getting loaded.

These days, instead of bring your own bottle, or joint, or blow, now it's bring your own dish. I've gained twelve pounds in the last two weeks! It's going to take a lot of 10K runs and early morning aerobics to sweat that off!

The last decade may not have made such a marked difference everywhere, but the indications are such that we can cautiously paraphrase Bob Dylan and say, "The times, they may be changin'."

The times may be changing, but the change isn't always easy. There can be casualties along the way if one is not careful. As fate, or the "Great Editor" would have it, we ran across the following letter this morning in the advice column of Abigail Van Buren:

Dear Abby: How can a man change so much in one year? My husband used to be a loving, caring, sexually alive man. We were considered an ideal couple who never argued.

He quit smoking a year ago (doctor's orders), and now he's turned into an arguing, complaining person who finds fault with everything I do. He goes to bed mad about something every night. He lies there like a log and never makes a move toward me—no hug, kiss, or even a caress.

He has eaten himself into clothes two sizes larger from snacking from the minute he comes home from work until he goes to bed.

I long for some love and companionship. If it weren't for the children, I would seriously consider leaving him.

He refuses to talk, so we can't even talk about what's bothering him. He wasn't this way before he quit smoking. I almost wish he'd start smoking again.

How do I get a conversation going with him? Please answer soon. My marriage depends on it. I love the guy, but he's not the man I married.

His Wife

This letter doesn't tell us everything. We don't know how old the man is, or his wife, or why his doctor told him to quit smoking. On the face of it, though, this sounds like a case of our old nemesis, white-knuckle sobriety. Maybe the guy was one step away from lung cancer or emphysema, and maybe the doctor saved his life by getting him off "coffin nails," but the job is obviously not complete. The poor guy is left gritting his teeth, hating the world, and holding onto tobacco sobriety through sheer force of will. In all likelihood, his only hope is that someone—maybe his wife—will say, "You've suffered enough. Here, have a cigarette, and another, and another."

As with anything else, quitting drugs works only if one is ready to quit. Without that readiness, the best-formulated detoxification, the most well-meaning reform is useless. That doesn't mean, however, that one should continue a despised habit, waiting for the quitting genius to bop him over the head with a Newtonian apple.

This did happen to a friend of ours, a "society" woman who directed a rehabilitation program at the Clinic, among many other activities. These included chain-smoking, a habit that she often said she was ready to quit as soon as someone gave her a good enough reason. One day she arrived at work with a big smile and minus her usual wreath of Pall Mall vapors.

"I finally quit!" she announced joyfully.

"How did you do it?"

"I saw my doctor yesterday, and he told me that if I kept smoking I would lose my right leg in less than a year. *That* was a good enough reason!"

Getting rid of an unwanted drug habit isn't usually that easy. Often it's a long process. Often, too, that process involves more than one attempt at stopping. And at some point you may have to seek outside help. The comedian says, "Quitting smoking is a snap. I've done it hundreds of times." The trick is to not get discouraged. Practice *does* make perfect, and if you've tried a hundred times, maybe on the hundred-and-first you'll succeed.

In this section, it happens that most of the examples involve the use of tobacco and chemical dependency on nicotine. The information, however, is applicable to dependence on any psychoactive substance. We don't recommend trying to kick a full-blown addiction to alcohol, other sedative-hypnotics, or any drug where the withdrawal can produce physical complications or does produce such psychological problems as intense depression or anxiety, without professional help. But otherwise, it doesn't hurt to try. Tobacco makes a good example in that it is high up on the chemical dependency and addiction scale. Dr. Andy Weil has called the machine-made cigarette "the most addictive substance on Earth," and he may well be right. On the other hand, quitting cigarettes, as quitting coffee, pep pills, habitual alcohol use and drunkenness short of full-blown alcoholism, glue or nitrate inhaling and other such habits on your own may be worth a try. There is professional help available if your own efforts don't work.

One of your authors started smoking at age twelve and remained a two-to-three-pack-a-day smoker for twenty-five years. He quit eleven years ago and, aside from a few one-cigarette slips in the first year, hasn't smoked since. Here's his story.

I started smoking on the way home from Boy Scout meetings. My dad, who had dark yellowish-brown nicotine stains on his fingers, smoked Phillip Morris. He bought his cigarettes by the carton, so there were always packs lying around the house. They were easy to take and share with my friends when I wanted to feel "grown up."

When I was a freshman in high school, an older boy taught me how to inhale. The first couple of times I tried it, I got sick. Within a few days, though, I was hooked. I liked my cigarettes strong, and when I started buying my own I alternated between Lucky Strikes, Camels, Fatimas and English Ovals. When filter cigarettes came into style, I settled on Marlboroughs because they had the right image. Although I thought I was smoking purely for the image, it's obvious now that I was chemically dependent on nicotine.

When I joined the Air Force, I got my food, clothes, a barracks bunk and very little money. The first thing I did every payday was go to the post exchange and buy enough cigarettes to last until the next check. Even at PX prices, that came to a lot of money, but once I had the cigarettes in my foot locker, I felt secure. For the next seventeen years I lived in fear that I would one day find myself without cigarettes.

I returned to civilian life during the Eisenhower recession. Jobs were hard to come by, especially for an ex-GI with only two years of college, but maintaining a supply of cigarettes remained a top priority. I remember coming back to my houseboat with a quarter in my pocket. I knew there was no food. I could either buy a pack of cigarettes or a loaf of bread. I opted for the nicotine. When times got tough, I bought Bugler or Top cigarette tobacco in the can and rolled my own. When times got really tough, I wasn't above collecting cigarette butts along the road.

I never seriously thought about quitting until I was a comparatively prosperous married graduate student. Frequent colds and waking up mornings in between with a chronic cough were facts of life. So was the financial drain of maintaining a three-pack-a-day habit for two while supporting a family on the G.I. Bill. Then my wife decided that we both should quit. I tried several times, but every time I tried was a disaster. I couldn't concentrate, and my temper flared. I lashed out at everyone—students, faculty, the kids and especially my wife. For a while I only smoked at school and cooled it at home, but even that didn't work. The next step was to keep a pack stashed outside and take a walk over the hill, out of sight of the house where I could sneak a smoke. In no time I was spending most of my time taking walks. Finally I told my wife what was happening, that I couldn't quit.

We eventually broke up. On my own once more, I forgot about quitting and smoked my way through the turn of the counterculture decade on a Mendocino commune. Again it was Top and Bugler. On a beautiful spring day fifteen years ago, I met my present wife. Shortly thereafter we moved to San Francisco. I went to work at the Haight Ashbury Free Medical Clinic and began learning about drug abuse and detoxification.

One day my wife, who smoked occasionally, suggested, "Let's both quit smoking."

"Oh, God!" I thought. "Here we go again!"

But working at the Clinic was having an effect on me. I was becoming health-conscious and becoming well aware that nicotine was doing me no good whatsoever. Also, every day at the Clinic there were people with much worse drug habits that I had getting off things like heroin, barbiturates, and amphetamines. Maybe I *could* stop smoking.

There was no longer any question of conscious denial. I knew that I wanted to quit. But I also knew from my experience working with addicts at the Clinic that deep down I was still convinced that cigarettes were good for me and fulfilled a deep-felt need. I went to work on changing my belief system, on reprogramming my attitudes about smoking.

I became hyper-aware of whenever I lit up a cigarette and developed a sense of self-disgust over the whole act of smoking tobacco. I talked to myself both verbally and mentally. I catalogued the times in the day when I smoked and became aware of the cues that signaled "nicotine hunger." There were many. Every time I lit a cigarette, I would say, "Oh, no! You're doing it again!"

Not all the programming was negative. In fact, most of it was positive. The truth was that in quitting smoking I was not giving up anything. Instead, I was opening a door to things I hadn't been able to do as a smoker. I made lists of these positive elements, such as:

- being able to run up a hill without gasping for breath at the top
- singing a song without going into a coughing fit
- tasting good food
- not getting colds all the time
- smelling good
- smelling well
- going wherever I wanted without worrying if I had enough cigarettes
- waking up and doing something other than lighting up the first one of the day

The list goes on and on. It includes not having to spend increasing amounts of money on a stupid, alienating and unhealthy habit. I have no idea what cigarettes cost now, but I know that I'm saving an awful lot of money. I have probably saved enough since then to pay for our whole first trip to Europe. Interestingly enough, when I was making those lists, I didn't know the half of it. A realistic list today of the things I've been able to do since I quit smoking that I couldn't have done otherwise would be at least twice as long.

Finally, I felt that I was ready to attempt detoxification again and make a go of it. All that was left was picking the time, place and circumstances. Seeing that, among other things, I had always used tobacco for dealing with stress, I figured that it was necessary to choose a stress-free stretch of time for withdrawal. That seemed reasonable. We were planning a trip East, and I figured that would be perfect. What could be more stress-free than a leisurely trip across country? I gave away my remaining cigarettes on the morning we left and did fine until the car stopped and wouldn't start again at a desert crossroads called Rye Patch, Nevada. Finally we got the car going, but not before I had bought a pack of Marlboroughs and smoked half of them, one after another. I was afraid to turn off the ignition again, so I bought two more packs and drove all night to the nearest Volkswagen dealer in Salt Lake City, chain-smoking and feeling very, very frustrated.

Over the next clutch of months I tried to quit several times. Something always came up to shatter my projected calm and drive me back to the pack. Finally, I was explaining the whole problem to one of the counselors at work when the truth came out.

"Rick," she said, "the problem is denial."

"How can that be?" I asked in exasperation. "I want to quit. I know that I have to quit. I've done lots of work on myself."

"But deep down, you're still in denial. You are afraid that you can't quit smoking, so you give yourself an out. You maintain the fiction that you can stop only in a stress-free environment. It doesn't work that way. Life is made of stress, and if it wasn't, the part of you that wants to keep smoking would create some. If you went to a mountaintop looking for peace to quit, and there wasn't another human or Volkswagen ignition system or management auditor for a hundred miles, you would still find some way to get stressed and reach for a cigarette."

She was right, of course. Waiting for a stress-free window in which to quit smoking would take literally forever. Instead, I would set a time and do it. I would set a goal—and there was a good one. The only other reservation I had about quitting was the knowledge that my temper still got nasty every time I tried. I wasn't worried about my coworkers at the Clinic. They were used to clients acting out all over the landscape. But there was no sense in losing a good wife along with a bad habit. And she was due to attend a week-long conference in New Orleans.

That was it. I'd see her off, and when she got back I'd meet her at the airport with a big, stink-free kiss and say, "Guess what I did while you were gone, darling!"

It was a worthy goal, and I kept it in mind as I smoked the last two cigarettes in the pack as I drove home after dropping her at the airport. Let the stress factor come, I thought, I'm ready for it! At home, I went right to bed and was up early and on my way to the office. There was a lot to do at the Clinic, and I dove into it eagerly. Later, the others said that I wasn't even as nasty as I'd said I'd be. At home in the evening there were a lot of odd jobs that needed doing. I had made a list of them, and they were enough to keep me busy until bedtime the first several evenings. The cues—those times when ordinarily I would light up—like getting up, going to bed, answering the phone, writing, sitting down to watch television—came, and I would note them, and they would pass. Nicotine desire came. Someone had recommended taking several deep breaths, really deep, heartfelt sighs, any time the hunger came on. I did and it worked.

On the fourth day I woke up and didn't want a cigarette. I felt good, very good. And I knew that, after twenty-five years of fearing it, I had gone several days without a cigarette, and the world hadn't come crashing in. As far as tobacco was concerned, I had turned about in the deepest seat of consciousness. The Hindus have a word for it, *ananda*, which means mastery over some element of self. In that week I had become nicotine*ananda*. In that sense, I was free!

"Guess what I did while you were gone, darling!"

There is a responsibility that goes with freedom. It needs to be protected. I know that I can never go back to smoking. It would just kick the whole process over again.

In the first year, I did slip. I broke down and lit cigarettes on several occasions. My conditioning held, and I never took more than a few puffs before throwing the thing away with my determination not to smoke reinforced by the experience. But recovery from tobacco smoking, like recovery from any psychoactive drug addiction, is a day-to-day thing. You may forget it for periods of time, but it's still there. The instances of nicotine hunger occur, but they become rarer with the passage of time. The slight twinge I felt while writing this personal case study is the first I remember in quite a long while. Deep breathing still works.

But I do understand the husband of the woman who wrote to Dear Abby. He is going through hell, and I hope he discovers where his devil is and gets help with it before it's too late.

Detoxification, whether accomplished with professional help or on your own, is just the beginning. The quality of the rest of your life depends on what you and others bring to it by way of recovery.

FINDING OUTSIDE HELP

Whether it's the inability to stop buying and sniffing cocaine by the gramful or drinking too much coffee, there's someone who can help.

Access to treatment is available through a variety of sources. Many businesses, professional organizations and sports leagues that have adopted the employee assistance program concept have EAP consultants on contract who will talk to you on a confidential basis and make a treatment referral if one seems appropriate. Your family doctor or medical group is another good source of information, treatment, or referral. Every state government has a substance-abuse coordinator working through either the state health or the state mental health office. These coordinators maintain information on treatment facilities within their jurisdiction. Further, many states have county-level coordinators who are even more directly familiar with what is available in their area. At the national level there is an organization called the American Medical Society on Alcoholism and Other Drug Dependencies, AMSAODD, that lists specialists in these fields. AMSAODD is currently working with other organizations in the treatment field to develop a national computerized treatment referral and consulting service. Anyone seeking treatment should learn as much as possible from these sources about the services available and try to choose one that is appropriate to his or her needs.

One does need to be careful in seeking help. Surprisingly, treatment and even diagnosis of substance-abuse and addiction are not part of the regular medical school curriculum. A few of these schools have had the benefit of "career teachers in substance abuse," experts in the field who were subsidized by the government to teach medical classes on diagnosis and treatment. The program was dropped, however, when the Reagan administration reorganized the National Institute on Drug Abuse and its sister institute on alcoholism in the early 1980s. Only a few of these career teachers have been kept on staff at their schools. One of these, John Chappel, M.D., at the University of Nevada Medical School at Reno has conducted nationwide attitudinal studies among doctors in conjunction with the Haight Ashbury Free Medical Clinic. These studies indicate that most practicing physicians not only have an abysmal ignorance about substance-abuse and addiction but are highly prejudiced against drug and alcohol misusers as well.

Doctors responding to Chappel's studies indicated that they would go out of their way *not* to treat anyone they suspected of abuse or addiction. Many current laws governing the practice of medicine reinforce this predilection by subjecting physicians who do treat abusers and addicts to intense scrutiny by enforcement agencies and peer review boards that often share the general lack of knowledge about abuse and addiction.

Acting out of fear, ignorance or prejudice, physicians will often miss a primary diagnosis involving drugs or alcohol. They may miss the *primary cause* of stress in the home or a history of accidents and minor illnesses. At times they will prescribe the very drugs that can lead to an exacerbation of the problem. Misprescription often results from a doctor losing touch or not keeping up with developments in pharmacology.

In recent years and in conjunction with many colleagues, your authors have developed and presented continuing medical education courses in prescribing practices that are aimed at the "dated" doctor. In many states, physicians are required to take a certain number of educational units per year as part of their license requirements. These courses include updates on the nature of all psychoactive drugs, guides to diagnosis, alternatives to chemical treatment, role play on dealing with drug abusers who try to "scam" prescriptions and attitudinal work. It is our belief that such courses, taken on a regular basis, should be a requirement for all practicing physicians.

WHAT TO LOOK FOR IN A PHYSICIAN

Attitude is probably the first thing to look for when seeking treatment. Is the physician open to your problem and willing to discuss it on a nonjudgmental basis? This doesn't mean you should seek out someone who will agree with all your wishes. You want someone who will help, not another enabler. Understanding what this means is relatively new to the medical profession. At a recent panel on "Chemical Dependency and the Twelve Step Recovery Process," John Chappel, M.D., introduced himself by saying, "My name is John Chappel, and I am a recovering enabler."

Look for someone who is knowledgeable. The treatment person should know something about the drug and its effects. Be wary of a physician who is all too ready to prescribe another psychoactive for your problem. An example of this is the physician who thinks he or she is solving a Valium dependency problem by shifting a patient to another benzodiazepine, such as Librium or Ativan. All sedative-hypnotics produce cross-dependency, and such a strategy is like prescribing vodka for an alcoholic whose drug of choice is gin.

Finally, does the physician seem well versed on the available treatment options? Can he or she go to appropriate sources, such as AMSAODD, or the local substance-abuse coordinator's office, or his own file for appropriate referrals? Does he or she know which recovery programs will be uniquely helpful for the particular patient? There is a lot of difference. For example, someone with a dual diagnosis, say an alcoholic who is taking lithium for a manic-depressive disorder, should not be sent to an AA group that will object to the patient's using the lithium necessary for treating that disorder.

All these guidelines are equally applicable to therapists, counselors, psychologists and other mental health professionals as well as to physicians and psychiatrists.

WHAT TO LOOK FOR IN TREATMENT PROGRAMS

If you are directly seeking treatment for yourself or another, the same criteria apply. While there are many legitimate treatment programs in the field, there are those that may border on the sadistic in their approach, as well as "country club" programs that are more enabling and reinforcing than treating. Learn what procedures have worked with your particular problem and what sorts of programs offer them. Know what is inappropriate. For example, someone with a low-dose, borderline codeine dependency shouldn't go into methadone maintenance, while a person with a chronic pain condition or who controls a seizure problem with phenobarbital probably shouldn't be in a drugfree therapeutic community. Working from a position of knowledge, try to find a program that is philosophically, attitudinally and practically in keeping with your needs.

Chronic pain may call for some specialized treatment or training on the therapist's part. There are pain clinics that teach individuals how to manage without resorting to narcotic drugs. We know, for example, that for some people acupuncture provides a rapid means of fighting drug hunger by stimulating production of the same peptides we get from running and other physical exercise. The only problem is that it may be much easier to find a running track than an acupuncturist when needed. Acupuncture also sometimes works for the withdrawal pain from kicking a number of drugs, including heroin, cocaine and tobacco.

Emotional pain and a need to develop emotional control may yield to training in biofeedback or a variety of meditational and yogic practices. Biofeedback works by channeling the mind into a state of relaxation. Similar results have come from creative activity, such as painting, crafts, music and do-it-yourself projects.

It's surprising how many things and activities in our world can be therapeutic if we let them, and we'll be discussing these in depth in the next two chapters. Often it's a question of being aware of what is right for you physically, emotionally, and psychologically, and acting on those feelings.

DETOXIFICATION

In discussing treatment, we must keep in mind that only a small portion of alcohol and other drug problems are represented by addiction. Further, the example discussed above shows an enlightened and progressive approach to substance-abuse treatment. Unfortunately, most people won't be able to count on that level of support. Most drug afflictions involve some degree of chemical dependency, and may even involve compulsive use, but they are not out of control. If there is a turning point from abuse to addiction, loss of control is the primary indicator for addiction. Often in these situations, denial is not a factor at all. Many of us are well aware that we have problems and would be happy to deal with them if only we knew where to go, whom to see or even just where to begin seeking help. Whether the problem is heroin, cocaine, cigarettes, Valium or coffee, the first step is usually some form of detoxification. This means ridding the body of the toxic substance.

The two most important factors in detoxification are time and the body's self-healing qualities. As self-perpetuating organisms, we are preprogrammed to achieve a physical balance. Drugs represent an intrusion onto the body's turf that forces it out of equilibrium. Many of the symptoms that we relate to drug withdrawal are simply the organism's overreaction as a preparation to reestablishing balance. These symptoms usually appear as the opposites of the drug's desired effects. For example, withdrawal from stimulants usually involves depression, while withdrawal from depressants usually involves overstimulation. Withdrawal from narcotics, which cause calmness, drying out of mucous membranes, chronic constipation and pain control, usually results in anxiety, a runny nose, diarrhea and pain.

Most of what we consider detoxification involves various means of mediating the withdrawal symptoms and helping the withdrawing individual to avoid relapse into drug use in the face of those symptoms. Each type of drug has its own effective form of detoxification, to some extent dictated by the nature and seriousness of the withdrawal symptoms.

There are many varieties of treatment available to people with alcohol and other drug problems. The best of these treatment programs involve an ongoing "continuity of care" and are long-term. In the substance-abuse treatment field, we have learned that addiction and abuse are not diseases that can be "cured" simply by detoxification, or ridding the addict's system of the drug. Detoxification may remove the drug, but it does nothing about drug hunger, the overwhelming desire to use again that most addicts experience both during withdrawal and sporadically after they are clean.

A good treatment program will start with detoxification but will continue from there into aftercare and, with addiction, recovery treatment.

SEDATIVE-HYPNOTICS

If one is detoxifying from a sedative-hypnotic, such as alcohol, benzodiazepines, or barbiturates, withdrawal can be life-threatening. In order to avoid dangerous seizures during the withdrawal, detoxification from these drugs is usually done in a hospital. The most common method is to substitute another, longer-acting drug, such as phenobarbital, and then decrease the dosage from the equivalent of what the patient is addicted to down to zero over a period of days or weeks. In that sedative-hypnotic drugs are also anticonvulsants, convulsions and seizures are often, but not always, a feature of their withdrawal. In that these can be life-threatening, another anticonvulsant, in this case a long-acting and easy-to-regulate drug, is used to ease the patient through the dangerous period. This substitution and withdrawal can be done on an outpatient basis, but that is not recommended. In a hospital, vital signs can be monitored at all times, and crises can be dealt with immediately.

NARCOTICS

Detoxification from narcotics, such as heroin or morphine, can often be accomplished on an outpatient basis. Withdrawal from these drugs can be uncomfortable, even painful, but it is not life-threatening, so there's greater leeway in handling it. Before the advent of heroin treatment centers in the 1960s, when treatment was provided only at federal correction facilities such as the one at Lexington, Kentucky, the options available to narcotics addicts were drug maintenance on methadone or detoxification in prison. This was done "cold turkey," or without any drugs. Counseling, aftercare and other treatment components that seem so important today were not offered, and the fact that prisoners released from these programs with little other support than "guidance" from parole officers quickly returned to drug-seeking and using behavior only added to the myth of irreversible addiction. Today there are more options available for narcotics withdrawal. Therapeutic communities, or TCs, are self-contained programs where the addicts may undergo withdrawal and live for a period. Some individuals in some of the more radical TCs, such as Synanon, held the opinion that the best period is the rest of one's life. Often, the TC philosophy and practice is for the individual to remain drugfree, even during withdrawal. This is chemical cold turkey, but the community usually maintains a high level of support to counter withdrawal and to create a healing atmosphere for aftercare and recovery.

Our own narcotics detoxification program at the Haight Ashbury Free Medical Clinic is a modified medical model that makes use of both counseling and "symptomatic medication." At intake, clients are given a physical examination, complete a personal medical history and are assigned to counseling teams. During withdrawal they come to the Clinic daily and spend an hour with a member of their counseling team. During that counseling session the client's withdrawal symptoms are assessed and the client is given one day's nonnarcotic medication. The medication is specific for the symptoms that the client is experiencing at that time or for symptoms he or she reports having experienced in the previous twenty-four hours. These medications don't totally suppress the withdrawal symptoms—anything that would do that would be as addictive as the drug he or she is trying to kick—but they do help, and they do keep the client coming in for counseling. At the Merritt-Peralta Institute, where David Smith, M.D., is the research director, clinicians are accomplishing inpatient opiate detoxification with the nonnarcotic drug clonidine. The aim, beyond detoxification, is to get the client into drug-free aftercare and then into abstinence and recovery.

STIMULANTS

Withdrawal from stimulants is rarely life-threatening and involves even less physical discomfort than withdrawal from either sedative-hypnotics or narcotic painkillers. There is, however, a high degree of drug hunger, especially with cocaine and amphetamines. This can be coupled with intense bouts of depression. The out-of-control stimulant addict often finds it very difficult to stop using when left to his or her own devices. For this reason, some period of inpatient treatment can be the best course to follow. The clinical criteria that are used in these cases include the degree of denial, the amount of physical and psychological toxicity to the drug, and the client's vulnerability to drug hunger. Cocaine addicts often respond well to social model detoxification in drugfree programs that offer direction, counseling and access to self-help without needing to provide the medical backup necessary in sedative-hypnotic detoxification.

Cocaine treatment is currently expanding at a great rate, partly because cocaine abuse and addiction are on the increase and partly because many cocaine abusers and addicts are of the middle and upper middle income groups and can afford a variety of innovative treatments. Programs range from expensive "country club spa-type" programs featuring massage, hot tubs, saunas and trendy cuisine in appropriately breathtaking rural settings, through equally expensive chemical dependency hospital units, to clinical outpatient counseling and support groups. Cocaine users tend to respond well to twelve-step programs, such as Alcoholics Anonymous chapters that will accept mixed drug addictions, and often go into these directly. There is now a Cocaine Anonymous twelve-step program with meetings in many parts of the country.

Some people can deal with detoxification in the midst of their day-to-day life. But many others respond best to a healing time away from work, family, friends and familiar, often painful surroundings. For these people, residence in therapeutic communities, live-in programs devoted to the transition from use to recovery, and even some time in a halfway facility may be best. In all forms of detoxification, appropriate and ongoing counseling is an important component of treatment.

There are some individuals—usually long-term high-dosage narcotics abusers—who seem to be either incapable of detoxification from their drug of choice or incapable of staying clean for more than a few days or weeks when they have detoxified. This handful has gone from treatment to treatment, failing with each in turn. The solution at present for these "permanent" addicts is maintenance of their narcotic addiction with a long-acting synthetic opioid called methadone. In Britain, a similar population was maintained on government-issued heroin until the abuses became too great. Methadone is used here because it can be taken orally and one dose lasts at least twenty-four hours. Also, we have a national fear of heroin. The reasoning is that addicts on methadone maintenance are at least out of the criminal underground in which heroin use would place them. With methadone they can lead fairly normal lives, hold down some types of jobs, and so on. But in fact methadone produces a stronger chemical dependency than does heroin and is harder to detoxify. Some people may, indeed, "need" methadone maintenance, but experience in areas that have cut back on this drug maintenance approach to addiction indicates that many people on methadone should move to recovery-oriented treatment approaches and learn to live comfortable and responsible lives without the use of psychoactive drugs.

At the other end of the scale, there are such borderline situations as those involving self-medication with drugs or alcohol for physical and emotional pain or such disorders as sleeplessness or depression. Often a potential drug problem can be nipped in the bud by a visit to a competent physician, by education or by an informed review of one's life-style in general. The worst thing anyone who thinks he or she has a problem can do, however, is nothing.

AFTERCARE

Aftercare is the process of returning a postdetoxification drug client to society. Recovery is the ongoing ability of an addict to live a productive and satisfying life without the use of psychoactive drugs. Recovery is not just being drug- or alcohol-free. It involves education, self-help and ongoing support for the recovering addict. The individual who attempts to maintain abstinence in the face of drug hunger without support is often a victim of white-knuckle sobriety, a stressful state that can lead to mental or physical illness and that usually results in relapse to active addiction.

More treatment programs are taking an active role in recovery, both within their own care structure by offering inpatient and outpatient aftercare services and by incorporating and referring to self-help organizations. The self-help movement, composed of such programs as Alcoholics Anonymous, Narcotics Anonymous, Cocaine Anonymous, Al-Anon, Alateen, and others, is one of the most effective recovery tools there is. These programs get results. They are responsible for keeping untold numbers—perhaps millions—of people in recovery and sobriety in many countries. The treatment community is coming to recognize this fact, and more treatment agencies are increasingly interacting with the self-help and recovering community, maintaining chapters within their treatment facilities and referring their graduating patients to these programs.

While it may be true that not all drug problems involve addiction, anyone who thinks he has a substance-related problem probably does. Treatment can be a full course, including intervention, detoxification, aftercare, recovery and self-help, or it can be any aspect of help that may be needed. Even when receiving treatment for problems with the same drug types, individuals may require different approaches. The same thing doesn't work for everybody.

Treatment can include individual psychological counseling, group therapy or family counseling. Support groups are often designated for specific drug problems, such as Valium abuse, or related to one's profession, such as nurses or professional football players, or may even represent a combination of both—for example, a support group for cocaine-abusing professional people composed of entertainers, stockbrokers, lawyers and so on. Detoxification may take place in a hospital (inpatient) or by appointment at a clinic or doctor's office (outpatient).

SEX AND DRUGS AND . . .

Long before the advent of rock 'n' roll, sex and drugs became inextricably mixed in the human imagination. On one hand, this probably had to do with the ability of both sex and drugs to bring about altered states of consciousness. The altered states produced involved a rapid onset and superficially similar effects. Those who inject stimulants or narcotics often describe in sexual terms the initial "rush" when the drug hits their systems. They describe this rush as being like a "full body orgasm." Various drugs have been seen through history as being capable of enhancing sexual experience. Other drugs have been seen as facilitating sexual performance either through the reduction of inhibitions or the actual increasing of potency, and, with men, the ability to maintain an erection when necessary.

In 1981 the Haight Ashbury Free Medical Clinic hosted a national conference on Sexological Aspects of Substance Use and Abuse. We learned that although some drugs may appear to enhance sexual activity, and at first may even facilitate performance to some extent, long-term or excessive use of any psychoactive substance usually leads to some form of sexual impairment.

With some drug patterns, the impairment is obvious and widespread. In the case of intravenous narcotics users, for example, the drug rush often replaces sex. Many habitual abusers are incapable of performing sexually, and couples instead shoot up together for a mutual rush experience. Sedative-hypnotic drugs, such as alcohol and barbiturates, may at first seem to facilitate sexual activities by breaking down social and psychological inhibitions, but their abuse often leads to impotency in men and a lack of sexual desire in both men and women. Such powerful stimulants as amphetamines and cocaine may actually facilitate male performance at first, but the abuse of these drugs can also result in impotency and decreasing libido.

Drugs can also become involved in a wide variety of psychological, physical, social and spiritual anomalies surrounding sexual activities. Some users discover that they can perform only while on a certain drug. Others find satisfaction only in sexual activities that for various reasons require total chemically induced disinhibition. The psychology of sex is very complex and has become a science in its own right. The effects of drugs play an important role in its study.

Unfortunately, sexual impairment is one symptom of drug abuse and addiction that may not automatically go away with abstinence and recovery. Counselors or peers who may not realize this pass off continuing impairment as a temporary problem. They may do a real disservice by advising patience and suggesting that the problem should go away by itself. A recovering person who is experiencing ongoing sexual problems should do something about them.

For men, impotence may be a complex matter with both organic and psychogenic components. Few, if any, simple assumptions should be made about its probable cause and duration in recovering men. Although some libido problems are common at the beginning of recovery, if you become concerned, we would recommend an examination and counseling specifically directed to sexual issues. Kathleen O'Connell points out that many men also have sexual insecurities and fears in early recovery, but most of these can be corrected by acknowledgment and education. On the positive side, men in recovery often are able to get more in touch with their own sexual needs. They can develop patterns of relaxing and taking care of themselves, of being vulnerable and feeling human beings. This can lead to greater intimacy and increased ability to respond to the needs of a sexual partner as well.

Women in early recovery may experience a period of obsession with sex or may spin romantic fantasies. O'Connell feels that knowing beforehand that this may be the case helps these women avoid embarrassing situations. She also points out that women entering recovery should see a gynecologist. Weight loss during addiction and abuse may interfere with the menstrual cycle. There may also be urinary tract infections and other problems resulting from poor hygiene and a rundown condition during the time of abuse.

Both men and women may develop sexual dysfunctions either before or during addiction. Often the abuse itself may have been an attempt to deal with overblown inhibitions or a personal sense of inadequacy that may rebound after withdrawal. Activities indulged in during addiction may have a major negative effect on one's self-image and sense of self-worth that are reflected in sexual concerns. Further, the taboo that many still adhere to about discussing sexual concerns with others can inhibit dealing with problems that arise in early recovery.

Sometimes sexual problems can be indicative of even more basic changes in the individuals involved. Recovering individuals may discover that they are no longer compatible with long-time partners, and vice versa. O'Connell cautions that people in early recovery should wait at least sixty days before making major decisions in their lives; making decisions about separation or divorce is probably not wise during this time. Among other things, such decisions may be based on guilt and could be regretted later. Often it is better to give things a chance to work themselves out.

"Often during early recovery couples get in touch with the knowledge that they really do love each other, and this is a time when they are able to rediscover their shared love. Early recovery is a rocky time, and it is important for couples to have faith in each other. Usually their old feelings of caring for each other will surface again as a result of abstinence."

Good sex, and love, are gifts of recovery and of abstinence that may take a little work to open and enjoy. Let us assure you, however, that the effort is worth the taking.

SECONDARY VICTIMS

Identification, intervention and treatment need to go beyond the addict. Help must also be extended to the secondary victims. These others are deeply and profoundly affected by the disease of addiction. The people whose lives are affected by addicts may be family members. They may be friends or business associates. Or they may be complete strangers. Strangers? The people who share a compulsive smoker's carcinogens in a close room are often strangers. So are the victims killed on our highways by drunk drivers.

The most likely way of helping the strangers who become secondary victims of addictive disease is by identifying and helping the primary victims. More may be necessary for those who are close to the primary victims, however. Al-Anon, Nar-Anon and the rapidly growing Adult Children of Alcoholics are all self-help programs that directly involve coalcoholics and coaddicts. These programs attempt to do for the families of addicts what their self-help counterparts, Alcoholics Anonymous, Narcotics Anonymous and Cocaine Anonymous, do for the addicts themselves, and that help is often sorely needed.

Families of dependent people often become victims of codependency. What is codependency? According to spokespersons at St. John's Hospital of Salina, Kansas, codependency is a set of maladaptive, compulsive behaviors learned by family members in order to survive in a family that is experiencing great emotional pain and stress. These behaviors are passed on from generation to generation whether alcoholism is present or not. In other words, the original alcoholic or drug-dependent person may have been a great-grandfather. No one else for three or four generations may actually become alcoholic, but most family members within those three or four generations have learned to use a set of behaviors that help them deal with the emotional pain and stress inherited from the original alcoholic family and which continues to create emotional pain and stress. This set of behaviors eventually becomes codependency or dependency disorders.

Some of these codependency or dependency disorders are: perfectionism, workaholism, procrastination, compulsive overeating, compulsive gambling, compulsive buying, compulsive lying, compulsive talking, dependent relationships. Other dependency disorders can be dependency on acquiring status, prestige, material possessions, power or control to the extent that one's behavior causes problems in social interactions with family members, coworkers, friends, authority figures and others. In addition, persons suffering from alcohol- or drug-related codependency or one of the other dependency disorders often experience themselves as being caught up in a kind of treadmill existence, so that whether or not goals are achieved, there is still a compulsion for more, an anxious feeling of incompleteness or emptiness that persists no matter what is accomplished.

Health problems can also exist, such as migraine headaches, gastrointestinal disturbances, colitis, ulcers, high blood pressure and many other stress-related physical illnesses. Emotional problems such as depression, anxiety, insomnia and hyperactivity are evident in many codependents.

Codependency and other dependency disorders result in:

1. Inability to know what is "normal" behavior.
2. Difficulty in following a project through.
3. Difficulty in knowing how to have fun.
4. Judging the self without mercy and having low self-esteem.
5. Difficulty in developing or sustaining meaningful relationships.
6. Overreacting to change.
7. Constantly seeking approval and affirmation, yet having no sense of self-identity.
8. Feelings of being different.
9. Confusion and sense of inadequacy.
10. Being either superresponsible or superirresponsible.
11. Lack of self-confidence in making decisions, no sense of power in making choices.
12. Feelings of fear, insecurity, inadequacy, guilt, hurt, and shame that are denied.
13. Inability to see alternatives to situations, thus responding very impulsively.
14. Isolation and fear of people, especially authority figures.
15. Fear of anger and criticism.
16. Being addicted to excitement.
17. Dependency upon others and fear of abandonment.
18. Confusion between love and pity.
19. Tendency to look for "victims" to help.
20. Rigidity and need to control.
21. Lying when it would be just as easy to tell the truth.

(St. John's Hospital Chemical Dependency Treatment Center, 1985.)

Although not everyone who encounters these symptoms is suffering from codependency, the symptoms do indicate the wide range of problems to which those close to addicted persons, including family three or four generations removed, may be vulnerable.

In her book, *Codependency, An Illness, Describable and Treatable*, Sharon Wegscheider-Cruse defines codependency as "a specific condition characterized by preoccupation and extreme dependence on another person—emotionally, socially, sometimes physically.

"This dependence, nurtured over a long period of time, becomes a pathological condition that affects the codependent in all other relationships."

Sharon and her husband, Joseph Cruse, M.D., who founded the Betty Ford Institute, are pioneers in recovery-oriented treatment for the drug- and alcohol-dependent. She has been especially active in the development of treatments for the codependent. As a champion for providing treatment for family members as well as for the dependent person, she points out that ignoring the people around the abuser is unfair not only to the codependent but to the addict as well.

In her frequent presentations on this theme to colleagues around the country, Sharon often makes use of a very effective tableau to show just how the dependent individuals can affect everyone around them, and vice versa. Using volunteers from the audience, she begins to construct her tableau. She starts with the dependent one. He or she can be a pillar of the community, perhaps a physician. As this person is larger than life to those around him or her, he or she stands on a chair. As other players are added—the spouse, his parents, her parents, the children—it's easy for us to get drawn into a family and a community drama.

The community is small, close-knit and Middle American, the kind of place Charles Kuralt loves to visit when he's on the road. Standing on the chair is John Arlington, and next to him, holding onto his jacket, is his wife, Betty. John's father, Matthew Arlington, is the town doctor, a pillar of the community. Next to Matthew is his wife, Martha. She adores him, as does his son John. John wishes that his father had played baseball with him some time, or at least had looked at the A papers he brought home from school. Sometimes it seems to John as though his father only payed attention when he did something wrong. Like the time he and Lenny stole a case of beer off the back of Tom Brady's delivery truck. He caught holy hell from his father for that one, while his good deeds brought only mild indifference as a response. But then, Matthew Arlington was the town doctor and a very busy, self-sacrificing man.

Across the street, in the house with the maple tree and the two dormers, live Marvin Bullard and his wife, Peg. Marvin owns the general dry goods store. Marvin is a hard worker and a good provider. He is also an alcoholic.

His daughter, Betty, doesn't know her father is an alcoholic. For years, Peg has done a masterful job of covering up and maintaining a household state of denial about Marvin's "problem." To Betty, then, everything is exactly as it should be. Hers is a normal family. Years later, she marries John Arlington, whom she has dated off and on in high school, after he finishes medical school; it is partly because he reminds her so much of her father.

The times are prosperous and the town is expanding. There's more than enough with the new population to overwork two town doctors. In fact, besides their private practices, both Matthew and John are on staff at the new municipal hospital over in the county seat. Every now and then they run into each other in the hall. When they do, Matthew pats John on the shoulder the way he did when John was a boy and says, "I hear you're doing well, son. Keep up the good work." Then he walks on before John can answer.

John and Betty have a pleasant ranch-style house that reflects his status as a physician and her ability as a homemaker and is more than adequate for them and their three children. It's out near the country club, where Betty, like her mother before her, is a leader in club and civic activities. She is also an adoring and supportive wife.

There isn't much love between them, but that seems natural to Betty. After all, she grew up in a house where love got lost early on among the blackouts, the accidents, the stumbling late-night urinations on the floor or in bed, the hushed-up scenes and the excuses. She knows that its her "duty" to keep the wraps on her husband's "problem." It's all very normal. It's the only life she knows.

With the virtual nonexistence of intimacy, Betty learned that, like her mother, she could exert power over her husband—and the rest of her family—through the manipulation of guilt and the use of emotional repression. In their own ways, each of her three children learned the same lesson.

In the spring of 1978, the club honored John and Betty with its "Model Family of the Year" award. The next day was their youngest daughter's birthday, but John had celebrated a little too much. He passed out face down in his daughter's birthday cake and was rushed to the hospital. Dr. Gray, John's colleague and family friend, explained that John was under tremendous stress from his medical work. That explained the car accidents and other accidental injuries that his medical records showed. He explained that John would be kept at the hospital for a few days for observation, although he assured the family that it was already hard to keep him in bed. He wanted to be up and treating the other patients in his ward. Dr. Gray prescribed 10 milligrams of Valium, as needed, for Betty, to see her through the stress brought on by John's "attack." She still takes five or six of the little blue pills daily, as needed. And she sleeps a lot.

Jeff, the oldest child, finished college and went on to Harvard Law School. He'd seen what the medical profession had done to his father and his grandfather and was having none of it. "I'm not going to be caught in that trap. I'm going to be the best damned corporate lawyer in the country. Make my pile early on and retire to a Greek island—or maybe get into politics. I don't have to be a workaholic doctor. I'm on my own, you know. Always have been. My father never paid any attention to me, and my mother? Ha!"

The middle child, Ella, was having trouble in school: running with the wrong crowd, cutting classes, probably using drugs. John was shocked and defensive when the principal called. He handed the phone to Betty and dashed out the door, muttering about being late for an appendectomy.

"What?" she said. "My little Ella? I don't believe it. There must be some mistake. She's quiet and well-behaved around here. If there's something wrong, it must be your fault. You're not doing your job!"

Fran, the youngest, is the family cutup. She's always doing something "cute" to get Mommy's and Daddy's attention. Her doctor is treating her hyperkinesis with Ritalin, but it doesn't seem to be doing much good.

If this were one of Sharon's tableaux, there would now be a number of people on the stage. First of all, there's John standing on his chair. Betty is a little to the front, looking up at him adoringly, holding his jacket and often keeping him from falling down. Next to her, Peg is doing the same for Marvin. Matthew and Martha are on the other side, with Matthew staring off into space. The children, Jeff, Ella and Fran, are all in front. Fran may be on the floor, throwing one of her tantrums. Betty may be looking a bit unsteady, but Dr. Gray is right there to hand her little blue Valiums, as needed.

As the family situation deteriorates, more volunteers are added. There's the principal from Ella's school, but by now Ella has run away and been arrested for possession and soliciting in Chicago. Add the policeman and the public defender whose phone call John hasn't gotten around to answering. Add others: Jeff's on-again, off-again girlfriend who can't understand why he can be cold and emotionless and then fly into rages over nothing. Add Fran's doctor and distracted teachers, kindergarten through third grade. We could go on. All these people, in one way or another, are holding onto the central figure, John.

Obviously, the chances are poor that these people could ever get it together to initiate an intervention. They have all adapted to the situation and are used to being part of the problem. However, let's say a miracle occurs and John enters a residential treatment program to deal with his alcoholism. Take him off the stage for three months. What do we have left? A lot of people leaning inward and clutching at an empty space above a chair.

John makes excellent progress. Say he's hit bottom and is highly motivated. The weeks pass, and he learns about addictive disease. He embraces the actuality of abstinence and recovery. Finally, the time is up and he comes home.

Up on stage, there's this mass of people, all off-balance, all clutching the space above the chair that John is about to reoccupy. He comes down the aisle of the auditorium waving his diploma, standing tall, smiling and shouting: "I'm free! I'm free!" Facing him in disbelief and incomprehension is the knot of grotesquely intertwined friends and loved ones leaning toward an empty chair.

Much of Sharon Wegscheider-Cruse's work has involved dramatically showing the impact of dependence on the family and community. Happily, the treatment community is beginning to take notice of these needs beyond the addicted or dependent individual. She has been instrumental in starting several treatment programs that include the family in the latter stages of residential treatment, while more and more programs are involving the family in their aftercare activities.

We believe that her work represents a wave of the future, a necessary step that treatment must take if it is to become effective. Ideally, such family-oriented treatment should also extend to the community. A key factor in accomplishing this is the destigmatizing of addiction. Once drug dependence becomes generally recognized as a disease, not unlike diabetes, that can be brought into remission, then it will become easier for the community at large to participate in both the rehabilitation of the victims and the prevention of the contagion. In addiction, we have a disease that has long lurked in the shadows. Feeding our fear and denial, it has affected succeeding generations of victims as well as those close to the victims. It needs to be brought into the light of human understanding and compassion if it is ever to be dealt with effectively.

The tide does appear to be turning. Many people in our culture have come forward to talk about their own personal battles with addiction. These include such role models as politicians, sports figures and media stars, as well as others whom our society admires. These people are heroes and heroines who in nonjudgmental and matter-of-fact ways have shared their own misfortunes so that we can learn from them. What they are doing helps move us all toward the light.

RECOVERY

BEING READY

The deciding factor can be developing an attitude that overrides one's perceived need for drugs. Attitude, or spirit, is, in the end, what sends many people who have gone through detoxification and aftercare and are in recovery back to drug use and a relapse into addiction. The attitudinal or spiritual basis for addiction is a deep-rooted conviction that alcohol and other drugs are good and provide temporary relief from emotional discomfort without negative aftereffects. Beyond detoxification comes the need to deal with the deep-seated reasons for drug use. This false conviction needs to be rooted out and replaced with the realization that in stopping the use of drugs we lose nothing. Instead, we stand to g in a world of new opportunities and experience.

RECOVERY'S GIFTS

Although it was written with cocaine abusers in mind, Dr. Kathleen R. O'Connell's recent book *End of the Line: Quitting Cocaine* has much in it that's applicable to recovery from other addictions as well. Dr. O'Connell, a licensed clinical psychologist who specializes in substance-abuse treatment, has treated well over two thousand people recovering from cocaine addiction and other abuse problems and brings that experience to bear when recommending courses of action to recovering individuals.

In her book she speaks of the "gifts in recovery." These are things that people who have suffered addiction may not have been open to receive earlier in their lives. She characterizes these gifts as "discoveries about themselves as human beings" that are available at the physical, mental, emotional, and spiritual planes.

Physically, she sees the recovering individuals gaining strength and competency in relation to their bodies. Recovery is a time of returning health and a sense of well-being. She points out that many addicts have been run down for so long that they've forgotten what good health is. There's also a freedom from the threat of drug-induced disease—the liver problems of the alcoholic, needle abscesses and other complications from the use of narcotics, sedative-hypnotic seizures. One is much less exposed to the possibility of sudden death through strokes and cardiac and respiratory arrest. There is comfort in knowing that you are contributing to better health rather than worse.

Mental gifts include a new sense of clarity, purpose and direction in life. One may become aware of an increasing ability to concentrate, to read and to remember information. Work often improves through increasing mental ability.

Emotionally, recovering people find that through being more honest with themselves they can also be more honest with others. Emotions used to mask denial or those caught up in wild drug and withdrawal mood swings become a thing of the past as recovery proceeds and a sense of emotional equanimity develops.

This is enhanced by a sense of spiritual calm that leads to peace and serenity. Often the cocaine addict and other addicts have led a life devoid of spirituality. They are surprised and pleased to learn, through recovery, that there is a spiritual side to existence.

Here is a list of specific experiences and understandings that Dr. O'Connell's patients have had in recovery. Many of the gains made by her patients involve things we touch on in this book. Others are worth including for the further insights that they provide:

My husband hasn't hit me since I have been clean.
I'm spending more time with my son.
I want to get up in the morning and go to work.
I'm able to eat now.
I have my health back.
I have my health for the first time in my life.

I don't have fainting spells anymore.
I don't use as easily anymore.
I'm looking good physically.
I have increased self-esteem.
I'm able to communicate with my husband.
We go out now as a family.
I read more, and my concentration is a lot better.
My memory has returned.
I have a more positive outlook on life.
I don't have those crusty rings around my nose anymore.
I can read the paper through now and my concentration is better.
I can think clearly now.
I'm able to leave town now without feeling paranoid about leaving
my dealer.
My self-esteem was so high in coming off the cocaine that I felt able to
get braces for the first time in my life.
I'm more focused on the present.
My income is higher, and my investments are better.
I can be around people and feel comfortable doing so.
I'm able to give and receive love.
I have a more positive view about relationships with the opposite sex.
Sex is much better.
I trust myself and my own intuition more.
I'm much more assertive.
I'm in sync with time now; I have a realistic perception of time.

Dr. O'Connell points out that "You can give yourself some of these gifts
by starting on your own recovery. And the best time to begin is right
now."

CURRENT DEVELOPMENTS IN TREATMENT

Just as there are strides being taken in the psychological and social
models of treatment and their relation to recovery, pharmacological
progress is also being made in medical adjuncts to detoxification aftercare
and recovery. If you have a substance-abuse problem, or if you are helping such a person, you should know about some of the most promising
new developments, since there's no guarantee that your physician will.
After all, you are responsible for your own recovery.

In addition to his activities as medical director of the Haight Ashbury
Free Medical Clinic and Professor of Toxicology at the University of

California Medical School at San Francisco, David E. Smith, M.D., is also the research director for the Merritt-Peralta Institute in Oakland, California. The Institute, directed by Barbara Stern, is a twelve-step and recovery-oriented chemical dependency treatment program that operates both inpatient and outpatient activities within Merritt-Peralta Hospital. Under the auspices of David and his colleagues there, it is also a site for medical innovation and experimental treatment.

OPIATE DETOXIFICATION WITH CLONIDINE

One of the new approaches they are taking is the use of clonidine for the detoxification of opiate-dependent clients. Clonidine has been marketed in the United States as Catapres since 1974. Its primary medical use is for the treatment of hypertension—high blood pressure. Within the central nervous system, clonidine apparently binds to "alpha 2" receptor sites. By so doing, it inhibits the release of norepinephrine, one of the brain's chemical messengers or neurotransmitters. The resultant lower levels produce a relaxing and dilation of peripheral blood vessels and decrease the heart rate.

While it doesn't appear to suppress the dull aches in muscles and joints that can appear in opiate withdrawal, clonidine does seem to provide rapid relief of anxiety, chilling, runny nose and gastrointestinal upset within thirty to sixty minutes after an oral dose has been administered. In order to deal with the aches, acetaminophen (Tylenol) is also administered. L-tryptophan, an amino acid, low levels of which are found in milk, is usually administered at higher doses (1 to 3 grams) in the evening to assist with sleep. Amino acids, such as l-tryptophan, as an aid for sleep dysfunction are also valuable alternatives for alcoholics who should avoid dependence-producing sedative-hypnotic medication.

These effects of clonidine seem to support the theory that opiate withdrawal symptoms are, in part, due to hyperactivity of the sympathetic nervous system. This view is supported by the observation that clonidine will partially block opiate-dependent individuals' symptoms of sympathetic hyperactivity that are precipitated by narcotic antagonists, such as naloxone (Narcan), which can throw an opiate-dependent person into instant withdrawal when it is applied.

Although clonidine does not bind to opiate receptor sites, nor does it produce euphoria, it does reduce many of the symptoms of opiate withdrawal. The value of this drug in the treatment of narcotic addiction is limited to the relief of symptoms during the detoxification phase, seven to ten days. It's not a drug for maintenance therapy.

OPIATE ANTAGONISTS

An alternative to methadone maintenance is also being developed that shows promise for recovering opiate addicts who want to guard against overwhelming attacks of drug hunger and yet not be subject to the ongoing use of a psychoactive drug. This alternative is the use of naltrexone (brand name Trexan). Like naloxone (brand name Narcan), naltrexone is a narcotic antagonist. It has no psychoactive effects whatsoever. It blocks the opiate receptor sites in the brain and so blocks all the effects of the narcotics that use these receptor sites. These substances are ineffective in blocking such other drugs as sedative-hypnotics (including alcohol), stimulants and psychedelic drugs.

Unlike naloxone, which needs to be injected in order to have its effects, naltrexone is effective when swallowed. It is also much longer-acting than naloxone. A dose of 50 milligrams effectively blocks the primary effects of a 25 milligram dose of heroin for twenty-four hours. A 150 milligram dose provides blockage for up to seventy-two hours. If a narcotic is used while the naltrexone dose is in effect, there is no euphoria, no respiratory depression, no relief of pain, no response whatsoever.

On the surface, then, naltrexone would seem an ideal means of warding off relapse among clean opiate abusers. Unlike the alcoholic who uses Antabuse, the opiate user doesn't get violently ill if he tries to use the drug. With naltrexone, there is no adverse reaction; there is no reaction at all. Drug-craving and drug-seeking behavior are reduced when the user knows that the drug will have no effect.

One drawback is immediately apparent. That is the difficulty of getting any but the most dedicated recovery-motivated patient to agree to this treatment in the first place. Naltrexone should be viewed as an adjunct to recovery and not a replacement for the many activities that can help one maintain a drugfree life-style. Those clients who use naltrexone are still encouraged to participate in self-help programs, aftercare and other recovery support groups in order to learn to live a comfortable and responsible life without the use of drugs.

Research has indicated that naltrexone can be an effective aid to recovery in narcotics addiction when used with certain highly motivated patients. Our colleague and fellow researcher, Donald R. Wesson, M.D., has characterized these as opiate abusers who:

1. do not meet criteria for methadone maintenance;
2. because of job considerations, cannot take methadone;
3. have done well on and want to withdraw from methadone; or
4. select naltrexone as an alternative to methadone.

He adds that programs involved in this therapy should be well monitored, with outpatient programs issuing the naltrexone in 72-hour-dosage pills as an adjunct to a full program of recovery.

Wesson also points out three basic difficulties in the clinical use of naltrexone. These are:

1. Acute narcotic withdrawal will occur if naltrexone is taken by an opiate-dependent person who has not been fully detoxified prior to its use. Symptoms may include drug craving, anxiety, drug-seeking behavior, yawning, perspiration, tearing, runny nose, broken sleep patterns, dilation of the pupils, gooseflesh, muscle twitches, hot flashes and chills, bone and muscle aches, loss of appetite, insomnia, low-grade fever, motor restlessness, weakness, abdominal cramps, nausea, vomiting, diarrhea, weight loss and increases in respiration, pulse and blood pressure—in other words, all the symptoms of narcotics withdrawal.
2. Acute pain management in injured naltrexone-maintained patients will require ingenuity by the treating physician, as the antagonist will block narcotic analgesic medication.
3. Maintenance patients having elective surgery need to stop their dose at least seventy-two hours before surgery and not start again for a minimum of seventy-two hours after their last dose of narcotic. To avoid relapse, naltrexone should be restarted before the patient leaves the hospital.

EARLY DIAGNOSIS

In that addiction and addictive disease are seen as a progressive disease, the goal of treatment is to diagnose and intervene as early as possible. The earlier that addictive disease is diagnosed, the easier it is to treat. For example, a sufferer of early onset alcoholism responds to treatment better than the long-term patient with such complications as medical problems arising from alcohol abuse and a diseased liver.

Addictionologists are learning that the long time linking of addiction with a preexisting character disorder exists only in a small number of cases. Addiction produces its own pathology. There is really no psychiatric profile of addiction. Diagnosis, therefore, is based on family history and early signs of vulnerability to addiction. Not all abuse is addiction, and the earlier the distinction can be made in a patient the better. Addiction and abuse call for different programs of treatment. For the addict, counseling and education on the disease and abstinence are called for. For the non-addiction prone abuser, education, counseling and development of control and responsibility can lead to a healthy life-style.

In diagnosing the individual who is having alcohol or drug problems, the first place to look is the family history. If at all possible, this should include grandparents. Overt addiction will often skip a generation, with the children of addicts becoming abstainers because of the childhood experience of living with addicted parents. However, the vulnerability continues even though the immediate parents may have been lifelong abstainers from psychoactive substances.

The other diagnostic clues will be biological and behavioral. The addiction-prone individual does not react to drugs and alcohol experimentation the way a nonprone individual does. For example, a group of teenagers have a party and get drunk. Some of them get sick, some of them pass out. One has a five-hour amnestic motor-functional blackout, which is not a normal first-time drinking reaction. On checking the teenager's family medical history, it is learned that although both parents are teetotalers, one grandparent on each side of the family underwent treatment for alcoholism.

If the situation is recognized for what it is, the teenager can be apprised of the danger this vulnerability poses and may opt for a recovering lifestyle involving abstinence, thus avoiding the onset of actual addiction. Not all cases are that successful, but such instances do point up the potential value of early identification and intervention.

Science may never find a "cure" for addiction. After all, we are dealing with a three-headed dragon and have been for centuries. But treatment does form a beginning on which recovery can be built, and more is being learned about treatment all the time. Beyond treatment is the second structure of self-help, which complements and helps lend form to recovery.

In these first four chapters, we've discussed the nature of addiction itself; the causes and the factors that contribute to addiction; why alcohol and other drugs do what they do and how people get hung up on them; intervention and the availability of treatment; and, finally, the nature of recovery through the use of recovery-oriented treatment and posttreatment programs. In essence, we have reviewed what help is available and what it can do. We have seen what can be done for us if we have alcohol and drug dependency problems.

THE ROLE OF NUTRITION IN ABSTINENCE AND RECOVERY

THE CORNERS OF THE MOUTH

Moving from dependency to recovery involves much more than simply not taking drugs. Improving your physical condition through nutrition, exercise, and relaxation also improves your attitude and general well-being.

One of the sixty-four hexagrams in the *I Ching* is devoted exclusively to the topic of nutrition. As happens in Eastern psychology, where the inclusive concept of "both/and" takes precedence over the limiting Western "and/or," "The Corners of the Mouth (Providing Nourishment)" goes beyond our usual notions of nutrition.

The oracular judgment of the hexagram instructs us, "Pay heed to the providing of nourishment and to what a man seeks to fill his own mouth with." The explication of this judgment gives nourishment a wider scope, including consideration of what in one's own nature is cultivated as well as one's interactions with others. In the Image, the "superior man," or one's higher nature, is described as, "careful of his words and temperate in eating and drinking." This thought is further detailed in the explanation: "Words are a movement going from within outward. Eating and drinking are movements from without inward. Both kinds of movement can be modified by tranquillity. For tranquillity keeps the words that come out of the mouth from exceeding proper measure, and keeps the food that goes into the mouth from exceeding its proper measure. Thus character is cultivated."

ANCIENT INDIAN FOOD GROUPS

Concern with proper nourishment is central to another ancient text. This one is the Hindu scripture known as the *Bhagavad Gita*. The *Gita* is part of a much longer cycle of epic poems collectively known as the *Mahabharata* and often thought of as the Indian *Iliad*. The cycle involves the efforts of a royal family, the Pandavas, to regain their kingdom from a group of treacherous half-brothers. Although part of this larger work, the *Gita* is thought to be the direct word of God, or at least a god, Krishna, giving humanity a code of ethics and a holy way of living.

The great and decisive battle is about to start and the forces of good and evil are deployed against one another before the city. Arjuna, prince of the Pandavas, rides his chariot out into the field between the two opposing armies. Because he knows all the warriors on both sides and, in fact, is related to many of them, he feels torn in his loyalties. How can he kill parts of himself?

In the face of this controversy, Arjuna's chariot driver, Krishna, reveals himself to be an avatar, or earthly incarnation of Vishnu, the god of preservation, and he proceeds to tell Arjuna, and through him the entire Indian subcontinent, the cosmic facts of life. One of the main things he talks about is nutrition.

Krishna divided everything into three qualities. These he called *sattva*, *rajas* and *tamas*. In his *Commentary on the Bhagavad Gita*, Sri Chinmoy translates these qualities as purity, passion and slumber. As with everything else, food was divided into these categories. Sattvic foods included fruits, vegetables, legumes, nuts and grains. These were considered pure substances. Meats and fiery spices excited the passions and were thought of as rajasic. Finally, tamasic substances were those that had no life. These included "dead" foods, things that had been processed or preserved and the substances used to preserve them. Today, most processed foods and such things as white flour and sugar would be considered tamasic.

In the Hindu scheme of things, as set down by Krishna, sattva is obviously the quality to be most cultivated. Yet all three qualities are to some degree intertwined, and total banishment of rajas and tamas in favor of sattva is not recommended. Eventual transcendence of all three qualities into a state of holy purity is the eventual goal in Krishna's scheme of spirituality. Short of that, balance between the three is the day-to-day goal of earthly humanity.

EATING RIGHT

Balance is also at the heart of *Eat Right!*, a germinal book on "psychonutrition" and the role of diet in abstention and recovery by Donald R. Land, Ph.D. Dr. Land, an internationally known educator and consultant in the areas of psychonutrition, stress management, food service design and corporate wellness programs, postulates three basic food categories. Although the basis of his work is a two-thousand-year-old Chinese healing treatise, the *Nei Jing*, his groups bear a striking resemblance to Krishna's *gunas*. They are:

1. Plant foods, including grains, fruits, legumes, nuts, vegetables and seeds.
2. Animal foods and salt.
3. Synthetic, extracted, stimulating food fragments, including sugar, alcohol and other drugs, caffeine, soft drinks and many "fruit juices."

Doctor Land pictures the three groups as being on a seesaw, with plant foods at the fulcrum and the two other groups at either end. He points out that many substance abusers violate nutritional balance by eating very little of the first group and taking wild swings between the other two. Often this means trying to balance their drug consumption, group three, by loading up on animal protein from group two, and vice versa. For example, a long alcohol or sweets binge is usually followed by a desire for meat, eggs or salty foods. Even in less extreme cases, a meal that is heavy in the meat department and contains a lot of salt results in a desire for dessert, coffee or alcohol. These swings tend to produce a perpetual state of dietary imbalance. His solution to this imbalance is expanding the fulcrum, making plant foods the major part of one's diet.

Balanced diet and nutrition are important for everyone, but they are especially important for anyone who is trying to abstain from alcohol and other drugs. Besides supported recovery work, improving your dietary and nutritional habits is one of the primary things you can do to promote your own wellness and safeguard your recovery. This may involve a basic change in eating habits not only for yourself, but for your whole family.

Poor nutrition and misguided eating habits may have more to do with our drug problems than we think. In his book, Dr. Land lists several interrelations between poor nutrition and chemical dependency. There are, for example, relationships between eating disorders and drinking disorders, alcoholism and food addiction, and metabolic imbalances that lead to blood sugar instability. Considering each individual's unique biochemical and metabolic makeup, it's clear that what we eat does matter.

All these are thought-provoking and lead us beyond the usual considerations of nutrition. One entire book has been written on the first two items. This is *The Solution*, by Karl Polak, a native of the Netherlands living in Hong Kong who discovered over time that his alcohol and other drug problems were a result of lifelong food allergies. Polak became involved in the Twelve Steps and Raja Yoga, and his book describes graphically his use of these and other means to successfully fight his own addictions and food disorders. His detailed backgrounds and descriptions of the alternatives used in his personal struggle make his book a good source for specific alternatives to drug abuse.

In general, our culture tends to think of nutrition in terms of calories, weight loss and cholesterol. Dr. Land considers this a most simplistic and negative approach, focusing as it does on dieting, or giving up something. In reality, good nutrition, like good recovery, means gaining a great deal rather than losing. Nutrition should never be just *adequate*. It should be optimal and do the best it can for each individual.

At best, nutrition should be part of a whole system approach to recovery. Each one of us is biochemically unique, so there is no one diet that will fit every individual. Instead, using some basic concepts, such as increasing the use of plant foods and decreasing the other two groups, each of us needs to develop a diet through carefully observing the effects that the things we eat and drink have on our health and feelings.

We very much are what we eat. While we may direct the "form" of our body/mind/spirit system in a number of ways, the "content," the raw material, is composed of what we "fill our mouths with."

Some food reactions are rapid and relatively apparent. Some foods, such as beef and other red meats, tend to sedate us. They give us a heavy feeling and, like alcohol and other sedative-hypnotic drugs, can produce a rosy glow. Others, including green vegetables, may seem to energize. (Look what spinach does for Popeye!) Other food reactions are much more subtle and occur over time. All food reactions require our continuing attention in choosing what dietary requirements are right for us as individuals.

EATING DISORDERS

It has become increasingly apparent that eating disorders bear a close similarity to substance abuse and addiction. Using a Twelve Step approach, Overeaters Anonymous has been successful in dealing with a number of problems, and some clinical ecologists, such as Theron G. Randolph and Ralph W. Moss, in their book *An Alternative Approach to Allergies: The New Field of Clinical Ecology Unravels the Environmental Causes of Mental and Physical Ills*, suggest that addiction to an alcoholic beverage may be a form of food addiction. Scientists studying anorexia nervosa and bulimia have seen close correlations between these puzzling diseases and addiction as well. In general, it can be said that there are relationships between nutrition, addiction and behavior.

These relationships can manifest themselves in a number of ways. Deficiencies in nutrients, for example, can cause problems and can result from both intake and utilization. An individual may have adequate intake of a needed vitamin or amino acid, but the substance is blocked from getting to the tissue that needs it by poor digestion, malabsorption or biochemical defects in the system. Scientists are now learning that proper digestion of one nutrient often depends on the presence of certain others.

Appetite control mechanisms in the brain have an effect on our intake of both food and drugs. To an extent, the action of these mechanisms is dependent on one's nutritional status. "Thus," as Dr. Land puts it, "what you eat and drink is determined by what you eat and drink."

Nutrition, however, doesn't exist in a vacuum any more than any other factor in abuse and addiction. It has to be considered along with everything else. Also, poor nutrition may be a cause for many problems that can exacerbate abuse and addiction or interfere with recovery. These problems can include sexual inadequacy, social inadequacy, chronic pain, inability to cope with stress, lack of control over thoughts, feelings or actions, depression, anxiety and poor self-esteem. These are symptoms that often involve unstable blood sugar, food allergy, nutrient deficiencies or other aspects of nutritional imbalance.

What can be done? Dr. Land suggests two ways of beginning a personal nutrition program. These are: (1) studying on your own, or (2) working with a nutritional therapist, holistic physician, or other practitioner. He recommends a combination of the two and lists twelve nutritional treatment goals:

1. ELIMINATION OF NUTRITIONAL DEFICIENCIES   Stress, history of poor diet, exposure to toxins, pollutants or allergens, chronic disease and recovery from disease, injury or surgery greatly increase our risk of deficiency and therefore increase our risk for sluggish functioning of the body's healing mechanisms. Deficiency is a relative matter, and large doses of certain nutrients are sometimes required to eliminate a deficiency.

2. TREATMENT OF HYPOGLYCEMIA Nearly all alcoholics in early recovery experience functional hypoglycemia; i.e., they experience blood sugar instability or low blood sugar to some extent. Dietary treatment of this condition is critical for optimum recovery.

3. IDENTIFICATION OF FOOD ALLERGIES, ADDICTIONS OR HYPER-SENSITIVITIES   Many foods trigger symptoms that lead to or intensify a desire to drink. For an alcoholic, these foods may be those from which his or her favorite beverage is made. Identification and elimination of such foods can be critical to easier sobriety and optimum recovery.

4. REPAIR OF DAMAGED TISSUES AND ORGANS   Certain tissues can either regenerate or repair themselves. The efficiency of this process depends upon optimum nutritional intake.

5. RESTORATION OF FUNCTION OF VITAL SYSTEMS   Stress, poor diet and chronic illness can affect vital systems in ways that are manifested through symptoms and in ways that are not. Restoration of these systems, which include the brain, heart, liver, endocrine system and immune system, is critical to High Level Recovery and depends on optimum nutrition more than on any other single factor.

6. REDUCTION OF CRAVINGS FOR ALCOHOL, SUGAR, CAFFEINE AND NICOTINE   Cravings, to a large extent, result from lack of nutritional integrity and from dietary intake that is neither balanced nor centered. A positive approach to reducing your cravings is based upon building nutritional integrity through nutrient supplementation and through a balanced and centered diet.

7. RESTORATION OF APPETITE   Ironically, your nutritional status is a determinant of your appetite, and appetite affects what you eat. That part of your brain known as the hypothalamus is generally understood to be the center of appetite control (it is also the center of emotional control, which is related to appetite). Brain function depends critically on nutritional status. In addition, imbalance in some nutrients can inhibit the senses of taste and smell. Thus, we can expect our appetite for nourishing food to increase as our nutritional status is improved.

8. RESTORATION OF INITIATIVE, CONFIDENCE AND WILLINGNESS TO COOPERATE The awakening of cognitive function, feelings, positive self-image and positive interpersonal interactions will result in varying degrees from nutritional therapy. These changes often lead to increased initiative, confidence and cooperation in the treatment process. No one, of course, can predict the extent of response to therapy, but I have rarely seen or known of a situation to the contrary.

9. INCREASED ABILITY TO HANDLE STRESS The strain on a person depends on the extent to which an event is *perceived* as stressful and on the extent to which the body's various systems—central nervous system, endocrine system—are taxed by the resulting stress. Our nutritional integrity is a factor in the experience of stress as well as in our body's defensive and restorative functions. Dietary intake itself can be a major source of stress (sugar, caffeine, toxins, allergens), or it can provide protection against stress.

10. CREATION OF LESS INTERNAL (DIGESTIVE, METABOLIC) STRESS The intake of harmful foods and chemicals and the resulting digestive and metabolic chaos can be as intense a source of stress as any that you experience. Digestive and metabolic stress lead to a vicious cycle. The more of this stress you experience, the less value is gotten from the very food and supplements necessary to improve functioning of your digestive and metabolic systems. Nutritional therapy can turn this downward spiral into an upward, healing cycle.

11. MINIMIZATION OF WITHDRAWAL SYMPTOMS A certain stress is associated with withdrawal from any addictive substance. Withdrawal symptoms are the most obvious part of the difficulties associated with abstinence and management of cravings. There is a growing body of evidence demonstrating that withdrawal symptoms in particular, and the experience of pain in general, are lessened by improving nutritional status. Withdrawal can be even easier if you prepare for it by building your nutritional status prior to withdrawal.

12. TREATMENT OF DISEASES ASSOCIATED WITH SUBSTANCE ABUSE Because of the general deterioration of all of the body's systems, including the immune system, there are endless possibilities for the occurrence of physical, mental and emotional dysfunction as a result of substance abuse. The function of nutritional therapy, again, is support of the body's own efforts to heal itself and restore balance.

Dr. Land's book *Eat Right!* is a good source of both detailed ways to implement nutrition therapy and references for further reading on the subject. He concludes his list by pointing out two central rules of nutritional therapy.

1. Minimize your consumption of highly processed food.
2. Balance and center your food intake.

IMPROVING YOUR DIET

The best way to start is by taking a good look at your present diet. Make a list of what you eat in the course of a week, and become aware of ingredients in any processed foods you use. Note that these ingredients appear on the label by order of quantity, the highest quantity listed first. You may be amazed at the number of products in which the first or second ingredient is sugar or salt.

If you do your own cooking, try to use fewer processed and preserved foods and more natural ingredients. It may increase your time in the kitchen, but the results are worth it. There are a number of good cookbooks on the market that emphasize easy-to-make dishes with fresh ingredients.

If you do your eating in restaurants and fast-food outlets, your task may be more difficult, but it is far from impossible. There is an increasing market for natural foods in our society, and the discriminating eater needs to find what is available. Watch for restaurants that emphasize the six plant food groups—grains, legumes (includes beans, lentils, peas and peanuts), vegetables, fruits, nuts and seeds—on their menus. Preparation is also important, and such things as foods deep-fried in animal fats should be avoided.

As ours has become more of an urban society in which most people buy their food in stores rather than growing it, foods have become increasingly processed and refined. In the interest of health, you may have to seek out less refined options. Instead of white bread or refined "whole wheat" bread, substitute whole-grain breads made from wheat, rye, rice, corn, millet, oats, buckwheat and/or barley. Whole-grain pastas are also available. Substitute brown rice for white and vegetable oils for animal fat in cooking and salad dressings. Eat salads! Try making your favorite dishes from scratch.

One bonus is that natural foods taste better. They may not seem to at first, especially if you are used to a steady diet of "pizazzed" fast food that is overloaded with flavor additives. Processed foods often contain chemicals that affect your tastebuds in the same way that drugs affect your brain, leaving them insensitive to natural flavors. Many drugs, such as nicotine, cocaine, caffeine and alcohol, also deaden our ability to smell and taste, and it may take us a while to regain these senses. As with other alternatives, the effects of natural foods may be subtle at first, but they are powerful, and in time you will discover a new world of variety and experience.

In the end, establishing the right diet with the right nutrition is a very personal matter. It depends often on your location and circumstances. Fresh and natural foods may be easier to find if you live on a full-service farm in the Imperial Valley than it is if you live in a hotel room downtown, surrounded by golden arches and plastic cups. Mainly it involves attention to what is available. Canned soups, for example, are often remarkably free from additives and preservatives, but there are exceptions. Read *all* labels. Seek out health food stores and restaurants, and don't be afraid to ask questions about nutrition. The people who work in these places are often there because they are interested in good nutrition and are more than willing to help. If nothing else, lean on the owners of restaurants where you regularly eat and stores where you buy food. They appreciate your business and will listen if you and others suggest products to them.

We'll be talking more about alternatives to drugs and food additives later in this book, but let us complete this discussion of diet and nutrition with the general reminder to learn what you can and, whenever possible, go to the fresh and go to the natural. *Bon appétit!*

Recovery: The First Day in the Rest of Your Life | 4

"The first day in the rest of your life" sounds like a greeting-card slogan, but it is a very real way to view recovery. Essentially, recovery is a starting over, starting from scratch in a whole new life. In this chapter we'll see what that means and learn what help is out there to see you through the dawn of that first day.

THE TWELVE STEPS

The self-help movement is responsible for developing the concept of recovery. The programs within this movement are often referred to as twelve-step programs because they follow the pattern originally laid out by the Twelve Step Program of Alcoholics Anonymous. These twelve steps represent a blueprint for recovery that has worked for thousands of people. There have been minor changes over the years. For example, as the realization that addiction is addiction, whatever the psychoactive substance, led to the establishment of Narcotics Anonymous and Cocaine Anonymous. Yet the gist of the document has remained the same and continues to be *very* effective.

Following are the twelve steps as they were originally presented in what is called the "Big Book," *Alcoholics Anonymous*. (Here quoted from the third edition, 1976, A.A. World Services, Inc., New York, reprinted with the permission of Alcoholics Anonymous World Services, Inc.)

1. We admitted we were powerless over alcohol, that our lives had become unmanageable.
2. Came to believe that a Power greater than ourselves could restore us to sanity.
3. Made a decision to turn our will and our lives over to the care of God *as we understood Him.*
4. Made a searching and fearless moral inventory of ourselves.
5. Admitted to God, to ourselves, and to another human being the exact nature of our wrongs.
6. Were entirely ready to have God remove all these defects of character.
7. Humbly asked Him to remove our shortcomings.
8. Made a list of all persons we had harmed, and became willing to make amends to them all.
9. Made direct amends to such people wherever possible, except when to do so would injure them or others.
10. Continued to take personal inventory and when we were wrong promptly admitted it.
11. Sought through prayer and meditation to improve our conscious contact with God *as we understood Him,* praying only for knowledge of His will for us and the power to carry that out.
12. Having had a spiritual awakening as the result of these steps, we tried to carry this message to alcoholics, and to practice these principles in all our affairs.

Many people have had problems with certain aspects of these steps and the program they represent. One of these has been a perceived religiosity. In truth, there are many chapters of AA and other self-help programs that do have a decided religious bent. On the basis of this and the many references to God and prayer in the twelve steps, some people have accused the self-help movement as a whole of being in some way related to the fundamentalist Christian movement. It is not. But those who cannot accept these aspects of a program should not categorically reject all self-help groups. There are meetings of self-help programs for agnostics, atheists and even secular humanists. These programs doubtless take a different interpretation of "God *as we understood Him,*" which is fine.

THE THREE-HEADED DRAGON

The Twelve Steps can be seen as comprising a living document, not unlike our national Constitution, that is flexible enough in interpretation to adapt to changing times and conditions. Like any blueprint, however, it may need some keys to promote understanding. One of the best of these insights was described recently by Chuck Brissette, associate director of Azure Acres, a recovery-oriented treatment program in Petaluma, California. Chuck was speaking at a class on the physiology and pharmacology of substance abuse, taught by Rick Seymour and other staff members of the Haight Ashbury Free Medical Clinic, at the California State University at Sonoma. Chuck's vision of the "three-headed dragon" has had a profound effect on our view of recovery and hence on the writing of this book. He has graciously allowed us to share his vision with you.

Chuck Brissette first envisioned the three-headed dragon when he was trying to turn a three-hundred-bed flophouse on Los Angeles's skid row into a "recovery community." He had been given a federal grant and instructions to convert the creaking, ancient hotel into the home of an organized substance-abuse treatment program. The three hundred assorted users, dealers and user-dealers who lived in the hotel were his patients.

Chuck had a staff of sorts. The Salvation Army was serving food and religion in the basement; there were visiting clinicians from the Los Angeles Department of Mental Health; and he had a group of other recovering folk from Alcoholics Anonymous. Actually, the staff seemed more like separate teams in a three-way tug-of-war than a cohesive staff. Each group had its own narrow and rigid idea of what the problem was and how to handle it.

The result of this mix was a total lack of cooperation. The anarchy that prevailed wasn't pernicious. As often happens when groups disagree about basic principles, each of the participants had created solutions that fit its own particular view of the problem. Unfortunately, although each group operated in good faith, none of their solutions appeared to be working. Despite the staff's best efforts, the users kept on using, the dealers kept on dealing and the user-dealers kept on doing both, all the while eating and singing with the Salvation Army, reviewing their childhood traumas with the L.A. Mental Health psychiatrists and listening to the Alcoholics Anonymous members saying, "My name is John, and I am an alcoholic and an addict." There had to be some way of looking at the problem that all three helping groups could buy. There had to be a common ground on which they all could agree.

In exasperation and frustration, Brissette prayed for guidance. It came in a vision, one of those flashes of inspiration that in the past have brought us the structure of DNA, the benzine cycle, Newton's Law, and Einstein's Theory of Relativity. In his vision, Chuck Brissette saw a three-headed dragon labled ADDICTION. Each of its three heads bore its own label. The labels read: PHYSICAL, PSYCHOLOGICAL and SPIRITUAL.

This was the answer! The dragon of addiction had three heads. Each helping group had gone after the only head it saw. Not only did the one head they severed soon grow back, but the two others remained. Addiction was a threefold problem, and the only way to fight it was to cut off all three heads at the same time. But each head had its own sources, its own problems, its own powers. So while all three would be cut off at once, it was a long process, and for each head that process was different. Even with all three heads gone, the dragon wouldn't die, but headless it could be immobilized.

THE PHYSICAL

PHYSICAL is the first head. In truth, chemical dependency as a component of addiction is an illness that involves physiological impairment. It is chronic, more like diabetes and other ongoing diseases than like short-term infections, and so its treatment requires a lifetime of attention. It is irreversible. The recovery community points out that once addiction takes hold, there's no way of going back to a preaddicted state. A cucumber can become a pickle, but once it's a pickle, it can never be a cucumber again. Finally, chemical dependency is progressive. Even when a person abstains, the disease of addiction paradoxically continues to grow. If an abstinent addict returns to use, even after a number of years, the symptoms of compulsion, loss of control and continued use in spite of adverse consequences will reemerge more quickly and more devastatingly than they did before. Chuck calls this image of addiction the "sleeping tiger." It may be a cub inside you when it's put to sleep, but it continues to grow, just as a tiger cub continues to grow even in sleep. If you wake it up, you'll discover that the cub you thought you had put to sleep forever reawakens as a full-grown tiger, larger, stronger and even harder to eradicate with every reawakening.

You cut off the first head by stopping use; but as critical as this step is, it is not enough. Detoxification is an important first step, and abstinence is absolutely necessary to recovery. But relying on abstinence alone is like taking a punch at a welterweight and then just standing there with your hands at your sides, thinking you've done all you have to do. That's suicide!

In the dragon image, as in reality, detoxification and abstinence are just the beginning. They cut off only one head. The dragon still has two heads, two thirds of its strength and mobility. And the first head can grow back very quickly.

Sobriety and recovery are two distinct processes. You can have sobriety or abstention without recovery, but you cannot have recovery without sobriety. The solution to addiction involves more than just not drinking or not taking drugs; it also involves getting well. To do that, you have to deal with the other two heads.

THE PSYCHOLOGICAL

PSYCHOLOGICAL is the second head. Addiction is also a disease of the mind, emotions and will. In a sense, people in recovery are recovering from a problem in living. Alcoholics Anonymous defines addiction as a "self-centered fear." Addiction as a psychological problem can be seen as a misdirected dependency on the self, a state of psychological narcissism. In essence, the alcoholic or addict has become his or her own higher power. He or she is in a state of emotional arrest, at an age of psychological dependency, and is incapable of hearing or acting on anything that comes from outside him or herself. The practicing addict doesn't believe that anything meaningful exists beyond that self and is therefore incapable of listening to anything outside that self. This total self-dependency lends to loss of control over use.

This concept was often graphically represented in the short term by psychedelic users in the 1960s. We remember the sudden travails of those tripping on LSD while driving down the freeway who suddenly became aware that they were responsible for all the other drivers on the road and had to maintain the overall pattern of traffic through sheer force of will. One interesting solution came from an acid tripper in Mendocino who, while watching the ocean, decided that he was responsible for the waves coming in and going out. As the shock of this realization passed he reasoned that the part of him that was responsible for the waves was not only greater than his own thinking self, but was also perfectly capable of dealing with the waves—and everything else, for that matter. With that he relaxed back into enjoying the seascape.

The second head is indeed the user's head, and when it goes out of control the results can be very frightening. This loss of control is often considered the hallmark of full-blown addiction. Bad enough from the outside, this loss of control for an individual who has cut off all outside input and has become totally self-dependent seems like the collapse of the universe. Everything that one can conceivably rely on is in a state of chaos and cataclysm.

If cutting off the dragon's first head relates to Step One of the Twelve Steps—i.e., "We admitted we were powerless, and that our lives had become unmanageable"—then cutting off the second head involves Step Two—"Came to believe that a Power greater than ourselves could restore us to sanity." The addict who has become totally dependent on a self, or soul, that is composed of mind, emotions and will must transfer dependence on himself to dependence on something outside that self, preferably something that will support recovery. In the self-help movement, this can be the recovering community itself, with its carefully constructed support system for the recovering addict.

THE SPIRITUAL

SPIRITUAL is the third head. In this sense, the spirit represents the heart, the gut, the hidden self, the eternal part, the undying part of you. It is what Buddhists call "your face before your parents were born," what AA's Big Book refers to as the "innermost self."

This is the hidden inner man or woman, and the problem lies with the belief system that is located there. The problem is that one's belief system is not discriminatory. It believes everything it is told. It receives all its programming directly from you. In other words, your own mouth programs your spirit, and your spirit has no capacity for editing what you tell it. It's like feeding data into a computer. You may have picked up the data here and there, or piled up a stack of research books to draw from, but you alone are responsible for what goes onto the keyboard.

Conversely, we are powerless over what we believe. Our beliefs are responsible for denial and are highly developed and integrated into every aspect of our being. This makes the task of an intervention specialist and a treatment counselor working with someone who has deep denial extremely difficult. In essence, you can't pressure someone into seeing what he cannot see.

Because of the unique reaction that the genetically addiction-prone individual experiences to his drug of choice, he or she programs his or her belief system with the deep conviction that that substance is "good" and that similar substances are "good." While essentially abstract, that belief might be expressed as something like this: "Drugs and alcohol are good and provide temporary relief from emotional discomfort without negative aftereffects." That testimonial could have come right off a top advertising copywriter's script sheet. And it did! We *sell* ourselves on the slogan that the *problem* is really the *solution*.

Is it any wonder, then, that the abstaining addict is drawn back into use? Even when the conscious self is convinced that addiction exists and that the worst thing it could possibly do is take a drink, or a snort, or a shot, the entrenched belief that using a particular drug is "good" can prevail.

How can one chop off this third, most subtle and probably most powerful head of the dragon? By reprogramming the belief system with the help of others. This is where self-help becomes intrinsic to recovery. Unless one deals with the third head, unless one changes the belief system and effects a turning-about in the deepest seat of consciousness, there is no recovery.

OVERCOMING DENIAL AFTER DETOXIFICATION

Denial is a vein that runs through all three dragon heads, directly from the heart of the beast. In the first head it's manifested as a refusal to recognize at a conscious level that a problem exists. Often, through cutting off the first and second heads, the user will accept that the problem exists but deny that there is a workable solution. Acting on the inner conviction that access to what he perceives as the "problem solving" drug must be maintained, the user hangs onto an escape: "The treatment system doesn't work," "The conditions weren't right." This is programming for failure. Such denial is like what Rick experienced in trying to find a stress-free time to quit cigarettes. Cutting through that denial involved the realization that as long as he was making the stress-free period an absolute condition for accomplishing nicotine detoxification, he was merely maintaining his addiction. Such a time would never occur. And deep inside he knew that. This was his "out."

You cut off the third head by reprogramming your belief system with the help of others. Chuck describes this process as the "spiritual law of hearing." This is not a religious activity but a spiritual activity. It deals with spirit as the site of your belief system. There are six stages involved, and they can act on each other like a row of dominoes. Basically, it's a question of hearing, as opposed to just listening. With hearing as the beginning, here are the stages:

1. Hearing (what you hear is what you see).
2. Seeing (what you see is what you do).
3. Doing (what you do is what you say).
4. Saying (what you say is what gets into your heart).
5. Receiving.
6. Keeping.

Through this process, the self-image begins to change. This is not the self-image that we usually think of, the face we put on for others that psychologists call the persona. This is the secret self-image that no one else sees, the grimy one. The real turning point is at the fourth stage, "saying." You are the one who did the programming in the first place, by what you said and thought, and therefore you are the one, with input from a "Power greater than ourselves," who has to do the reprogramming.

All this was summed up about 2,300 years ago in *The Dhammapada*, a compilation of teachings by Gautama Buddha:

> What we are today comes from our thoughts of yesterday, and our present thoughts build our life of tomorrow: our life is the creation of our mind.
> If a man speaks or acts with an impure mind, suffering follows him as the wheel of the cart follows the beast that draws the cart.
> What we are today comes from our thoughts of yesterday, and our present thoughts build our life of tomorrow: our life is the creation of our mind.
> If a man speaks or acts with a pure mind, joy follows him as his own shadow.

This has been stated even more succinctly in a Buddhist mantra. A mantra is a statement that can be chanted for spiritual purposes, on the basis that "what you say is what you get in your heart." This one translates as: "You are what you think, having become what you thought."

So runs the lesson of the three-headed dragon. A true vision is one that goes beyond a simple metaphor and grows with the evolution of understanding. C. G. Jung would have called this an "archetype," a powerful image from the mass unconscious that can be another manifestation of "a Power greater than ourselves," that continues to evolve as needed.

In summarizing our description of Chuck Brissette's powerful metaphor we have called up the words of Gautama Buddha, the very words that, in Buddhist parlance, set the wheel of *dharma*, or law, in motion. This is no coincidence. We are beginning here to weave a tapestry, to borrow threads from ancient and far-spread medicine to adequately approach and deal with the current realities of substance abuse and addiction.

Although this chapter opened with the evocation of a blueprint that was first developed by Alcoholics Anonymous and then adopted by a variety of other self-help groups, what we are talking about goes back much, much further and is basic to human life. In his *Twelve Steps to Happiness*, Joe Klaas states that the first step may apply to any situation where one is powerless. It may apply to "compulsive overeating, drug addiction, alcoholism, schizophrenia, neuroses, compulsive gambling, habitual smoking, chronic child beating and other self-destructive maladies."

Although we have so far couched the discussion of recovery in terms of recovery from addiction, our sense is that recovery is in no way limited to the addicted or even to the addiction-prone. In speaking of recovery and self-help we are alluding to the much broader range seen by Klaas—all of us who are afflicted with self-destructive maladies.

Addiction to psychoactive substances is one manifestation of a "living problem" that nearly all of us share. We seek a sense of meaning, of pleasure and fulfillment in a world that often seems to hold out little hope for these. This is not a new condition brought on by the burden of present-day technology or the fear of nuclear havoc. Over a hundred and thirty years ago, in *Walden*, his account of a voluntary therapeutic withdrawal from society, Henry David Thoreau wrote:

> The mass of men lead lives of quiet desperation. What is called resignation is confirmed desperation. From the desperate city you go into the desperate country, and have to console yourself with the bravery of minks and muskrats. A stereotyped but unconscious despair is concealed even under what are called the games and amusements of mankind. There is no play in them, for this comes after work. But it is a characteristic of wisdom not to do desperate things.

Thousands of years before Thoreau built his hut on Walden Pond and tried to simplify his life away from desperation, thinkers and healers, prophets and sages addressed the "human condition." No, we didn't invent addiction in the twentieth century. We know that we didn't even invent alcohol and other drugs in the twentieth century. Why then do we feel that we need to start from wheelless zero and invent solutions to problems that have been with us in one form or another since the dawn?

REPROGRAMMING OUR COMPUTER

Chuck Brissette invoked a dragon, a most ancient and venerable archetype, in order to simplify and direct our thinking about addiction. He also invoked a much more modern simile for what Japan's Zen Buddhists call the "mind" and what we have referred to as the spirit, the site of our belief system—the computer.

The computer is a marvelous machine. It does what we want it to do most of the time. The one this book is being written on displays a smiling and receptive face every time it is turned on and a program disk is fed into it. Doesn't matter what the program says—same smiling face. You can feed it 2 + 2 = 4, and it will smile. You can feed it 2 + 2 = 10, and it will smile. As far as the computer is concerned, 2 + 2 = 10, if you—the programmer—say so. And the next time someone goes to the computer for information and asks "What's 2 + 2?" and the computer says "10," that person will say, "Hey! There's something wrong with this computer!" But there's nothing wrong with the computer. It's just been fed the wrong information, a bad program.

Our belief system is very much like that computer. It can't tell us anything that it has not been programmed to tell us. The major difference between our belief system—our spirit—and the computer is that it is programmed by and communicates that program to only one person. When it reflects on the "fact" that "alcohol and other drugs are good and provide temporary relief from emotional discomfort without negative aftereffects," it's not that the spirit is out of whack. The information it's been fed is out of whack. Stronger terms could be used.

Many mental-health specialists believe that substance abuse and addiction are the result of either "addictive personality" or "underlying psychopathology." Therefore, they conclude, the correct approach to abuse and addiction is psychotherapy. Health professionals and others in the recovery community reply that addiction is a pathological state in and of itself and the psychopathology that appears during active addiction is a symptom of the addiction rather than vice versa. In other words, the problem is in the program, not in the computer. If faulty information has been fed into the best, most perfect information processor in the business, faulty information will come out.

In a demystified sense, the process of recovery is a process of reprogramming, of replacing faulty, damaging information with information that can lead toward maturity and a meaningful, satisfying life. It's as simple as that.

The self-help programs run on that premise.

HOW THE SELF-HELP PROGRAMS WORK

Many individuals are put off by the twelve-step self-help programs because they don't understand how they work. The system doesn't make any sense. A bunch of people get together and they take turns getting up and talking about their helplessness. Just what good does that do?

As is true with many of the important things in life, one gets out of a program what one puts into it. The effectiveness of self-help programs directly involves the process of cutting off the third head of the dragon. They work through the six dominolike stages of hearing, seeing, doing, saying, receiving and keeping. But it takes involvement in all six stages for the process to work.

You can go to any number of Alcoholics Anonymous, Narcotics Anonymous, Cocaine Anonymous or Overeaters Anonymous meetings, one a week, two a week, every day. You can be super-virtuous and go three times a day, and yet those meetings may have as much effect on you as religiously watching the morning and evening news every day. What did Dan Rather say between 7:05 and 7:10 last night?

Don't feel alone if you can't remember. In a culture where we are talked at and proselytized through every waking hour, we have become experts at listening without hearing. This condition may have become exacerbated in our own time, but it is nothing new. Christ's parable of the sowing of seed speaks to the same human condition. More recently, the Canadian sociologist Marshall McLuhan described reading and watching and listening as primarily means of massaging our eyes and ears without any meaningful exchange of ideas taking place.

We have become used to having everything from the Super Bowl to Shakespeare wash over us, but change is not brought about by a media massage. It takes action on our part. Listening to other people describe their problem doesn't reach the parts of us that need to be reached. Our own voice is the one we must hear to reprogram our belief system. The moment when one gets up in a self-help, twelve-step meeting and says, "My name is———,and I am a———," is a moment of great importance in the course of beginning recovery. In its own way, this moment is analogous to the Buddhist exercise of "turning about in the deepest seat of consciousness." At that moment, one's personal wheel of *dharma* is set in motion. The group's acceptance acknowledges the sanctity of the moment and the turning about, anchoring it in the temporal and spatial reality of the meeting and the group. It's all very magical, and it can happen again and again as a moment of affirmation and reaffirmation.

This moment of turning about is not, however, isolated. It is rather part of a continuum that includes recognition of the problem, whether it's drug addiction, alcoholism or any other compulsive infirmity, intervention if necessary and treatment if necessary. Exercising the twelve steps within a nurturing and anonymous fellowship is often preceded by and interlaced with a course of treatment that is becoming more and more aware of the role of self-help and long-term support in its own effective outcome.

In reviewing the history of substance abuse and addiction treatment we have discussed the problems that arise from treatment philosophies and techniques that do not take into consideration the chronic nature of abuse and addiction. It has been all too easy to limit our attention as health professionals to the acute problem at hand. After all, that's been medicine's role in our society—to intervene when illness strikes, treat the symptoms of that illness with medicines or remove the seat of that illness with a scalpel, and then return the patient to normal life until the next crisis strikes.

At the other extreme, one finds some "cult" groups and even long-term inpatient programs in which charismatic leaders have interpreted a need for extended treatment as a need for cutting the entire program off from the world at large. Such isolation, especially in situations where all those involved are ex-users and there is neither professional supervision nor contact with a greater continuity of care, can result in group aberration and paranoia in which the client's dependence on a drug of choice is merely traded for a dependence on the program itself. The more extreme of these programs have made national headlines in recent years.

Many forms of long-term community commitments can be very helpful for the addict in early recovery. These include religious as well as secular groups. The overwhelming majority of therapeutic communities are conscientious, are professionally run and belong to national organizations that preclude such self-absorption, but one should always investigate a program carefully before entering it or recommending it to a client or loved one.

Because the Haight Ashbury Free Medical Clinic has an international reputation in the treatment of substance abuse, we are often visited by treatment specialists and government officials from overseas. One recent visitor was the mental health director of a Northern European country noted for its forward thinking and humanistic attitudes. Years earlier this country had instituted an "enlightened" program for dealing with opiate addiction. They viewed it as a disease calling for humane detoxification coupled with intense psychotherapy and counseling for the "underlying causes of the addiction." In essence, the national treatment program was a model of therapy as conceived in the 1960s and early 1970s.

In his capacity as director of the Clinic's Public Information Project, Rick Seymour met with the mental health director and listened to a familiar story. Over the years that government had poured money and effort into the detoxification and rehabilitation of its opiate addicts, only to see the addicted population relapse time and again into active addiction. Frustration had mounted to the point where everyone working in government and treatment who had anything to do with opiate addiction treatment were suffering what seemed to be a national systematic burnout. As a result, the government was considering a basic overhaul of its addiction treatment procedures. The minister had come to the United States seeking confirmation and moral support for a national shift of all opiate addiction treatment over to methadone maintenance.

Rick ascertained that quite possibly the problem wasn't that the minister's programs had gone too far with their social model of treatment. In all probability, they hadn't gone far enough. The minister's answers to Rick's questions, revealed that treatment had concentrated on physical withdrawal from the opiate drugs and psychoanalysis. Once clients were drug-free and supposedly in abstinence, they were quickly discharged from treatment and returned to society. The national treatment programs, competent as they may have been within their short-term scope, did very little to provide the crucial long-term support. They had no direct interaction with Narcotics Anonymous, nor with any other twelve-step setup. What aftercare did take place was basically ongoing psychotherapy. Good psychotherapy will bring to the fore other "problems" for which the addict may consider drugs as a solution. These painful past experiences may even serve as triggers for more drug usage. But the therapy doesn't address the addict's addiction.

In discussion with the minister, Rick didn't try to talk him out of adopting methadone maintenance. Instead he outlined some of the basic tenets of addictionology. He pointed out that all addiction, including opiate addiction, produces its own psychopathology. With the exception of the handful of "dual diagnosis" cases, or cases of addiction *and* mental illness together, most addicted clients respond much better to extended and supported abstention from psychoactive drugs than they do to extended psychotherapy. He shared our experience that addiction is a chronic condition wherein episodes of drug hunger can lead to repeated relapses into active abuse when its victims do not have long-term support for their abstinence. Finally, he took the minister out to Forest Farm and introduced him to Paul Ehrlich.

FOREST FARM

Forest Farm is a substance abuse treatment center for adolescents and young adults about two hours northwest of San Francisco. It occupies a pine- and redwood-studded ridge above the sparsely populated valley that extends from central Marin County out to the wild coast where Sir Francis Drake once beached his ship, the *Golden Hind*, for repairs while circling the globe on a privateer's mission. The farm itself could be in Switzerland or Tibet. Clouds often swirl in the upper branches of the tallest trees, and buildings look out on lines of tree-capped ridges to the north and south. Like the *aesklepions*, the original Greek hospitals of classic times in Cos and Epidaurus, the farm is built on "healthy" ground. The earth itself exudes a peacefulness and serenity that are in keeping with the farm's therapeutic nature.

Paul Ehrlich, the treatment director for Forest Farm, developed its treatment procedures with long-term recovery in mind. Although he has worked in the substance-abuse treatment field for many years, Paul is a relative newcomer to the disease concept of addiction. As he puts it, "I was always intrigued by the failures, that ten or so percent of clients that didn't respond to basic counseling aftercare. We could detoxify them, but sooner or later, and most often sooner, they would be back. It took me a long time to even begin learning how to deal with that population, but they're the people Forest Farm is mainly set up to help."

He talked at length to the minister from Northern Europe as one who had approached the whole concept of addiction and self-help through twelve-step programs with considerable personal skepticism. "But it works, and that's what's important!"

Like other recovery-oriented treatment programs, Forest Farm integrates counseling, facilitated peer groups and attendance at local twelve-step meetings. The facility has extensive grounds and a swimming pool, and many forms of exercise and outdoor activities are integrated into the clients' overall treatment schedule. The stay at Forest Farm is long-term, usually months rather than weeks. In some ways, however, Paul is as interested in what happens after treatment as he is in what happens during the client's stay.

"Recovery is a lifelong undertaking. Addiction doesn't end with detoxification and abstinence. That's merely the beginning. There are issues of making up for arrested maturity to be dealt with over time. Also, the recovering addict is subject to flare-ups of delayed withdrawal on down the road. These can happen months—even years—after the addict enters into abstinence, and they require support."

He talked to the minister about the role the community can play in furthering abstinence and recovery. The minister's country, with its long history of social responsibility, had an excellent opportunity to develop a truly therapeutic society by supporting efforts at the community level for helping not only opiate addicts completing formal treatment but all people experiencing problems with alcohol and other psychoactive drugs.

After years of doing almost the right thing, the minister remained skeptical, but Paul and the rest of us gave him and those he represented a lot to think about. Here in the United States we are a long way from the kind of therapeutic community involvement that could in time wipe out most drug abuse and addiction. Often we find ourselves still fighting the basic stigmas and denials that surround substance abuse in our culture.

THE VISION QUEST

Occasionally there is a community effort that is noteworthy not only for what it attempts and accomplishes, but for what it could mean for the future. In this category are programs for young people that accentuate the positive. These are programs that don't necessarily address the issues of substance abuse but rather the root causes of abuse, such as feelings of helplessness, low self-esteem, and boredom. Many of the "Outward Bound"-type programs fit into this category. One program that has interested us a great deal is the "vision quest."

The vision quest began as a therapeutic program for "troubled" high school-age youngsters. It now involves a wide range of young people and includes parents and other adults, most of whom wish the vision quest had been developed when they were younger.

At its core, the vision quest is a rite of passage based on coming-of-age ceremonies practiced in the past by many American Indian tribes. In ancient times, most cultures had nurturing ceremonies to mark the coming of age and other important steps in the maturation of the young. These ceremonies are still practiced in so-called primitive societies, and their echoes can be found in the Jewish bar mitzvah and Catholic confirmation ceremonies. The Arthurian tales of the quest for the Holy Grail are depictions of such rites in a more magical form.

At their best, these rites of passage are powerful maturing agents for the young and provide a means of integrating young people into the life of the community as emerging adults. They not only provide initiation but test the mettle of the young, often providing them with some idea of their own inner resources by pitting them against the implacable forces of nature and society after sufficient preparation.

It may be argued that our culture has developed its own more subtle markers on the road to maturity, but if it has, they seem to be singularly ineffectual for a number of young people who find themselves helpless and bewildered by the world they live in. Many twentieth-century Western philosophers have pointed out that today people all too often lead lives of existential isolation within society.

In a way, the vision quest addresses existential isolation by embracing physical isolation. A group of young people gather together with experienced facilitators in order to prepare for an adventure. The adventure is a trip into the wilderness, in the course of which each of them is expected to spend several days completely on his or her own, alone.

Once the preparations are completed and the group is ready, they travel to a wilderness area where civilization may not be far behind in miles but the chance of encountering others is virtually nil. Once there, they spend several more days in preparation at a group campsite. There they are separated into pairs, and each pair establishes a camp a distance from the group site. At a prearranged time, after they have established a rendezvous point, the pairs separate, and each individual establishes his or her own camp at some distance from all the others. Each participant has enough water and supplies. This is not a physical survival test. The survival skills being tested are spiritual. As was the case in Indian vision quests, the climax of this time alone is an all-night vigil during which each participant, in isolation, asks for a vision.

The next morning the pairs rendezvous and return to the group camp. After a reorientation and much tale swapping, the group returns home. The quest doesn't end there, any more than addiction treatment ends with detoxification or the turning about in the deepest seat of consciousness. The participants are expected to act upon their experience. For many, this involves taking steps toward their personal future. One example is a system of mentorships. Business people in the community where the vision quest was developed may have volunteered to accept questers as interns, working with them after school. Others may enter into community service and learn the ways of adulthood in that manner. Whatever path they follow, many of them have forged strong friendships not only with other questers but with themselves. They complete the quest with a better understanding of who they are and what they can do.

DEALING WITH THE CHANGES

Young people are not the only ones who may need rites of passage. The adults who undergo long-term treatment and enter recovery often face bewildering changes in their lives, changes that they cannot deal with on their own. The attitudes friends and family hold toward you may change drastically, and not always for the better. These people are used to you being one way, and although they are usually pleased that you have given up your destructive habits, they may find the new you more than a little disconcerting. An example is the spouse who has spent years taking care of you and may now feel as though you no longer need him or her. Especially acute problems can arise, for example, when you go into abstention and recovery and your wife or husband continues to abuse drugs.

The fellowship found in twelve-step programs can be especially helpful at these times, as can other forms of support. There are programs and individual therapists who can encourage the necessary realignment of relationships.

There are times when a recovering person needs to separate from everything around him or her, find new friends, a new job, a new place to live. In these situations one is virtually starting from scratch, and it can be hell or a great adventure, often depending on the support that you can find.

SUPPORT GROUP THERAPY

At its best, treatment has many of the qualities of a vision quest. It acts as a doorway into a better life for those who experience it. Paul has brought many of the vision quest's qualities to the treatment techniques in which he has a hand. Besides Forest Farm, an inpatient facility, Paul has been instrumental in developing recovery support groups for cocaine abusers. The first of these groups was developed in March 1981 as a response to a compelling increase in cocaine abuse in the San Francisco Bay Area. In August 1982 Paul began cofacilitating a cocaine recovery support group at the Haight Ashbury Free Medical Clinic along with David Smith, Millicent Buxton, Joe McCarthy, M.D., and Maureen McGeehan, M.S.W.

According to Paul's and Maureen's description, "Each cocaine recovery support group has eight to twelve members, ranging in age from nineteen to fifty-eight years. Most are in their late twenties and early thirties. About sixty percent of each group is male. The minimum level of education is high school, and several members are currently students or hold graduate and professional degrees. All group members are employed at least part-time, including occupations in law, music, medicine, business, homemaking and the skilled trades."

These group members, who apparently represent a wide range of middle-class backgrounds and occupations, generally came to the groups as a result of life crises, "financial problems, arrest, pressure from family or significant others." Frightening or life-threatening experiences had led a number of them to seek treatment. Many of them had tried to limit or stop the use of cocaine on their own without much success and had learned of the groups in a variety of ways.

Paul and the other facilitators (each group is cofacilitated by a male and a female counselor) established three basic ground rules for group membership:

1. They agreed that the identities of members and the content of group discussions are to be held in strict confidence by all members and not discussed with anyone outside the groups.
2. They agreed that, with the exception of certain prescription medications when a proper medical diagnosis has indicated their necessity, no group member would attend a session while under the influence of any psychoactive substance or use such a substance within the twenty-four hours preceding a session.
3. They agreed that each group member would have an expressed desire for recovery, defined as "the ability to live comfortably and responsibly without the use of any psychoactive substance."

Abstinence isn't a prerequisite for entry into the support groups. However, group members are expected to embrace abstinence as the initial treatment goal and are challenged to this end. Those who don't achieve it usually drop out of the group within the first several months.

The goal of these cocaine support groups is recovery. Ehrlich and McGeehan see recovery as a reversal of the processes at work in addiction itself, such as the deterioration of physical health and the decline of one's ability to function in work and relationships, the damage to self-esteem as compulsive use leads to loss of control and the inability to curtail use, even when the consequences are obviously dire. In recovery, the chemically dependent person is able to abstain from psychoactive drugs, demonstrate personal freedom and responsibility, realize personal growth and change, and maintain meaningful and effective relationships with others.

This view of recovery is dynamic. Not only is it a reversal of the processes we see taking place in addictive disease, it is also the antithesis of the static abstinence found in white-knuckle sobriety. The life-embracing nature of this paradigm runs counter to the kind of statements one hears from WKS sufferers, who maintain that their ultimate goal is the elimination of all chemical processes in the brain. In the medical books we have read, that condition is also known as "death."

Therapeutic techniques and practices that are used in the cocaine groups are built on three basic tenets. These are:

1. Addiction is a disease that has its basis in genetic factors, learned experience and environmental conditioning.
2. Recovery is possible.
3. While people may not be responsible for their addiction (due to genetic predisposition or extreme compulsion produced by the drug itself), they *are* responsible for their recovery.

These cocaine recovery support groups encourage clients to achieve four long-term goals:

1. Abstinence from mood-altering chemicals.
2. Development of a comfortable drugfree life-style.
3. Understanding the process of addiction and recovery.
4. Establishing and maintaining a program that supports lasting recovery.

To these ends, the groups are seen as part of a continuity of care that can include outpatient treatment, long-term residential treatment, detoxification and crisis intervention. Clients attending the groups are strongly encouraged to participate in Alcoholics Anonymous, Narcotics Anonymous, Cocaine Anonymous and any other self-help programs that support a chemical-free life-style and promote emotional, social and spiritual growth. Group participants' families are encouraged to involve themselves in the treatment process by joining in family sessions, couples' sessions, Al-Anon and Nar-Anon meetings.

The cocaine recovery support groups are seen in part as an introduction to the language of recovery. While the cofacilitators of the groups may not actually "work the steps," they introduce the group members to the concepts that vitalize the self-help movement and help them to change their concept of addiction. By introducing the clients to the true nature of dependency and addictive disease, they help to negate feelings of guilt and recrimination over past failures to cope with the problem through the exercise of will.

Although a comparatively recent convert to the self-help movement and disease concept of addiction, Paul has come to believe very strongly in the importance of the first step, "We admitted we were powerless and that our lives had become unmanageable," to successful recovery. His study of such Eastern disciplines as Zen Buddhism leads him to a deep appreciation of that step's paradoxical nature.

Lecturing to Rick Seymour's physiology and pharmacology class at the California State University at Sonoma, Paul pointed out that the first step provides a key that unlocks the addictive trap. Compulsion is the flip side of willpower and really can't be stopped by an exercise of will. On the other hand, with the admission of powerlessness over psychoactive drugs, one gains power over the rest of one's life. We'll be discussing this paradox at greater length in the next chapter.

To illustrate the paradoxical nature of this turning about, Paul described the children's toy known as the Chinese finger puzzle. You've probably seen these for sale in Chinese shops around the country. The device is simple, a small tube of basket material that fits over the index fingers of both hands. Once in place, however, no amount of tugging the fingers apart will release them. In fact, the more you pull on it, the tighter the puzzle becomes. The trick of getting free is to give up. You have to relax and push slightly in the opposite direction. Then the puzzle comes loose. In addiction willpower and attempts at controlled use have the same effect as trying to pull both fingers away from the basket. They merely tighten the grip of addiction.

This concept runs counter to many of the precepts that we hold dear in Western civilization, with all its emphasis on responsibility and self-reliance. However, it is found again and again in Eastern tracts. The *I Ching*, for example, points out that obstructions in life are overcome "not by pressing forward into danger nor by idly keeping still, but by retreating, yielding." Elsewhere it says that evil should not be fought directly, but by tending to that which is good.

Forest Farm, the cocaine recovery support groups and many other treatment entities with which we have become involved through the Haight Ashbury Free Medical Clinic and through the growing self-help movement, represent a growing continuum of care that is based on physical, mental and spiritual precepts. As we have seen, these have been synthesized from a number of sources ranging from breakthroughs in medical science to ancient wisdom as interpreted by personal experiences of those intent on helping themselves and others become well. All of this focuses on that moment that can be seen variously as the loosening of denial, the adopting of the first step or the turning about in the deepest seat of consciousness. In one way or another, it is in a very true sense the first day in the rest of our lives.

We have seen the opening door, the realization that comes with exploding the myth of helplessness, the myth that nothing can be done to end our drug dependency. The sun is rising on the first day of our drugfree lives, and that is exciting. But what about tomorrow, and the next day, and the next?

It's all too easy to lose faith in recovery and fall into a slough of despondency and self-pity. It's all too easy to apply a coating of rigidity on what should be a flexible and growing edifice. As we react to the stresses of a new life-style or recoil from instances of delayed withdrawal and drug hunger, we can find ourselves, if we are not careful, trapped in the living rigor mortis of white-knuckle sobriety. When the door is open, are we going to walk boldly through it? Or are we going to huddle there in misery and fear?

And what of the many people who may not be addicted but are looking to rid themselves of unwanted habits, who want to gain a new sense of maturity, self-worth and health without this excess baggage? This book isn't just about addiction. It's about growth and fulfillment and a maturing capability for dealing with life. All these things are related, part of a whole that we can either deal with in this life or leave to chance in the future.

As we now know, abstinence in and of itself is not the final goal. You don't want to detoxify just so you can sit around for the rest of your life, wishing you had a line of coke, a joint or a very dry martini. That's white-knuckle sobriety. Real recovery is a positive state, a time of personal growth. Dependencies are put behind. There are more exciting and rewarding things to do.

The Next Day,
and the Next:
Alternatives to
Drugs and
Alcohol | 5

In this chapter we move beyond both addiction and recovery. The first day in the rest of your life has come, and you have rejected alcohol and any other psychoactive drug as a solution and are ready to get on with your life. This is an exciting time, a time of great potential for personal development and growth. There is no gray and featureless plain stretching through the years in front of you. You don't have to give up all pleasure or happiness just because you've given up your drug or alcohol habit. On the contrary, the doors are opening in your life to new experiences, opening to a new, varied and exciting landscape.

There are many ways besides using alcohol and other drugs to be high, to experience alternate states of consciousness. Human beings have sought these experiences throughout history, to have them is a right, perhaps a need. This chapter will explore and explain the many positive ways of achieving these states without using drugs, alcohol or any other substance.

Many of these alternatives represent a marriage of Western know-how with elements of Eastern medicine that we are only now beginning to understand on our own terms. They are ways of helping us realize that recovery really isn't a closing door. It's opening doors to worlds of life experience that are denied us by the disabling effects of drugs.

Our bodies, minds and spirits can heal and rebound from drug-induced physical and mental disability, from sexual dysfunction and social dysfunctions that we may not even have been aware of. With new resolution and strength we can resume our development as human beings.

KNOWING WHY WE STARTED

It's time to look at the problems because of which we got involved in alcohol and other drugs in the first place and do something about them. Addressing these problems, we move to a greater focus than that of the addict, the coaddict or even the nonaddicted but in some way dependent and face problems that are common to virtually all humanity. These are the problems we may have set out to deal with by turning to alcohol and other drugs. These are the problems that are manifested in our perceptions as "emotional discomfort," and they have many, many forms. This emotional discomfort is not new. Twenty-five hundred years ago Gautama Buddha based his entire philosophy on his recognition that life is filled with pain and suffering and on his conviction that this pain and suffering could be surmounted by following an "eightfold path" that bears many interesting similarities to the Twelve Steps. A hundred years ago Henry David Thoreau restated this "pain and suffering" as "quiet desperation." Many thinkers before, after and between these two have grappled with the "human condition." Students of the human interaction with psychoactive substances often point out that the interaction usually begins with the best of intentions—a search for meaning in life, a desire for enhanced consciousness, the yearning for a sense of well-being—in short, in individual attempts to deal with the human condition. The instincts are basically good, but the wrong path is taken.

When the drugs or alcohol are removed from one's life, the human condition remains. After the first day in the rest of one's life there is the next day and the next. At this positive and auspicious point one is free to grow and to explore, free to find personal solutions to the problems that were temporarily worsened by the negative effects and aftereffects of drugs. In this chapter we will be looking at other forks in the road, paths to well-being that, with drugs and alcohol left behind, one is free to explore.

HOW NEW DISCOVERIES LEAD TO OLD SOLUTIONS FOR TIMELESS PROBLEMS

Recent medical and scientific breakthroughs in the study of dependence and addiction support the contention that the physical, spiritual and psychological aspects of human beings all interact, that none is separate. One example of this interaction can be seen in current studies by Ken Blum, Ph.D., and others on the locus ceruleus. The locus ceruleus is a portion of the brain that acts as a biological pathway for all drug effects in that organ. Blum and his colleagues have discovered that when a recovering addict or a postwithdrawal dependent person experiences drug hunger, a hypersympathetic electrochemical discharge occurs in the brain. This discovery indicates that drug hunger, which has long been considered a purely psychological occurrence, has a physiological component; in other words, it is "real," not just "in the mind" of the dependent person. There is probably an as-yet undefined connection linking the electrochemical discharge and the psychological drug hunger to the deep-seated spiritual mechanisms of dependency and addiction.

Research on the locus ceruleus is in its infancy, and for now it is producing more questions than answers. It's not yet known whether the psychological occurrence of drug hunger triggers the physical discharge in the brain or vice versa. Drug hunger often seems related to external cues, such as seeing or talking about drugs, or being in a place or situation where one used drugs in the past. We know that persons with alcohol and other drug dependency often respond to these environmental cues, and that ex-smokers, for example, may experience tobacco hunger at those times or in those places where they used to smoke. However, there are also many instances when drug hunger seems to arise of its own volition. The Alcoholics Anonymous "Big Book" is filled with accounts of alcoholics who relapsed into abuse and didn't have the faintest idea why.

The concept of a human nature made up of three interacting realms may remind us of Chuck Brissette's three-headed dragon, and well it should. In this view the dragon is a parasite that takes on the form of its host. Is it any wonder, then, that addiction is such a tenacious disease, or that we have to go outside of ourselves in order to fight it? In the immortal words of the cartoon character Pogo, "We have met the enemy, and he is us!" Recognizing this aspect of dependence and addiction is enough to send a shiver of horror through any one of us. Yet it's that recognition that gives us hope for release and the ability to come to grips with the problems of dependency.

Literature is filled with examples of parasitic villainy, from Robert Louis Stevenson's *Dr. Jekyll and Mr. Hyde* to the recent movie *Aliens*. Can anything be more repugnant to our nature than an evil that hides within our-

selves, that can feed on our belief systems and be protected and nour-
ished by our own souls? And yet the tide turns when the victim sees the
parasite for what it is.

In Chapter 4 we discussed the turning about that can lead to sobriety
and recovery. We discussed the importance of casting away the belief that
alcohol and other drugs are good and provide temporary relief from emotional discomfort without negative aftereffects. Participation in self-help
and support programs leads us to the realization that we have mistaken
another kind of problem for the solution, and it helps us to erase such
deep-seated beliefs. But once we begin to believe that alcohol and other
drugs are *not* good and that they do *not* provide relief from emotional
discomfort, what then? Those of us who have come to realize that use of
any psychoactive substance is not good for us physically, psychologically
or spiritually must look elsewhere for relief.

One approach to these following days is that of replacing them with an
ongoing series of "first days." Many recovering people speak of maintaining sobriety "one day at a time." In this scheme of things, *every* day is the
first day in the rest of your life. This sounds great as a slogan, but it may
not always go the distance once the first excitement of recovery begins to
wane and horrible memories of withdrawal are replaced by rosy glimpses
of "the good old times." Often more is needed to build a lifelong recovery.

Just as the problem of dependence and addiction is composed of three
interlinking parts and we are composed of three interlinking natures, it
follows that any viable approach to the rest of our lives must be made in all
three realms—the physical, the mental and the spiritual. The self-help
movement approaches the breadth of this through the Twelve Steps to
self-improvement. As with any living document, the Twelve Steps don't
go into great detail. Instead, they form a framework, an outline of exercises that can lead to greater personal maturity. The individual working
the steps provides the means of fulfilling them.

Self-help places great emphasis on fellowship, and much discussion of
working the steps and trading individual experience of them takes place
at the meetings. After all, the constituency is ideally composed of men
and women of good will working together to solve a mutual problem.

The problem is not a new one, nor is it specific to alcohol and other
drugs. The abuse of these psychoactive substances is but one among
many blind alleys down which humanity has blundered in its search for
relief. The greater problem has many names. Some thinkers call it the
"existential problem." Buddhists call it *dukkha*, and others refer to it
within the many manifestations of pain. Basically, we are talking about
the difficulty of finding meaning and fulfillment in a universe that often
seems devoid of both. Throughout history and prehistory, solutions have
been sought.

Within this cosmic issue is the question of how to deal with the more or
less mundane issues of day-to-day living. There is an old Zen saying that

the way to walk ten thousand miles is one step at a time. In this chapter we are looking at some of those steps, looking at what you as an individual can do to make life more enjoyable for yourself.

As a means of gaining satisfaction and fulfillment, the "Big Book" emphasizes the role of "giving." In its interpretation, this is literally going out and, through discussing your own experience with addiction and what the program has done for you, bringing others into sobriety and into the movement. The theory, which appears to have much merit, is that helping others in this way keeps your own addiction at bay.

The concept of receiving by giving is not new, nor did it originate with Alcoholics Anonymous. The self-help movement has applied an ancient truth to a practical problem.

The discovery of central nervous system receptor sites is another scientific breakthrough that helps us understand the nature of dependency and addiction. First, it is a misrepresentation and a misunderstanding to think of these as "drug" receptor sites. No, the various receptor sites that are in the process of being identified are there to interact with the body's own neurotransmitters, electrochemical substances that occur naturally within the human brain and nervous system. The existence of these substances has been postulated for all psychoactive effects and has been verified in some cases. Today there is little doubt, for example, that such internally produced peptides as endorphins and enkephalons manage pain and produce euphoria in much the same ways that opiate and opioid narcotic drugs do. Stimulant drugs both resemble and interact with such neurotransmitters as epinephrine, norepinephrine and adrenaline. A form of the psychedelic drug dimethyltriptamine, or DMT, has been identified as an internal psychedelic that occurs naturally within both human and rat brains. The enzyme responsible for its synthesis and the receptor sites where it is absorbed by nerve terminals have also been discovered. One suspects that it is only a matter of time until sedative-hypnotic enzymes are discovered. The recent identification of the benzodiazepine receptor sites and specific benzodiazepine antagonists are a major step in that direction for the entire sedative-hypnotic drug class.

One inference that can be drawn from these discoveries is the likelihood that all psychoactive drugs affect us by mimicking the action of naturally occurring enzymes produced by our own bodies. If that's the case, what need is there for any dependence on drugs? Can we not learn to use our own minds, bodies and spirits to gain the positive effects that we tried to achieve and maintain through the use of alcohol and other drugs?

In some instances, many of us have learned to do just that. Running and aerobic exercise are examples of ways we have consciously used our bodies to help deal with pain and produce feelings of energized euphoria. A number of disciplines that have been used in other cultures and specialized segments of Western Culture work to similar ends. In this chapter we will explore with you many of these means of naturally developing positive effects within our mind/body/spirit system without the use of drugs.

THE EASTERN CONNECTION

As we noted at the beginning of this chapter, new discoveries can lead to old means of dealing with timeless problems. We know that we are not the first culture to have dealt with the problems of emotional, physical and spiritual pain that led us to seek solutions through the use of drugs. Many cultures have wrestled with these same problems and have developed solutions. Among these are the societies that gave rise to the "psychological" religions of antiquity, such as Hinduism and Buddhism. The doctrines and writings of these religions have been shrouded by differences in language and cultural points of reference, but often when they are adequately translated into Western terms, what is being said and practiced becomes startingly modern and relevant.

People who are familiar with both realms have noted a distinct similarity between the twelve-step movement and certain Eastern psycho-philosophic disciplines. Some have even called Alcoholics Anonymous "American Buddhism." A look at the history and nature of Buddhism and a comparison between Buddhism and the Twelve Step principles may show whether there is a similarity and, if there is, what Buddhism and other Eastern religions can teach us about learning to cope with dependence and addiction.

About 2,500 years ago, in India, a high-born prince named Siddhartha Gautama came face-to-face with a conviction that much of life involves suffering. Besides being a prince, he was a member of the Kshatruja, the aristocratic military class, who were equal in social standing to the priestly Brahmins but less involved in sacerdotal affairs. Within his caste, withdrawal from worldly affairs in order to contemplate the "great secrets" was an accepted practice, even for a prince. Siddhartha spent a number of years studying with many Hindu holy men and following a variety of ascetic disciplines such as fasting and devotional exercises. In time, he decided that what he had been doing was spiritual hogwash. According to legend, he sat down beneath a bodhi tree at Buddha Gaya (Bodh Gaya) and vowed he wouldn't move until he had unraveled the great secret.

This he did, to his own satisfaction. Under the bodhi tree he developed two related concepts, the "four noble truths" and the "eightfold path." The first of these noble truths he already knew before he sat down. It was the reason he had set out on his quest in the first place, namely that life involves a great deal of suffering. The word he used, however, is *dukkha*, which we may have translated as "suffering," but which means much more than what we usually consider suffering—just as the term "pain" as we have used it in this book encompasses more than what happens when you bang your thumb with a hammer.

In Pali, the language of Buddhist scripture, *dukkha* ordinarily means "suffering," "pain," "sorrow" or "misery," as opposed to the word *sukha*, meaning "happiness," "comfort" or "ease." As used to signify the first noble truth, however, *dukkha* also includes such deeper ideas as "imperfection," "impermanence," "emptiness" and "insubstantiality."

Because of its primary focus on suffering, Buddhism has often been seen in the West as an essentially pessimistic religion. Actually, Buddhism is neither pessimistic nor optimistic. Buddha has been referred to as the "third physician." One physician may gravely exaggerate an illness and give up hope altogether. Another may ignorantly declare that there is no illness and that no treatment is necessary. Both are deceiving the patient; both are equally dangerous. But the third physician diagnoses the symptoms correctly, understands the cause and the nature of the illness, sees clearly that it can be cured and courageously administers a course of treatment, thus saving his patient. For Siddhartha Gautama, or Doctor Sid, the focus is not on suffering, but on the means of eliminating suffering. Happiness, in its broadest sense, is the goal of Buddhism. One gets there by recognizing the four noble truths.

The second noble truth is that suffering is caused by the delusion that the self exists independently of nature and the universe, and that one can live an egocentric life. Buddha is identifying the cause of suffering as that selfsame spiritual and psychological narcissism that we found at the heart of addiction and denial. The individual's ego is his or her own higher power, and he or she is literally incapable of hearing or acting on anything that comes from outside.

The third noble truth is that there is emancipation. Liberation from suffering is possible, and the state of liberation is called *nirvana*. What is involved is essentially admitting that we are powerless and that our lives are unmanageable, and coming to believe that a power greater than ourselves can bring us to sanity. After all, it was the Buddhists who coined the phrase "turning about in the deepest seat of consciousness."

The fourth noble truth is that emancipation can be accomplished by following the eightfold path, composed of the following attributes. (As you read this list, try to think of each instruction in the most literal sense. There is really no simple explanation for any of the stages, a fact evidenced by the thousands of years and millions of pages Buddhist commentators have already devoted to the task.)

1. Right Understanding
2. Right Thought

3. Right Speech
4. Right Action
5. Right Livelihood
6. Right Effort
7. Right Mindfulness
8. Right Concentration

The realization of all the above, the four truths and the eightfold path, was part of Siddhartha Gautama's enlightenment. When he got up from under the bodhi tree, he was the Buddha, "the enlightened one," and he spent the rest of his life teaching the truths and the path. He explained it in different ways and in different words to different people, according to each listener's stage of development and capacity to understand and follow him. The essence of what he had to say, however, consistently involved realizing the truth about suffering and following the path to liberation.

Through the centuries millions of words have been spoken and written about the path, but its essence more than a little resembles the Twelve Steps developed by the pioneers of Alcoholics Anonymous. It should not be thought that the steps of the path are to be picked up and set down in numerical order, any more than are the individual Twelve Steps. As with their modern counterpart, they are all linked together, and the practice of each helps in the cultivation of all the others.

Having established a link between Buddhism and self-help that appears to be based on the universality of basic problems faced by both those who suffer overtly from addictive disease and the rest of humanity, let us note that similar doctrines appear in a variety of other religions and psychological paradigms as well. Each one of these has developed specific systems for furthering the individual's progress on the road from suffering to happiness, and each has developed coping mechanisms.

The most successful of these mechanisms involve a dynamic quality for personal growth and development. The least successful of these, such as drug abuse and addiction, overeating, gambling and other attachments to the material, operate from a philosophy that things are never going to get any better and merely *appear* to provide *temporary* relief from suffering.

Let's look at some of the successful ones.

MEDITATION AND YOGA

Meditation and yoga are dealt with here under one heading because, in practice, meditation is a form of yoga. As a whole, yoga involves all three interacting realms—physical, mental and spiritual—while meditation is usually thought of as mental development of one's spiritual nature. In practice, however, all forms of yoga involve a meditative state of mind, while not all forms of meditation involve physical activity. These distinctions may seem confusing at first, but they should become clearer as we discuss the history and nature of disciplines and see where they fit into recovery and how they can enhance a drugfree state.

THE "MAGICAL" EFFECTS OF YOGA AND MEDITATION

In the esoteric literatures of Tibet, India and other countries where these disciplines have been developed for centuries, extravagant claims have been made for what can be accomplished through the practice of yoga and meditation. Books on Tibetan yoga translated by the Northern California Oxonian, Walter Yeeling Evans-Wentz, describe such disciplines as the "yoga of psychic heat," in the practice of which devotees can generate enough heat in their bodies to dry a succession of wet sheets wrapped around their naked bodies in near-freezing temperatures after they have swum in an icy lake. He also describes *lum-gompa*, a discipline in which the devotees become capable of leaping about the precarious Himalayan crags like Tibetan mountain goats without ever losing their footing. These devotees learn the arts of *lum-gompa* while sealed in caves that can be exited only by floating straight up through a chimney hole.

Ancient scriptures indicate that the masters of advanced yoga disciplines were fully capable of controlling *all* the forces of nature and turning them to their own ends. Most of them hasten to add that such masters had become so totally in harmony with the universe and its forces that the one thing they were incapable of doing was using their powers for selfish or evil purposes.

Certain Zen Buddhist monastic orders are supposed to have developed greatly heightened perceptions, including extrasensory perceptions, from the practice of directed meditation. These orders account for the stories of expert blind archers and swordsmen who can duel while blindfolded.

Even the usually understating Maharishi Mahesh Yogi at one point claimed that advanced practitioners of Transcendental Meditation could be trained to levitate. People who had tacitly accepted his doctrine that if even one percent of a population took up TM it would change the whole population's consciousness for the better balked at meditators floating in the air, and TM's reputation suffered a setback.

Although many of the claims for these disciplines verge on the miraculous, we should remember that often miracles are scientific phenomena that are not yet understood. Claims that meditators and yogins could take control of and change their involuntary bodily processes were also discounted until some of these people were tested with Western scientific instruments. It was found that some of them could control such things as their own pulse rate, heartbeat, brain waves and body temperature. Once the amazement died down, Western scientists and nonscientists as well realized that just about everybody can elevate their pulse rate. You can do it involuntarily by almost hitting the Mercedes that pulls into the passing lane in front of you, or you can do it deliberately by running a hundred yards or doing fifty jumping jacks.

One can also rapidly lower pulse rate with a yoga breathing exercise. Yogins often speak of concentration on the *hara* or breathing through the *hara*. The *hara* is your abdomen or gut or, more specifically, the area just below your breastbone and above your navel. But you don't just contemplate your navel, you breathe through it. You take several deep breaths, expanding your stomach, and hold each breath at the point of maximum expansion. What this accomplishes is the stimulation of the vagus nerve, a cranial nerve arising in the medulla oblongata and innervating the larynx, lungs, heart, esophagus and most of the abdominal organs. When the vagus nerve is stimulated in the *hara*, it automatically reacts by slowing heart rate.

"So," you may say, "that's a great parlor trick, but what's so great about a reduced pulse rate?"

When one is stressed the pulse is elevated, and when one is relaxed and content it is lower. Apparently it doesn't matter which is changed, the stress or the pulse; in either case, the system goes along with the change. Tests have indicated that when this slowing down takes place, changes occur in the brain waves as well. Here we have a good example of the interrelated nature of body, mind and spirit. Consciously change any one of them and the other two most likely will go along.

This is just one example in which we now know the physiological pathways taken by a yoga "miracle." The chances are good that other effects that have reportedly been achieved by Eastern yogins will, in time, yield their secrets to Western science.

A meditation teacher of our acquaintance remembers that in the early 1970s, when many young people were going from psychedelic drugs to meditation and yoga under the influence of Baba Ram Dass and other interpreters of Eastern disciplines, the general aim in learning these disciplines was the gaining of supernatural powers. That was the growth era for a variety of self-realization movements. Many of these seemed to be syntheses of Eastern disciplines, self-aggrandizement and high-pressure sales techniques, and they contributed greatly to dubbing the 1970s as the era of the "Me Generation."

Our meditation-teaching friend thinks that the power era of meditation and yoga is behind us now, and most people practice what she refers to as "mindfulness" in order to gain true peace of mind, compassionate sensitivity and spiritual development. The most discernible product of these practices is peace of mind. We should point out that this can be a dynamic peace of mind that includes a good measure of euphoria—that elusive ingredient that many find fleetingly in drugs and for which they may seek through drugs well beyond the point where tolerance and abuse have wiped out all traces of it. It doesn't come with a hammer blow as it can early in drug use, but it does come in time and is more lasting, repeatable and controllable. With yoga and meditation, the high that results is not from a waste of neurotransmitters. In time, other advantages and features of these disciplines present themselves. There can be great joy in exploring these as they come. For now, we offer a few insights and our own conviction that what used to be said in error about alcohol and other drugs is actually true about yoga and meditation: They work.

The practice of meditation and yoga has been well known to the Far East for many centuries, and it forms the core practices of several Eastern religions. For example, meditation has been a part of Buddhism since its inception. It was in a state of meditation under the bodhi tree that Siddhartha Gautama became aware of the "four noble truths" and the "eightfold path."

Although some forms of meditation and yoga have been used by Christian mystics since the beginnings of Christianity, our Western concept of these practices has often been based on simplistic stereotypes: the bearded holy man sitting cross-legged on a mountaintop; the Indian fakir walking across glowing coals or lying on a bed of nails. These visions led us to view meditation and yoga as inexplicably exotic activities, not untinged with charlatanism, with no apparent purpose beyond inspiring the awe of onlookers and prompting the passing tourist to toss a few coins in appreciation. To the bulk of Western humanity, such activity was a part of "ancient night." Even the language used to describe what was happening was inexplicable and untranslatable.

MEDITATION

In 1969, Lama Anagarika Govinda visited several college and university campuses in the United States. Born in Germany in 1898 and describing himself as "an Indian National of European descent and Buddhist faith, belonging to a Tibetan Order and believing in the Brotherhood of Man," Lama Govinda was perhaps an ideal person to expound on the deeper mysteries of Eastern thought to a Western audience. He did, in fact, consider himself a "point man" for what he saw as an increasing migration of Eastern philosophy to the West. He saw the takeover of Tibet and the persecution of Tibetan religious leaders by the Chinese as having a potential impact on today's world analogous to the impact of Judeo-Christian beliefs two thousand years ago following Rome's sacking of Jerusalem.

He believed strongly that "the future of the world lies in a combining of Western technology and Eastern psychology."

A man of power and deep thought, Lama Govinda carried a simple message. When asked what could be done to further world peace, when asked what one could do to improve the quality of life, he had one answer. It was, "Sit down, cross your legs, compose your mind and meditate."

Even in 1969, with an audience that had some familiarity with Eastern psychology and great familiarity with consciousness effect through psychedelic drugs, his statement was often met with incredulity. How could such a simple exercise, if one could even call it an exercise, affect such major arenas as world peace and quality of life? Just what was meditation, anyway? And what did it do?

Although various forms of mental discipline are doubtless much older, the earliest body of yogic tradition that is still with us was synthesized and taught by the Hindu yogin Patanjali in India about 3,000 B.C. Called Raja Yoga, Patanjali's doctrine called for the use of meditative concentration to discipline the mind into a state of holiness. It was this Raja Yoga that Ralph Waldo Emerson, Henry David Thoreau and other American "transcendentalists" practiced in New England in the 1800s. Although they greatly influenced the culture of their day, the transcendentalists and their philosophy were out of synch with a rapidly industrializing and expanding culture, and they became little more than an American philosophic footnote in an era that looked on the East as inexplicable, a terra incognita whose main value was in supplying cheap labor and overseas markets for goods and Christianity.

At the end of World War II, many soldiers serving with occupation forces in Japan became interested in the meditation practices of Zen Buddhism. While the monks' explanations of what they were doing seemed inexplicable to the soldiers' Western minds, the practice of sitting was itself relatively simple, and the resulting calm and happiness were obvious. When a Zen master, D. T. Suzuki began writing in English about Zen, which is the Japanese form of Dhyana or C'han Buddhism, the concepts were still confusing, but his words found a receptive audience. In his book *An Introduction to Zen Buddhism*, Suzuki gave the following explanation:

> What is dhyana? Dhyana literally means, in Sanskrit, pacification, equilibration, or tranquillization, but as a religious discipline it is rather self-examination or introspection. It is not necessary to cogitate on the deep subjects of metaphysics, nor is it to contemplate the virtues of a deity, or the transitoriness of mundane life. To define its import in Buddhism, roughly and practically, it is the habit of withdrawing occasionally from the turbulence of worldliness and devoting some time to a

quiet inspection of one's own consciousness. When this habit is thoroughly established, a man can keep serenity of mind and cheerfulness of disposition, even in the midst of his whirlwind-like course of daily life. Dhyana is, then, a discipline in tranquillization. It aims at giving to the mind the time for deliberation, and saving it from running wild; it directs the vain and vulgar to the path of earnestness and reality; it makes us feel interest in higher things which are above the senses; it discovers the presence in us of a spiritual faculty which bridges the chasm between the finite and the infinite; and it finally delivers us from the bondage and torture of ignorance, safely leading us to the other shore of Nirvana.

Regular meditation, called *zazen*, is a key discipline in the practice of dhyana, or Zen. Followers of Zen often gather in retreats, or sesshins, and meditate for days at a time. This meditation may take any of several forms. The two most common are a directed form that involves concentration on a paradoxical conundrum, or koan, such as the question "What is the sound of one hand clapping?" and a variety of nondirected contemplations of the infinite void where the object is to obtain clarity of mind. The latter is called *shikan-taza*. These various practices do not in any way represent an escape from reality or a spacing-out. As Dr. Suzuki explains:

> The practice of dhyana is often confounded with a trance or self-hypnotism—a grave error which I here propose to refute. The difference between the two is patent to every clear-sighted mind, for a trance is a pathological disturbance of consciousness, while dhyana is a perfectly normal state of it. Trance is a kind of self-illusion, which is entirely subjective and cannot be objectively verified; but dhyana is a state of consciousness in which all mental powers are kept in equilibrium, so that no one thought or faculty is made predominant over others. It is like the pacification of turbulent waters by pouring oil over them. In a smooth, glossy mirror of immense dimension no waves are roaring, no foam is boiling, no splashes are spattering. And it is in this perfect mirror of consciousness that myriads of reflections, as it were, come and go without ever disturbing its serenity. In trances certain mental and physiological functions are unduly accelerated while others are kept altogether in abeyance, the whole system of consciousness thus being thrown into disorder; and its outcome is the loss of equilibrium in the organism, which is the very opposite to what is attained through the practice of dhyana.

It could be said that the eventual goal of Zen meditation is the attainment of a state of enlightenment every bit as exalted as that achieved by the Buddha. A Zen practitioner, however, would answer that anyone who is trying to gain enlightenment or reach Nirvana is attempting the impossible. Many of the Zen koans involve the paradoxical nature of life and lead one to the realization that most paradox is engendered by the individual insisting on dealing with spiritual matters from a standpoint of egocentricity. Far from going nowhere, Zen meditation can produce some startling results.

Philip Kapleau, an American businessman who became a Zen devotee and spent five years in Japan, describes his personal experience with *kensho* in his book *The Three Pillars of Zen: Teaching, Practice and Enlightenment.* Part of his realization, however, was that *kensho*, or enlightenment—or whatever you want to call it—is not an end but a beginning. Understanding oneself and one's place in the universe is an ongoing process. The enlightened one doesn't stop and say, "Okay, here I am." He continues traveling on a road marked by surprises and delights.

TM, or Transcendental Meditation

Not everyone has such dramatic results from meditation. It must be remembered that what Kapleau describes is the result of years of diligent practice. Not all of us have the time, the motivation or even the desire to devote that kind of intensity to meditative practices. To the average person who is searching for alternatives to alcohol and other drugs, such a commitment is not practical. What was needed was an approach to meditation that would provide benefits for Western humanity without totally disrupting the Western way of day-to-day living. In the 1960s, such a procedure arrived here from India.

The Maharishi Mahesh Yogi has been called the Henry Ford of meditation. Transcendental Meditation, or TM, as his doctrine is called, is a stripped-down, assembly-line, mass-production model of meditation. There is no religious practice attached to TM. It is based on the premise that if we sit quietly for twenty minutes twice a day and allow our minds to empty their chaotic garbage, we will naturally feel better and do a better job of living our lives. Eventually TM added frills, including long training sessions in France and Switzerland for its teachers and promises of such skills as the ability to levitate for its devoted students, but the basic vehicle was soundly tailored for Western needs and capabilities.

Initiation could be accomplished in a few hours. It consisted mainly of practical discussion on the mechanics of meditation. Practitioners of TM were instructed to sit with their eyes closed *regularly* for twenty minutes in the morning and evening. Maintenance of this schedule was stressed with the explanation that many of the good effects are cumulative and only regular practice ensures maximum benefits. Aside from the twenty-minute, twice-a-day requirement, practitioners could meditate on their own, wherever and whenever it was convenient for them. TM could be done in any posture, from the full lotus, which many Westerners find anatomically impossible, to sitting in a chair. Some TMers we know do their meditation while lying in bed.

TM meditation requires the use of a *mantra*. This is a sound of several syllables that is repeated silently during meditation. Many Eastern techniques use religious phrases or chants to this same purpose, but unlike these, the TM mantras have no meaning beyond being euphonic syllables that are easy to repeat throughout a meditation session. One's mantra is formally "invested" by a teacher at the end of a twelve-day abstention from all psychoactive substances. It was explained that this drug fast would purify the body and mind and make the mantra-enforced meditation more effective from the get-go. This makes good sense, especially to anyone in drug recovery. As with acupuncture and other mind-affective activities, the kindling effect of meditation is cumulative.

Since the advent of Transcendental Meditation, a number of other meditation techniques have been introduced into our society. Many of them have more or less religious overtones. Others are nonsectarian hybrids, often offered as courses at community colleges and similar forums of continuing education.

Using Meditation in Recovery

Like acupuncture, meditation has been a subject of much interpretation and misinterpretation in the West. One meditation teacher recently pointed out that whenever you sit, you are saying to God, "Here I am, do what you want with me." In a way, this is the same conduit system used in most Western notions of prayer, but with an opposite flow pattern. In prayer, we are usually trying to talk to God and communicate what we want. In meditation, we are trying to listen to God and find out what He wants. Seen in this way, illumination, *kensho*, realization, enlightenment—whatever we want to call it—is a path toward total communication with God, "as we understand Him," and acceptance of God's will.

In the 1960s, when Eastern psychology was flooding the Western world in the wake of psychedelic consciousness, people came to meditation for a wide variety of reasons. The concentration generated by meditation practices was considered a major ingredient in magic. There were Eastern pundits who supposedly could materialize objects out of thin air. Others could read minds, or communicate telepathically, or move large objects effortlessly, or change the very fabric of reality. Those were magic times, and many Westerners indulging in "cosmic consciousness" felt that with a little applied meditation, they, too, could operate beyond the laws of physics.

A good case can be made for profound psychological effects caused by meditation, but many of us who have continued to meditate on a regular basis have discovered a far more pragmatic result from the practice. In day-to-day life, the mind is in a state of frequent agitation. We are pulled this way and that by conflicting emotions and priorities. We are like pools that are constantly being stirred up and muddied. But have you ever watched what happens to a pond when it is allowed to sit for a period? In time the mud settles to the bottom and the water becomes clear. Quite simply, this is what happens to our minds in meditation.

This settling-out process may not be apparent at first. It's a developed skill, but in time one learns to relax the mind as one sits, and the cares of the day settle like mud. After a while we wonder what all the uproar was about and realize that whatever was getting to us is not really all that important.

One meditation teacher at a nearby community college reports that she may be really agitated when she gets to school; maybe she's had a fight with one of her kids. She gets to class and sits, and in a while the cause of agitation evaporates. After the first class she calls home and says, "We can work it out."

Best of all, there's nothing you have to do. You don't have to press a special calm button. It just happens.

YOGA

In his book *Great Systems of Yoga*, Ernest Wood states that yoga means "union." He elaborates that yoga is "the practice of occult powers—or rather the discovery and use of those powers residing unseen in the depths of the human mind. . . . Yoga means union—with the latent possibilities and unseen actualities of and beyond the mind. The Introspectional Psychology, all ancient teachers asserted, is justified by its results; it works."

Like meditation, which it includes, yoga has a very pragmatic bottom line. A lot of high-flown metaphysical terminology has been used through the millennia to describe yoga, but the final consideration is: either it works, or it doesn't work. Americans and other Westerners who have taken to practicing yoga on a regular basis have discovered that when it is done correctly, it works.

As we said at the beginning of this section, there are many forms of yoga. Wood recognized ten original Oriental yogas and classified them into two basic groups. These are Raja Yoga and Hatha Yoga. Although they do tend to overlap, Raja Yoga concentrates its practice on the mind, while Hatha Yoga concentrates its practice on the body. The division with which we have become most familiar in the West is Hatha Yoga. Hatha Yoga is primarily concerned with exercise. A strict interpretation of the doctrine, however, limits this exercise to breathing. *Ha* represents the incoming breath, while *tha* is the exhalation. In general, Hatha Yoga also involves the performing of certain *asanas*, or yogic postures. Many of us have become familiar with at least a few of these *asanas*, such as the cobra, the plow and the lion. There are many pictorial books on the market that show step-by-step how to do yogic *asanas*.

One must keep in mind, however, that there are some fundamental differences between Hatha Yoga and traditional Western exercise. The person who tries to execute a yoga *asana* as though he were doing Marine Corps calisthenics is apt to injure more than his pride. The best approach is to find a yoga course with an experienced teacher, which you can do on most community college campuses and in many community centers.

One quality of Hatha Yoga is that none of the movement is to be forced. Every *asana* is to be relaxed into. The body's natural inclinations are gently guided by the mind into developing the flexibility necessary to perform the exercises. Rather than forcing the body to perform, in yoga one concentrates on allowing the body to do what it can easily do at any given time.

Yoga teachers are dealing with powerful forces that can do good but can also do damage, and accordingly they need to take care. Rick Seymour remembers one occasion at California State University at Sonoma in the late 1960s when Hatha Yoga was first coming into vogue on college campuses.

> I was sitting in front of the student union when I saw a line of young men and women in gym shorts and T-shirts following an older man, similarly dressed, who was twisted and grimacing. The line of students copied his tortured form and features while they all shuffled across the campus. I thought that it might be a mass rehearsal for crippled beggars in some biblical passion play but later learned that it was the morning yoga class headed for the school infirmary. All of them, including the teacher, had simultaneously wrenched their backs while attempting an *asana* they were unprepared for.

The most important thing to remember in any form of Hatha Yoga is not to force anything. If it isn't easy, don't do it. Any *asana* should be mastered by relaxing into it, not by force of will or muscle. As in any discipline that involves exercise, some soreness is to be expected, especially at the beginning. You may need to adopt modified exercises and positions if the standard ones are impossible. For example, some Western folks never do manage to recondition their bodies so they can sit cross-legged on a cushion in meditation for long periods of time. While certain meditation masters insist that the legs must be in a full or half lotus, or at least crossed, while one sits erect on a low cushion, others recognize that most Westerners grew up sitting in chairs, and they reason that the stress and pain of trying to adopt a totally unfamiliar sitting posture far outweighs any benefit derived from using the orthodox postures.

The specific goal of Hatha Yoga is the development of strength, balance and flexibility. Although the visible manifestation of these is physical, it should be noted that these exercises affect the full tripartite nature of our being. As the body moves in new ways the mind follows and moves in new ways as well.

ENLIGHTENMENT

It has many names. In Japanese Zen practices, it's *kensho*. In Eastern Orthodox Christianity, it may be called "going to God." The followers of Buddha called it *parinirvana*. These names and their different shades of meaning have been collectively termed "enlightenment" in our Western culture.

Personal enlightenment has been considered an important life goal in a number of societies. People who have studied such disciplines point out that the Twelve Steps of the self-help programs can be seen as a pathway to enlightenment. They cite especially the eleventh step, "Sought through prayer and meditation to improve our conscious contact with God as we understand Him, praying only for knowledge of His will for us and the power to carry that out." Others consider such spiritual paths to be illusory and a waste of time in our modern, materialist and competitive world. Whichever your opinion may be, however, some form of enlightenment has represented the ultimate goal for many of the disciplines we have been discussing. Therefore, a few words on the subject may help clarify that potential aspect of our recovery and personal development.

Psychedelic drug users talked a lot about enlightenment in the "psychedelic sixties." At a time when many believed that world peace was just around the corner and justice could be gained by developing group consciousness, the mass enlightenment of all humanity seemed just ahead on humanity's evolutionary trail. The new American and European mystics read gnostic and other metaphysical scriptures that contained a bewildering variety of mystical religious experience. Many thought that if they took enough LSD, they would become every bit as enlightened as Lama Anagarika Govinda, Meher Baba, Sri Yukteswar, Baba Ram Dass, Yogananda, and Timothy Leary, to name only a few.

It all seemed very simple at first: a clap of thunder, or a Zen roshi slapping his hand on a table at the right moment, or reciting the correct number of mantras, and there it would be, nirvana, the "Big E!"

The more reading, practicing and/or taking psychedelics that the "explorers of inner space" did, however, the more confusing, fleeting and downright ephemeral enlightenment became. There were disturbing questions. For example, the Buddhist saints—great beings called *Bodhi*-

sattvas—were obviously enlightened but took an oath not to enter nirvana "so long as one blade of grass remained unenlightened."

In the sixties, religious gurus flocked to the Western limelight. Many of them guaranteed instant, or at least very rapid, enlightenment to their followers, usually in exchange for money or extensive "services." One so-called guru conferred enlightenment with a certificate, suitable for framing; you could fill in your name and hang it on the wall. The requirement for that particular brand of enlightenment was the ability to send twenty dollars through the mail to the "guru's" post-office box.

Other mystical religious leaders either described enlightenment as something gained after many years, or even lifetimes, of devotion and practice or maintained that there really was no such thing as enlightenment, no matter what you called it. Most of these did not seek to establish large followings or get Rolls-Royces but concentrated on speaking and writing what they considered to be the truth.

One problem that may be at the root of much enlightenment controversy is the lack of any clear definitions. By its very nature, the concept of enlightenment is as ineffable and personal as one's concept of God. The truth of what enlightenment means may only be shared by truly enlightened people—if any such actually exist. Then again, the truly enlightened may be sure only of their own state of being. It all can get very confusing.

MINDFULNESS

Sylvia Boorstein, a teacher of what she calls "practice in mindfulness," has been practicing meditation and following a spiritual path for most of her life. She recalls the attitudes about meditation and enlightenment that were prevalent in the 1960s and comments that many people were looking for magical powers then. She feels that has changed, and those who continue to practice today have far different or at least more practical goals.

She views enlightenment not as a sudden, life-changing revelation, but more as a process of personal evolution that involves increasing sensitivity and compassion. If there is such a thing as enlightenment, it's not something that comes all at once and changes us forever. It consists of small glimpses that prompt small changes in consciousness that help us to become better human beings over time.

The process of enlightenment, even as depicted in the Ox panels, can be seen as a cyclic event. In practice, at any given time, we are somewhere on the circle of panels. The Zen Buddhists have a saying, "Before enlightenment, chop wood, carry water. After enlightenment, chop wood, carry water." Human activities continue, no matter what the state of mind, but the state of mind itself can change.

One can come to the realization that the only thing in life that can be controlled is one's attitude toward it. At first this may seem like a negative and very deterministic view but, all things taken into consideration, a realistic one. Genetic and environmental factors, family, society, health—all the multitude of interactions—form the web of our lives. And yet we may control our attitude to it all, and that, as the sage may say, can be the difference between nirvana and samsara, or heaven and hell. Even though we may be caught in a web of circumstance, that web is finely tuned to our attitudes and paradoxically will change as our attitudes affect it.

Sometimes a stage may be a momentary flash, leaving in its wake a sense of buoyancy, of bliss, the fleeting veil of a loving presence. At other times the experience may cause lasting changes, may begin opening a road to a higher state of consciousness. This state—call it bliss—is an active, dynamic state not to be compared to the blitzed-out chemically induced inactivity that one experiences when drunk on alcohol or stoned on other drugs. Those who have stopped using drugs report that the experience of bliss slowly returns, like a thing of beauty that has been chased away by blight. The enlightened state colors our being and our actions. As it grows, the enlightened state can bring delight and a sense of wonder to the most mundane of activities—even those of chopping wood and hauling water.

EASTERN ODDS AND ENDS

Before we leave the decreasingly mysterious Far East, let's look briefly at a few of the other possible alternatives abounding in that part of the world. As we pointed out, many forms of experimental and participatory psychology developed in the East lend themselves especially well to dealing with the human desires and problematic mysteries that lead many to the path of drugs. The basic practices of Hatha Yoga and meditation are perhaps the best known of these formats, but they by no means represent the entirety. These have not been greatly studied in the West, nor has Western science shed any real light of understanding on them, as it has with the more familiar forms of yoga and meditation. But there is ever-increasing evidence that these methods do work and can help the recovering person. Let us therefore review some of the other practices, paths that may in time become clearer to the Western mind.

MANTRA, YANTRA AND TANTRA

Although rooted in Hindu and Buddhist tradition, tantra and tantric yoga have developed several unique aspects that are little understood in

the West. The tantra tradition, as a whole, flowered within the development of Tibetan Lamaism. Lamaism is the result of a Buddhist overlay on
the pre-Buddhist magical religions that early missionaries from India
found in the Himalayan mountains. The hybrid that resulted has excited
Western minds with its iconography and complex yogas ever since Tibet
was first opened to Western scrutiny by the British Younghusband expedition of 1904. Even before then, that mysterious highland was considered an almost mythic omphalos of world mysticism. The lamas and the
people of Tibet kept to themselves, and only a few Westerners, such as
Alexandra David-Neel, who disguised herself as a man in order to enter
the country, and Walter Yeeling Evans-Wentz were able to gain the trust
and cooperation of the Tibetans in order to study their world.

Evans-Wentz was an American, a Californian who grew up in the
shadow of Mount Shasta, the holy spirit mountain of the California Indians, went to Oxford and then to Sikkim to study Vajrayana, as the
Tibetan tantric discipline is called. There he was asked by Lama Kazi
Dawa-Samdup to edit and introduce in the West a series of Tibetan holy
books that had previously been forbidden to anyone but practicing lamas.
Among these were the *Bardo Thodol*, translated as *The Tibetan Book of the
Dead*, and *Tibetan Yoga and Secret Doctrines*. Even in translation, these
books were highly esoteric and considered of little more than scholarly
interest until the 1960s.

In 1964, in the midst of their experimentation with LSD, Timothy Leary
and his colleagues at Harvard University read *The Tibetan Book of the Dead*.
On the basis of their personal experience, they decided that it was not an
esoteric mythology involving life after death, but a manual for dealing
with altered states of consciousness. They published a loose revision of
Evans-Wentz's book titled *The Psychedelic Experience: A Manual Based on the
Tibetan Book of the Dead*. This served as an introduction to the effects of
psychedelic drugs for many in the 1960s.

Tibetan yoga books may have described altered states of consciousness,
but what they described was based on hundreds of years of yogic experience rather than on the use of drugs. Once readers get beyond the pyro-
technic descriptions of experience, they can see the methods used to gain
these states of consciousness through the practice of tantra and Vajrayana
yoga.

Many tantric practices make use of mantras and yantras. Mantras we
have encountered before in the Transcendental Meditation of the
Maharishi Mahesh Yogi. These are chanted or thought sound syllables,
sometimes religious sayings, that are used in meditation to interrupt the
flow of irrelevant thought and enhance concentration by ordering the
mind. One of the most well-known of these is the *"Aum mani padme hum,"*
chanted by many Buddhists. Chants are used by disciplines in most
religions, including Christianity.

Yantras are visual aids to meditation. Unless one's practice calls for closed eyes, one has to look at something. The simplest of these devices may just be a lighted candle. Many yantras are circular in design and are called mandalas. Others may depict symbolic religious motifs, gods and goddesses or saints, but these are not merely religious paintings. They serve a specific yogic function in drawing the eyes through certain patterns that help order the mind through sight just as mantras do through sound.

An aspect of tantric yoga that has brought it much attention and more than a little misinterpretation in the West is that it makes use of physical activities in its practice that are not ordinarily considered spiritual, including coitus. We don't ordinarily think of sex as a religious activity, but in tantra it is formalized, venerated and performed in a ritualistic context in such ways that the erotic physiochemical experience of coupling and orgasm act to further the self-discovery and spiritual advancement of the practitioner.

This use of sex should not be too surprising. When one considers what an integral part of consciousness sex represents, it's surprising that other practices don't involve it more. Sex is certainly a major factor in the use of drugs. Several years ago, the Haight Ashbury Free Medical Clinic presented a national conference on drugs and sex that revealed a wide range of concerns involving both dysfunction during drug use and sex as a factor in abuse. Perhaps in time a clearer understanding of the spiritual use of sex in tantra and in the earlier Buddhist and Hindu practices will help us to heal sexual problems caused or at least exacerbated by the abuse of alcohol and other drugs.

MAN TOLD ME TO FIND HAPPINESS FILL THE LUNGS
MAN TOLD ME TO FIND HAPPINESS EMPTY LUNGS
—R. Singer (Surya)

Underlying virtually all yoga and meditation is the understanding that breath represents the interchange between man and the universe. Most of the religions that form bases for these practices recognize that all consciousness is divine, and further, that the natural habitat of consciousness is the air we breathe. Therefore, when we breathe we are breathing pure consciousness, or God as they conceive him. It behooves us to breathe correctly, and behind all the *asanas* or postures of yoga and behind the concentration of both yoga and meditation is attention to correct breathing.

According to most of these doctrines, man is endowed with a "subtle" body that processes consciousness at the same time our material body is processing oxygen. This *prana* passes through two channels, the *ida* and the *pingala*. These intertwine with each other, following roughly the same course as our spinal column. At each point where they cross is an energy center, called in some disciplines a *chakra*, or wheel. These *chakras* and the channels are involved in *kundalini*, or serpent energy, which, when activated, can travel up and out of the body, connecting our consciousness directly with cosmic consciousness. Yogins who are involved with *kundalini* practices warn that it is a powerful energy that no one should mess with unless he or she has had thorough training and supervision. They say activating this energy would be like going into a power station and pulling switches at random. You don't know what might happen. Kundalini yoga, however, is a complex discipline far removed from the "watching the breath," or breathing exercises that most forms of meditation or yoga call for. In other words, be aware of it, but don't worry about it.

WHIRLING

In *The Natural Mind*, Andrew Weil, M.D., points out that many children first experience altered states of consciousness by deliberately whirling. "Anyone who watches very young children without revealing his presence will find them regularly practicing techniques that induce striking changes in mental states. Three- and four-year-olds, for example, commonly whirl themselves into vertiginous stupors."

It's no wonder, then, that there are adults in this world who persist in doing similar things. Perhaps the best known whirlers are the Near Eastern whirling dervishes, who follow a yogic practice that involves protracted periods of spinning about. One presumes that their concentration prevents wobbling off and into one another like so many skipping tops and instead keeps them on their feet, more or less in place, and in an increasing state of vertiginous bliss.

Many peoples perform religious dances. In fact, it may well be that dance in general has its origins in yogalike practices. For our own purposes, vigorous dancing can be a form of aerobic exercise. As with other such exercises, it seems to create a sense of exhilaration. Besides, it can be a lot of fun.

FULL CIRCLE TO WHAT'S BEHIND THE STEREOTYPES

At the beginning of the section on meditation and yoga we mentioned some of the stereotypes Westerners have held regarding the activities of Eastern holy men. These images are not merely figments of our Western imagination. They actually exist. But are they useful for any purpose beyond inspiring awe and prompting donations?

Many religious figures, including Christ, spent some time in isolation on a mountaintop, or in a cave, or off in the desert wilderness. Much of early monasticism is based on the spirituality engendered by solitude and the cloistered practice of meditation. Many people seem just as capable of concentration in the midst of life. The Buddha center in Benares, for example, the holiest meditation site, is located right on the main street, where traffic—including cars, buses, camels and elephants—is constantly passing noisily by.

Many forms of asceticism are practiced in the name of improving concentration and gaining spiritual power. From time to time one of these practices gains a foothold in Western fashion. Currently there appears to be a lot of interest in walking across glowing coals; it has become trendy, so to speak. We have talked to several individuals who have attempted this practice with training and claim that successful coal walking has done great things for their concentration and self-esteem. We don't recommend it, however.

These and other practices seem curious to us now, and they don't appear to have any direct application to recovery or growth in the West. We must remember, however, that up until a few years ago acupuncture was considered Eastern mumbo-jumbo, a placebo practice with no application in Western treatment. Yoga and meditation were likewise considered mere curiosities until recent decades. The world out there is full of mysteries, and some of them could be tomorrow's viable paths to health and fulfillment.

EXERCISE

Although we may be what we think, as the Buddha has stated, there are many possible stages between the thought and the state of being, all of them related. Mood, which is the outward manifestation of one's state of mind, can affect one's state of mind and vice versa. Physical health and brain chemistry can, in turn, have a profound effect on both mood and state of mind. Essentially, what we do with our bodies can have a profound and long-term effect on our minds, and what we do with our minds can likewise have a profound and long-term effect on our bodies. All these interactions can be involved with our desires to use or not to use drugs, since they involve our totality of being in relation to our living experience. In recent times we have turned to science in our attempts to understand these interactions.

Science has often been described as our means of discovering and explaining the obvious. Such appears to be the case with exercise. It is common knowledge that at least certain kinds of physical activity help us to feel good. In recent years it has become increasingly apparent that certain regimens of physical exercise, practiced on a regular basis, can improve both our physical and our mental well-being. Even though it may be hard work and temporarily exhausting, the end result is usually positive. There are many reasons for this: the development of self-esteem, feelings of accomplishment, physical enhancement involving both weight loss and muscle development. A good exercise regimen, continued over time, will produce distinct improvements. Exercise will at least improve one's ability to exercise. Now science has indicated that there are unseen, subtle ways in which exercise can help us. For example, we are starting to learn how various types of exercise affect the neurotransmission system in ways that bear a direct relationship to recovery and abstinence from drugs.

Aerobic exercise of various kinds seems especially helpful to the individual seeking alternatives to alcohol and other drugs. This is exercise that involves the raising of both heartbeat and respiratory rate for sustained periods. Aerobic exercise has come into fashion and can be practiced at gymnasiums, health spas, universities and colleges, community centers and even in your own living room with a videocassette made by your favorite show-business personality. The most popular form of aerobic exercise is jogging. Perhaps this is because jogging can be done just about anywhere, doesn't require any special equipment besides a pair of good shoes and can be done at one's own pace without special training.

RUNNING FOR YOUR LIFE

In the late 1970s, Arnold J. Mandell, M.D., the cochairman of the Department of Psychiatry at the University of California Medical School at San Diego and a prominent researcher in brain chemistry and psychopharmacology, was one of the scientists who "discovered" the benefits of running. In his own words, "I was thirty-nine when my coronary arteries were used up." Mandell took up running as an attempt to stay alive. His book *Coming of (Middle) Age: A Journey,* describes his embarrassment at putting on a green running suit and red Adidas and his fear at the warnings about "sudden deaths in middle-aged men during Saturday-picnic sack races."

Mandell had grown up as an "intellectual." His circle denigrated physical exercise and all those who indulged in it. Like many American boys, he dreamed of glory on the playing field but knew that he didn't have the physical wherewithal to make the team, any team. He knew that getting into condition and not making the team would be humiliating, so he never got into condition, never even knew what getting into condition meant. As a consequence, he approached middle age as an overworking, hyperactive, overweight and fairly typical American adult, strongly attached to cigarette smoking and overeating. Arnold's problem wasn't addiction. Like many of us, however, his life was cluttered with bad habits, and there were very few good ones to offset them. There was very little motivation to exercise beyond the occasional round of golf that comprised his middle-class society's token physical activity. It took a failing cardiovascular system to change his way of living.

He started out running fifty yards slowly and then walking fifty yards briskly; checking his pulse. In about sixteen months, when he had reached the point of running ten miles in a hundred minutes and coming to a resting pulse of fifty-four beats, "the secret that deprecating gym teachers had kept from me was revealed: being in condition is a drug for the mind."

You'll notice he didn't say that running is a drug for the mind. He said that being in condition is a drug for the mind. That is an important distinction. Exercise is not like taking a pill, or smoking a cigarette, or downing a drink. In the scheme of things, the effects of alcohol and other drugs are nearly instantaneous. Aerobic exercise is much slower and more subtle in its effects on our body and mind; it's more like acupuncture or yoga. The effects take a while to build up a head of steam. However, its effects are no less powerful in their cumulative force than are the short-term, fleeting effects of alcohol and other drugs.

Like many people who have discovered the rapture of running, Dr. Mandell got into it in a big way. He ran long distances, savoring the psychoactive effect. In *Coming of (Middle) Age: A Journey*, he describes the "spooky time" in the second hour of running when "colors are bright and beautiful, water sparkles, clouds breathe, and my body, swimming, detaches from the earth. A loving contentment invades the basement of my mind, and thoughts bubble up without trails."

As a neuroscientist, he not only could appreciate the effects of running on his consciousness, he could begin to understand them as well. He lost weight and developed a stamina he had never had before. His cardiovascular problems came under control. But these were all more or less expected outcomes of long-term, intense physical activity. The changes in consciousness were a not-altogether-expected bonus. In explaining the effects of running, he describes running as a language, a means of communication: "Until relatively recently the only way to talk to the brain was with words."

As we saw in earlier chapters, words are not the most effective way of talking to the brain. Alcohol and other drugs speak much more directly, conveying solutions to problems that work for a while. Aerobic exercise is a way of talking to the brain in the same way that drugs do, but with much more positive results. These ways of communicating speak directly to our neurotransmitter systems, bringing about emotional and conceptual as well as physiological change.

The running literature, when it waxes philosophical, may talk about running in terms startlingly similar to those used with drugs. Mandell cites the literature as saying that "if you run six miles a day for two months, you are addicted forever." A recent News America Syndicate feature by Fred Moody, titled "When Jogging Becomes an Addiction" and describing a twelve-step meeting of addicted runners, was not entirely tongue in cheek. In truth, running can become a compulsive pursuit. There are instances in which the runners can and have gotten carried away, devoting long hours to the pursuit of "runner's high."

It is a truth of addictive behavior that anything that makes one feel good can become a focus of compulsion. Many activities have their dark side. Weight management may turn compulsive and become anorexia or bulimia. A desire to succeed can become a blind obsession with power. Love of God can become a destructive fanaticism. Let's face it, human beings are capable of getting carried away, and many things can be dangerous when taken to their extremes.

The causes of runner's high appear similar to what happens in acupuncture. Experiments have shown that sustained running increases levels of brain endorphins, those internal peptides that give us euphoria and pain management. Like acupuncture, running seems to do more of a positive nature than can be rightfully attributed to internal "opiates." The discovery that running increases endorphin production indicates that it may do other positive things for us as well.

The effect, as experience would lead us to believe, is not immediate. It's as though one has to be turned on to running over time. The desired results from running are cumulative, but once they develop, they are real.

In addition to the production of internal opioids, running and aerobic exercise in general appear to have a dampening effect on the locus ceruleus discharges that various researchers connect to the onset of drug hunger in addicts. Running also seems highly effective in stress reduction on a regular basis. Whatever the mechanism, we have begun prescribing running as a means of decreasing drug hunger during early recovery. The results have been sufficiently promising for us to recommend a regular regimen of running and/or other aerobic exercise to anyone in recovery or otherwise seeking alternatives to alcohol and other drugs. The effects are cumulative, and they are subtle at first, but in a surprisingly short time you may find very tangible returns for the investment of time and energy.

Running and the Immune System

Since we began working on this book, scientific evidence has come to light indicating that running and other aerobic exercise not only increases endorphins but may enhance the functioning of the immune system as well. Research is showing that the presence of T lymphocytes, prime components in the body's ability to fight off disease, is markedly greater in individuals who are engaged in regular aerobic exercise. Anecdotal evidence seems to back up these findings, indicating that folks who exercise regularly get sick less often than those who do not. The evidence is strong enough that AIDS treatment and prevention programs are now recommending regular exercise to those who are in early stages or may have been exposed to the disease as well as abstinence from drugs that may suppress the immune system.

General Safeguards

Anyone taking up running, especially someone who has been away from strenuous exercise for a long time, should get a comprehensive physical examination before getting into it. Even if you are physically fit, take it easy at first and slowly increase your distance. In fact, it pays to take it easy as long as you are running. As one long-term runner advises, "Start off slow and slack off from there." Another refers to what she does as "LSD"—that is, "long, slow distance." Keep in mind that sports medicine is one of the biggest therapeutic growth industries, and a lot of the injuries treated by sports medicine specialists are running injuries.

Most running injuries are a result of pushing beyond one's limits. It's fine to set a goal of eventually running in a ten-kilometer race or a marathon, but don't try to do it the first week out. The best way is to slowly increase your running to an optimum cardiovascular level. There are differences of opinion as to just what that level is. We recommend about twenty minutes of elevated heartbeat, which for most of us equates to about two miles of running. Twenty minutes of any cardiovascular exercise, or enough to get you sweaty and breathing hard, four or five times a week should satisfy all basic exercise needs. If you want to do more, you could try longer runs once or twice a week. Or you could alternate running with other forms of aerobic exercise through the week.

Of course, if you really want to, you can build yourself up to entering the "iron man" competitions, go into exercise ecstasy with Arnold Mandell or do equivalents of the Sierra hundred-mile run. Remember, however, running itself can be a focus of "compulsion, loss of control and continued exertion in spite of adverse consequences." We have known people who continued running with acute tendonitis or other worsening injuries with as much denial as they ever applied to their drinking or drug addiction. Keep running and the pain will go away? Don't bet on it. The endorphins may mask the pain of a running injury for a while, but they won't mend a torn ligament or a pulled tendon.

Runners must also guard against the mistaken belief that because they are exercising they can indulge in bad eating habits and other physical excesses with impunity. Running may help keep the pounds down, but it has no effect on such potentially destructive things as cholesterol buildup in the cardiovascular system from eating too many animal fats and other rich foods.

As with anything that helps us feel good, running can produce its own compulsive behavior. We must, therefore, take care, even if injuries don't take place, that we're not spending time on the track or trail that is needed elsewhere. Used wisely, running can be a rewarding activity, able to do more for us than just decrease drug hunger. Runners often develop a sense of self-worth and accomplishment that can help to dismantle the poor self-image that many abusers and addicts have, especially in the early stages of recovery. If not overdone, running provides a basis for physical improvement and well-being.

THE AEROBIC CONNECTION

Virtually everything that we have had to say about running is true for other forms of aerobic exercise as well. Exercise can take many forms, but the most effective regimens include a warm-up period, about twenty minutes of elevated heartbeat and a cool-down at the end. Some aerobic programs include Hatha Yoga *asanas* and/or variations of t'ai chi chuan and other Eastern forms of exercise. In that many exercise teachers seem to have studied ballet or other forms of dance, ballet exercises are often integral to their programs. Often these programs are more strenuous and demanding than running.

They can also be dangerous, especially if a teacher is inexperienced or insensitive to the limitations of those who have not had access to long-term exercise. A good exercise teacher will be aware that members of the group will be at different levels of proficiency, suppleness and ability. There should be frequent reminders to take things at your own pace and not to overdo.

Aerobic exercise has become an "in" thing to do in every part of the world that is touched by Euro-American culture, and it's as easy to find a class in Tokyo, Japan or Papeete, Tahiti as it is in Marbella, Spain or Kent-field, California. Books and videocassettes are being produced by exercise buffs and movie stars, each with the "secret" of good exercise. Some people are calling aerobic exercise the "American Hatha Yoga."

With everyone and his sister putting together an exercise program and marketing it, it is hard to tell whether aerobic exercise is evolving or merely diversifying. As serious teachers continue to involve themselves in the field and to interact with health professionals in sports medicine a few things are being learned about how the human body reacts to exercise, and exercise is being modified accordingly. One example of this is the development of "nonimpact aerobics."

Generally, basic aerobic exercise involves a great amount of jumping around, and as more and more neo-Nijinskys became aerobic teachers the vertical impact quotient of the exercise increased. Nonimpact aerobics came about as a means of dealing with an increasing number of foot and leg injuries suffered by students and teachers alike. Advisers in the sports medicine field studied the dynamics of the exercise to find out why such problems as shin splints and pulled muscles occur. Once they identified as culprits exercises that involved jarring impact with thin mats or hardwood floors, they worked with influential teachers to promote specific exercises that provide the cardiovascular and other desired effects of higher-impact exercises while minimizing the wear and tear on one's skeletomuscular structure.

Even though safer forms of exercise are catching on, it is wise to choose the teacher and group with great care. Listen to signals from your body and react accordingly. Some stiffness and aches are to be expected, especially when one is beginning an exercise regimen, but excessive soreness or specific inflammation should be checked out by a doctor. If you have any sort of physical problem or injury, you should discuss it with your exercise teacher. A good one will be able to tell you what you can do and what exercises to sit out.

BESIDES RUNNING AND AEROBIC EXERCISE

Running and aerobic exercise are just two of many activities that will improve cardiovascular health and stimulate the production of endorphins and other peptides. Others include swimming (which is the original "nonimpact" exercise), tennis and such active team sports as basketball and soccer. Many people have taken up walking, and an increasing number of health professionals are calling a good swift walk of several miles one of the better forms of cardiovascular exercise.

Although we now know some of the scientific reasons why exercise helps in recovery from substance abuse and addiction, those of us who indulge in it have known for a long time that exercise makes us feel good. The greatest danger is that of injury from trying to do too much too quickly. Those who are used to compulsive behavior need to avoid the tendency to go from zero to twenty miles in the first week of running or to exercise for three hours straight the first time they get on a gymnasium floor. Start slowly and slack off from there.

Those who are used to fast—fast—fast relief need to remember that the good effects of exercise are cumulative. They don't hit you over the head like a shot of heroin or vodka. They may be slow, but they are sure.

TO SLEEP, PERCHANCE TO DREAM

Current research indicates that the major psychoactive drug groups are able to cause changes in our consciousness because their molecular structures and effects mimic in part those of internally produced substances. If this is true, it would follow that any of the desired effects that we have sought through the use of drugs can be obtained by other, less dangerous, less enslaving means. The initial motivations for using drugs are often positive in their inception. As Andy Weil has pointed out, "People use drugs because they work." These motivations may include the desire for wisdom and truth, for mastery over pain or negative emotions, for improvement of work performance, for relaxation and for improvement of social skills. Unfortunately, in seeking to self-medicate our ills and shortcomings we have unconsciously bought the slogan, "Alcohol and other drugs are good and provide temporary relief from emotional discomfort without negative aftereffects."

Many people have a great fascination for altered states of consciousness. Since the 1960s, a great many young people have indulged in cosmic-scale alteration of consciousness with such drugs as LSD, mescaline and MDA. Even today, the exploration of inner space through the use of MDMA and other phenethylamines continues to be a focus for a theoretically conservative younger generation. Many who today decry the use of any drugs still maintain that the "psychedelic" experience that they may have undergone while fledgling seekers was of profound value to them. Baba Ram Dass, the former Dr. Richard Alpert, once pointed out to Meher Baba that, given the nature of Western culture, he and many others would never have started upon a spiritual path had it not been for their introduction to holy consciousness through psychedelic drugs.

According to various ethnopharmacologists, many of the roads to deep mysticism either started with or were enhanced by the use of psychedelic substances. R. Gordon Wasson linked the use of both ergotamine and the psychedelic mushroom *Amanita muscaria* to the classical mystery religions. In a foreword to his two-volume compendium *The Greek Myths*, the British historian and poet Robert Graves suggests that much in Greek mythology may have resulted from the use of psychedelic substances. In particular, he mentions both *Amanita muscaria* and the dung mushroom, *Panaeolus papilionaceus*, as bases for the divine "ambrosia and nectar" used by the gods and demigods. He cites a variety of references in the myths themselves and emblematic motifs in ancient statuary and votive paraphernalia to support his theory that many of the demigods and goddesses were actually sacred kings and queens of the pre-Classical era who used these substances to gain deep religious insights and an understanding of the gods.

The psychedelic link is not limited to the Classical Greek and Roman cosmogony. Wasson, for example, believes that European ideas of heaven and hell may have derived from experiences similar to those encountered by both him and Graves in psilocybin rites of the Mazatec Indians of Oaxaca. Other commentators have pointed out the use of potent psychedelics by mystically oriented religious groups in many parts of the world.

Of course, this is not to say that psychedelic drugs are the only means by which one can achieve transcendental experience. Such a statement is not only totally inaccurate, but would run counter to the thesis of this book. Psychedelic drug experience, fleeting and confusing as it is, is not the stuff of long-term inner development. Proper and lasting spiritual growth and the development of personal maturity requires practice and insights that no drug can provide over the long haul. Yet for many, psychedelic drugs provided a taste, an introduction, to transcendental experience that has led them into a variety of spiritual practices that have solidified the beginnings encountered with the use of LSD and other consciousness-effective drugs. Many others have taken other turns in their lives and look back on their psychedelic experiences with feelings ranging from nostalgia to sheer horror.

We now know that psychedelic drugs, like any other psychoactive substances, can be dangerous. Indeed, the drugs in this category that have been involved in nonmedical use are nearly all included in Schedule 1 of the Federal Controlled Substances Act and are therefore considered to have a high abuse potential and no medical usefulness. Even without the laws against their use, taking psychedelic drugs is a chancy proposition for anyone, particularly someone who is practicing abstention and a life of recovery. Does this mean that those of us who do not wish to use psychoactive substances are cut off from psychedelic experience? Not at all.

Life in our society makes many demands upon us. Most of us simply don't have the time or the inclination to indulge in many of the nondrug accesses to psychedelic experience. Most of us aren't inclined to run twenty-five miles a day and experience the raptures described by Arnold Mandell, nor do we have the inclination to drop everything and spend half a decade in Japanese monasteries in order to experience Kapleau's Zen enlightenment. There is no doubt that these experiences and their side effects would do many of us a world of good, but that degree of dedication is hard to come by. Besides, who would feed the canary, raise the kids, pay the mortgage and get the next chapter to the editor? Gee! It was a lot easier to just take 500 micrograms of "Windowpane" LSD and sit down under a eucalyptus tree.

What if we were to tell you that you don't need to run 175 miles a week, or sit in zendo for months at a time, or eat mushrooms with shamans in Oaxaca, or smoke exotic herbs in the high Himalayas in order to have transcendent psychedelic experiences? What if we were to tell you that many of us have profound and vivid psychedelic visions on a regular basis without either using drugs or resorting to arduous and time-consuming activities? What if we were to tell you that you probably do it yourself, often, without even thinking about it?

The access to profound psychedelic experiences is so matter-of-fact, so common to our collective experience, that we don't think of it as such. However, J. C. Callaway of the University of California at San Francisco School of Pharmacy has, and he has shared the results of his research with us.

Callaway points out that few publications have considered the psychedelic experience as a natural state of mind. He suggests that through dreams the mind experiences alternate states of consciousness on a regular basis, whether the ego wants to or not. Further, the purpose of dream occurrence may be to gain perspective and insight into waking reality.

Most human beings spend about a third of their lives in the rest and rejuvenation process we call sleep. To the best of our knowledge, less than a quarter of this time is spent dreaming, or what is often referred to as "rapid eye movement sleep," or REMS. REMS is one of five qualitatively different stages of sleep as characterized by electroencephalographic, or EEG, activity. According to Callaway, the REM stage usually increases in length during the sleep cycle, often reaching a period of approximately two hours in length prior to waking. Dreams also increase in length and intensity throughout the sleep cycle. The longest, most vivid and emotionally charged dreams tend to occur just before we get up. These are the dreams we are most likely to remember.

Since dreaming is considered to be a brain-mind phenomenon, one may be inclined to suggest a chemical mechanism to describe the event. Callaway suggests that the dream-producing mechanism is similar in nature to what occurs when one takes a psychedelic drug, and that it involves essentially the same system of neurotransmitters. The primary chemical agents may be carbolines that are produced naturally in the brain during sleep in conjunction with psychoactive, eudogenous tryptamines, such as dimethyltryptamine (DMT) and 5-methoxy DMT.

Similar alkaloids are the active ingredients in the psychedelic preparation *ayahuasca*, which is used by South American shamans to produce visions. Unlike the hallucinations produced by LSD, these drugs don't produce distortions in form, depth-movement perception or color. The primary function of these drugs has been the production of out-of-body experiences, clairvoyance, simultaneous group visions, remote viewing and divination. The medical anthropologist Claudio Naranjo reports that the most frequently occurring phenomena with these drugs are the appearance of images on flat surfaces and the coexistence of visions with an ongoing and undistorted perception of one's surroundings. Abundant bright and vivid colors were reported by users with their eyes closed. Naranjo also noted "rapid lateral vibration in the vision field" of those experiencing visions. The vibration could be interpreted as an awake version of REM. To further confirm a possible harmala alkaloid—REM dream sleep connection, it's been found that both produce similar "alpha"-type brain waves.

Callaway postulates that a group of beta-Carbolines and psychoactive tryptamines are produced in our brains during REM sleep and facilitate the psychedelic visions that we call dreams. These internal tryptamines interact with another key actor in this drama of the night, a neurotransmitter called melatonin that is produced in the pineal gland. Interestingly enough, the pineal gland is identified in many schools of mysticism as the mysterious "third eye," the seat of inner vision. Recent scientific evidence also suggests that this gland may play some role in clairvoyance and clairvoyant trance.

The production of melatonin seems to be inhibited when the eyes are open but increases during sleep and in some meditative states. This chemical action involves a reaction, the production of serotonin, a chemical that alternately produces both melatonin and pinoline, a chemical that inhibits monoamine oxidase (MAOA), which activates the dimethyltryptamines. Callaway says that this seesaw of chemical effects may account for the cycles of dream and nondream sleep that we experience. Because the concentrations of pinoline and DMT increase, our dreams become longer and more memorable through the night. Callaway concludes that these substances may well be "the stuff of which dreams are made."

"It may be that the syntax of thought in dreams is different from the visions of dreams. This difference also occurs between the thought processes of day dreams and the visions of night dreams. Such neurotransmitters could also be responsible for other naturally occurring alternative states of consciousness, as are experienced in some meditative states. . . . The neurotransmitters responsible for inducing dream sleep may be psychedelic when administered in the waking phase."

THE UTILITY OF DREAMS

Although Callaway has given us a model for the chemical mechanism of dreams and hinted that their content may well reflect thought prompted by their visionary quality, conjecture on the content of dreams is still wide open. We are left with the questions: What do dreams mean and of what importance are they in our lives?

While prophetic dreams play an important role in some of the Bible's Old Testament stories, and dreams may have sparked such creative endeavors as Mary Shelly's novel *Frankenstein*, our Western culture has tended to view the dream state as an interesting but ultimately unimportant enigma. One recent commentator dismissed dreams as a form of mental housecleaning wherein the brain takes advantage of sleep time to clear out the files, as it were. There are enclaves within our culture, however, that attach more meaning to dreams than that of a mere chaos of excess sensory input.

Since the late nineteenth century, several schools of psychology have looked on dreams as portals to rich unconscious activity. Perhaps the most notable of these is the Zurich school, based on the precepts of the Swiss psychologist and anthropologist Dr. Carl Gustav Jung. Jung and his associates postulated a complex unconscious structure based on the existence of a "mass unconscious." This could be seen as a vast memory bank shared collectively by all humanity, or even all creation. Jungian analysis is to a great extent based on facilitated self-interpretation of the client's dreams.

Many preindustrial cultures took dreams very seriously indeed. Some of these granted dream-state experience equal status with waking experience and devoted a lot of time to relating and discussing dreams in full tribal councils. Others saw dreams as direct communication with the gods, prophetic visions, journeys to other worlds or ways of exploring the depths of their own minds.

Generally speaking, the same motives that led certain psychologists and preindustrial peoples to look seriously at their dreams led twentieth-century seekers to the use of psychedelic drugs. In dreams, therefore, we may find an alternative to psychedelic drug use that provides experiences comparable to the positive effects of these drugs.

One could argue that dreams don't follow any rules, that they are both capricious and chaotic, they may be euphoric or frightening or just plain inexplicable. The same could be said for the effects of psychedelic drugs.

The subjective experience of dreaming comes in many different forms. There are nightmares that frighten us, erotic and sensual dreams that excite us, symbolic dreams that may provide us with valuable insight into our lives and our relations with others. Sometimes dreams are like movies in which we may or may not have active roles. We may be emotionally involved or we may be mere spectators of the action. In some dreams we may find ourselves fully conscious and aware that we are within a dream. Such dreams have been called many things and probably include such psychic phenomena as "astral travel" and "out-of-body experiences."

The realness of these lucid types of dreams can produce reactions ranging from transcendent delight to stark terror. Some peoples and philosophies have concluded that they are not dreams at all but actual experiences of an astral or spiritual body operating outside our physical body, i.e., out-of-body experiences. These experiences have been cited as proof of life after death, but those who have them are warned that they may be trapped outside their bodies. Adding to the fearsome quality of these experiences is the sense that what is happening is somehow external to the astral body and therefore could be dangerous. Recent studies may help to dispel our fears, however.

BEING AWAKE AND IN CONTROL HERE IN DREAMLAND

In his book *Lucid Dreaming: The Power of Being Awake and Aware in Your Dreams*, Stephen LaBerge, Ph.D., a fellow at the Stanford University Sleep Research Center, cites the experiences that he and others have had with lucid dreaming and describes the research they have done to show that such dreaming is indeed more than a figment of our sleeping imagination. Their studies indicate that "astral travel" creates an environment within our sleeping consciousness that is so real and so detailed that those who experience it are convinced that they are fully awake in some external scene. Further, they have found that lucid dreaming, often considered a capricious and rare accident, can be learned and practiced on a regular basis.

LaBerge, who has personally experienced lucid dreaming since childhood, has no doubts as to its utility. He states early on that "lucid dreaming has considerable potential for promoting personal growth and self-development, enhancing self-confidence, improving mental and physical health, facilitating creative problem-solving, and helping you to progress on the path to self-mastery."

Lucid dreaming is simply the act of being conscious within one's dream. There is no real paradox involved between "asleep" and "conscious"—you are awake in your dream. You have brought your waking consciousness, with all its access to memory and identity, into the dream state. This can be frightening, especially if you are convinced that you have become some defenseless out-of-body self in a hobgoblin-filled "astral world." But that can be dispelled if part of the knowledge you bring to the dream is that all of it is within your own head and that you are participating in a drama of your own making.

With the element of fear removed, one is often filled with elation and wonder at the beauty and detail of the inner world that is being experienced. One is capable of performing feats that are impossible in the waking world, such as flying, traveling in time and space—all the things you can't really do on psychedelic drugs. Also, unlike most psychedelic trips intense enough to produce somewhat similar experiences, the feeling felt and lessons learned in lucid dreams can be taken back into waking consciousness to produce profound changes in overall consciousness.

Your coauthor Rick Seymour has had occasional lucid dreams since childhood and reports these as among his most vivid experiences. One of these dreams took place while he was living in a commune near the Mendocino coast in the early 1970s.

> I had gone to the city with my ex-wife and some other folks and had gotten separated from the group. There I was at about four A.M. on Market Street, cold and broke. There were no cars, no traffic, I couldn't hitch back to the commune. Then I thought, "Hey, wait a minute. I'm not really here. I'm asleep in my tent up at the commune!" I cranked open one eye, and sure enough, there I was in my sleeping bag. I closed the eye, and there I was back on Market Street.
>
> "Let's have some fun with this dream," I thought, and I pulled a big roll of bills out of my pocket. I went into the all-night diner that had appeared behind me and ordered a deluxe burger, fries and a chocolate shake. I ordered the same for the beautiful young lady sitting next to me. When we finished, we both walked outside and joined the crowd watching a gala parade.

Rick learned something important from that dream. He discovered that dream states could be controlled through knowledge and through attitude toward the experience. By paying attention to it, life may be as changeable as dreams are through conscious will. Since that time Rick has often approached a seemingly unpleasant situation with a memory of the night on Market Street and an attitude of "Let's have some fun with this dream."

LaBerge expands on this concept, pointing out that we are "more or less" conscious when we are awake. Lessons in consciousness learned in dream states can be applied to waking states as well. Much in current philosophy and scientific studies on perception indicates that what we gain from the world often depends on the amount of attention that we give to it.

In his book *Tibetan Yoga and Secret Doctrines*, W. Y. Evans-Wentz points out that Tibetan lamas practiced dream control, in which they could will anything to happen in their dreams, toward the end of learning to control waking experience as well:

> In other words, the *yogin* learns by actual experience, resulting from psychic experimentation, that the character of any dream can be changed or transformed by willing that it shall be. A step further and he learns that form, in the dream-state, and all the multitudinous content of dreams, are merely playthings of mind, and, therefore, as unstable as mirage. A further step leads him to the knowledge that the essential nature of form and of all things perceived by the senses in the waking-state are equally as unreal as their reflexes in the dream-state, both

states alike being *sangsaric*. The final step leads to the Great Realization, that nothing within the *Sangsara* is or can be other than unreal like dreams.

To the yogin, everything is part of a great illusion, or sangsara, and seeing through that illusion is nirvana. Short of this great realization, however, we can always profit by greater consciousness in our daily lives. One of the aims of meditation, for example, is the sharpening of concentration or mindfulness in our daily experience. LaBerge concludes that there is no reason why lucid dreaming should not result in a higher development of the human mind, and, we might add, a greater appreciation and sense of wonder in our daily lives.

But how does one go about learning to be awake in a dream?

HOW TO DREAM LUCIDLY

Most of us are fortunate enough to have had a few memorable dreams in our lives. Short of running off to the mystic mountains, joining a Don Juan or indulging in sustained ascetic or athletic disciplines that may not be in keeping with making it to the office on Monday morning, dreams provide a viable access to altered states of consciousness.

For many, however, dreams are fleeting and incoherent experiences that are often forgotten at the moment of awakening. Are there ways of enhancing one's dream life? Yes. Richard Bach said in his second book that things tend to increase when you pay attention to them. Just as we send messages to the endorphin enkephalon system when we run and do aerobic exercise, we can send messages to our dream center. Bach provides the basic key to this message sending: it's a question of *paying attention*.

One of the simplest ways of paying attention to dreams is to write them down. Keep a dream journal next to your bed, or in the bathroom, if you don't want to disturb your sleeping partner, and write down what you remember of your dreams when you wake up. At first these notes may be scattered or chaotic impressions: "face of a cliff," "fish in the living room and grapes in the light." These may make no sense at first, but persevere. As a beginning dreamer, you are like the beginning runner who takes it a few hundred feet at a time. As the impressions increase you'll find the dreams themselves taking on increasing vividness and complexity. You'll find yourself looking forward to them the way you used to look forward to your next acid trip.

In the course of his research at the Stanford University Sleep Research Center, Dr. LaBerge has investigated and experimented with a number of methods of waking up in a dream. This can happen naturally when the dreamer is struck with a logical inconsistency within the dream, such as Rick's realization that he could not possibly be in San Francisco. Most often, however, the realization that one is dreaming triggers awakening rather than dream lucidity. It helps to preconsider the realization and prepare for it by suggesting some activity within the dream state to solidify one's position there. In 1938, Moers-Messmer suggested looking at the ground. Don Juan, in the books by Carlos Castaneda, recommended looking at one's hands.

LaBerge puts forth a number of suggestions, the easiest of which is presetting the mind for lucid dreaming the same way you tell yourself to wake up at a given time or to remember to stop at the bank on the way to work. This is done by visualizing yourself doing what you intend to remember and verbalizing the desire. The best time to do this is toward morning, when your dreams are getting longer and more intense. Suggest to yourself during a waking phase that "the next time I'm dreaming I want to remember to recognize that I'm dreaming." LaBerge calls this "mnemonic induction of lucid dreams" or MILD.

The experience of full lucidity, when it blossoms, can include marveling at what your mind has created and a sense of great elation. As the director of your dream, you can will many experiences to take place. LaBerge recommends getting beyond these willed experiences and going with the dream to see what it can teach us.

As with bad psychedelic trips, there may be some bad dreams. As you become involved in dreaming the landscape, varied as it can be, becomes more real, and bad dreams, when they do occur, can be momentarily frightening. Even the bad dreams, however, can provide a learning and growing experience. Often they help us to understand some of our deeper concerns, the ones that we tend to gloss over when we are awake. In sleep, as in life, one learns to maintain a state of equanimity. Meditation is a good way to establish emotional equilibrium, and recognition of dream content will do much more to defuse our fears than suppression will. Finally, in learning to enjoy and profit from our dreams we may be opening another door to a whole realm of life that was wasted on us before, bringing us closer to being whole human beings.

LUCID DREAMING AND RECOVERY

Many dreams can be healing dreams, and an individual can use lucid dreams to strengthen abstention and recovery. Dreaming tends to be a very direct way of getting at the third head of the dragon, where our deepest convictions are held. Many individuals in recovery have reported having dreams in which they relapsed into use and feeling great remorse on awakening. These dreams indicate the continuing presence of that "drugs are good for you" value impacted in your spiritual level.

In a lucid dream, one is consciously aware of being in recovery. When you are offered a drink, or a joint, or a cigarette, you can turn it down. "No thanks. I don't do that anymore." Not only will you feel positive on awakening, but you will also have sent a direct message to your spiritual self that you do not do that anymore. In time, the presence of a chemical temptation can act as a cue to initiate lucid dreaming rather than a spiritual counterattack capable of eroding your resolve.

HARDWARE-ASSISTED TAKEOFF

In the history of flight, some of the fastest, most powerful and highest-flying vehicles have paradoxically needed assistance in getting off the ground. Carrier-based airplanes are thrown aloft by a catapult. The rocket planes, such as the X-1 and the X-15, are carried into the stratosphere by high-flying long-range planes designed to carry a heavy payload. Space shuttles and other space vehicles get beyond the earth mounted on massive booster rockets. These booster systems were originally called "Jet Assisted Takeoff," or JATO.

Psychoactive drugs have provided a function similar to JATO in boosting human consciousness toward where it wants to go. We have learned, however, that alcohol and other drugs leave a lot to be desired as a booster system. Although they may perform initially in kicking our consciousness into whatever orbit we wish it to obtain, in the long run they are totally disastrous to the payload, our minds and bodies. There may be nothing quite as stultifying as heading boldly for the moon and stars, only to fall in pieces onto the launching pad.

Drugs have proven to be a most dangerous booster system, and their widespread use has led many people to reject the whole concept of outside help in maintaining personal growth in recovery or in any form of abstinence. It was generally felt that anything meaningful had to come from within. An enunciated goal of alcohol and other drug treatment centers was, and still is helping the client stand on his or her own two feet and effectively reenter society without "crutches."

There are, however, viable booster systems that can help one deal with abstinence and walk through the opening door to growth and expansion beyond alcohol and other drugs. These systems provide an alternative to the self-medication individuals may have felt they needed for the control of emotions and social interaction. These involve the use of special machines in order to train the mind-body-spirit vehicle in continuing the journey on its own. They provide a hardware-assisted takeoff.

We first became interested in these systems during the early 1970s. At that time, a previously hidden population of substance abusers was being identified around the United States. Unlike the drug users spotlighted in the 1960s, these were not countercultural acidheads or marginal street people. This population resided within the American mainstream and included businesspeople, white collar workers and housewives. Unlike the street drug abusers, this population was not in revolt against anything except perhaps its own psychic pain, neurotic fears and negative emotions.

In many ways, the population represented a throwback to the turn-of-the-century opiate abuser described by John P. Morgan, M.D., as "a middle-aged, middle-class housewife with two children." The attitude that these people took toward the drugs they used was similar to that of Morgan's addicts with their elixirs, tinctures and tonics. The drugs they took were legitimate pharmaceuticals. Usually these had been prescribed, at least in the beginning, by well-meaning physicians for what they interpreted as legitimate medical indications. Often, drugs from different psychoactive types had been prescribed for different ailments: Valium for anxiety, amphetamines for obesity and/or performance, and codeine for pain. Their patients may not have had a drug of choice but used each one according to the symptoms they were experiencing or the needs that they felt at any given time. In light of their pattern of use, these people were labeled "poly (or multiple) drug abusers."

Polydrug abusers do not see themselves as criminals or thrill-seekers. To their minds, they are merely normal citizens using the wonders of modern chemistry to control a variety of symptoms and to enhance their quality of life. Consequently, their level of denial can be extremely high. Unlike their street counterparts, middle-class polydrug abusers tend to be drug-naive. If they do come to perceive their use of a drug as a problem and try to quit, they may confuse withdrawal from a drug with the reemergence of the symptoms for which they took the drug in the first place. As a consequence, they may find themselves in a state of total helplessness and inability to deal with their compulsive use in any form.

When we started the West Coast Polydrug Research and Treatment Project, under the auspices of the Haight Ashbury Free Medical Clinic, in 1972, most of its clients were these middle-class polydrug abusers. They were so far removed from our usual Clinic clientele that we could not see them at the Clinic's Drug Abuse Treatment, Rehabilitation and Aftercare Project building. Instead, we set up facilities in an anonymous-looking three-story building in a middle-class residential area near the University of California Medical School at San Francisco. No shingle was hung out, so there was no way, other than the periodic arrival and departure of clients, of telling that the place was anything but the residence it appeared to be.

The clients themselves presented us with many enigmas. More than any street drug abuser, they were convinced that they needed the prescription drugs they were using in order to maintain health, sanity or both. In treating them, the bottom line often was the problem of symptom reemergence as a complication to withdrawal. Symptom reemergence is simply the reappearance of the condition for which the drug was prescribed in the first place. Psychoactive drugs may help with acute pain and other short-term problems, but they don't make chronic problems go away; they just mask the symptoms.

The problem that faced our treatment professionals was that these clients not only needed to get off the drugs that they were using, they also needed alternative means for dealing with the original problems. You could detoxify a polydrug client from a sedative-hypnotic and an opiate and an anorexiant, or appetite-suppressing stimulant, but abstinence from these drugs wouldn't last if the client found him or herself again facing a combination of anxiety, chronic lower-back pain and rapid weight gain. The only way we could help them was through providing alternative means for controlling their multiple dysphorias.

Drug maintenance had been tried with most of these people and had resulted in escalating tolerance and compulsive use. We needed procedures that would effectively retrain the client's own body and mind to deal with his or her problems without drugs, procedures that would phase themselves out as the retraining was accomplished. One of the first that we tried was biofeedback.

BIOFEEDBACK

Defined in the most general terms, feedback takes place when part of an energy flow returns to or is directed back to its point of origin. In information systems, feedback is usually thought of as that information that returns to the sender. For example, one of the reasons a teacher will give a quiz is to see if the information being sent out is getting across to the students. Evaluation forms are another way of gauging performance by feedback from others.

All living organisms constantly give off information in a number of ways. The bio-broadcasting with which we are most familiar is the spoken or written word, but there are many other channels. While psychologists and other mental health practitioners tend to rely heavily on our verbal and body-language signals, physicians take a number of other broadcasting systems into account. They check our pulse, they listen to our hearts and lungs through a stethescope, they can even measure the minute electrical waves that come from our brains, with an EEG, or electroencephalogram.

With biofeedback, some of the information coming from you is directed back to you as the action causing the information is taking place. It's like holding up a biological mirror, and like looking in a mirror, it gives us the opportunity to correct anything that seems out of order—pat the stray psychic hairs back in place, flick the piece of spinach off our emotional front teeth. Biofeedback is, therefore, a means of monitoring our own biological processes, and for many practitioners it also involves ways of modifying those processes for our own betterment.

In the late 1960s a number of scientists in different parts of the United States and the world became interested in biofeedback. One of these was Barbara B. Brown, Ph.D., whose book *New Mind, New Body Bio-Feedback: New Directions for the Mind* appeared in 1974 and represents a primary source for information on the field. She was instrumental in starting the Bio-Feedback Research Society, which held its first annual meeting in 1969 with 142 participants and has grown ever since. Dr. Brown became interested in biofeedback while performing research on whether cats respond to color.

Although the development of biofeedback in its current form is recent, the roots go all the way back to medieval "trials" in which guilt might be assessed on whether a person's tongue was burned when touched by a hot iron, and to the ancient Chinese practice of giving a suspected wrong-doer a handful of dry rice to swallow. If the suspect could chew and swallow the rice, he was judged innocent. If he choked on the rice, he was assumed guilty. Our first impulse may be to smile at these "primitive" beliefs, but they made use of principles similar to those employed in biofeedback.

The basic principle at work in these early forms of "lie detection" is that inner emotions are manifested in physiological reactions. In both cases there was a primitive awareness that such emotions as fear and guilt affected the salivary gland functions and resulted in a dry mouth. In the absence of such powerful negative emotions, the tongue has a coating of saliva that could protect it during a brief contact with a hot iron. An innocent Chinese could perhaps moisten the dry rice sufficiently to swallow it.

In the mid-1700s Luigi Galvani accidentally discovered that electrical energy could be conducted through living tissue. In 1888, Fere discovered that the resistance of the skin to a small electric current changed in response to changes in emotion. These discoveries led to the modern polygraph, which operates by measuring differences in the electrical conductivity of the skin. The accuracy of such instruments anywhere from forty-five percent to seventy-three percent, has so far kept courts from admitting them as evidence. There is, in fact, a great deal of controversy over whether the polygraph has any role in law enforcement at all, or if it represents a gross and inaccurate invasion of personal and constitutional rights.

The use of similar principles in biofeedback is much less controversial but much more exciting. There are today a number of different instruments involved in biofeedback research and treatment. These include enhancement of signals from a variety of bodily sources, including skin galvanometry, named for Luigi Galvani's discovery, and EEG brain-wave measurement. Dr. Brown points out that unlike the measuring of heartbeat or brain waves, where cognizance of emotion and mind functions are not the primary objective, when one reads the skin, "it is not the skin that the skin talk is talking about primarily; the skin is talking about the *mind*."

Biofeedback training represents one more example of the communication between you and your self that we have been discussing throughout this chapter. It may be one of the most direct methods of learning to fine-tune the emotions and mental states to produce a feeling of well-being at will. In our polydrug research and treatment program it provided a means of dealing with the reappearance of the problem for which many patients began taking drugs in the first place. As polydrug abusers were weaned off their drugs of choice often the original problems, such as chronic depression or anxiety, that these drugs were prescribed to deal with would reassert themselves and form a dangerous postwithdrawal cause of relapse.

Used in substance-abuse aftercare, biofeedback training usually involves identifying the appearance of brain "alpha" waves. These are related to meditative states and other states of relaxed well-being. Other brain waves, theta and beta, are necessary for overall functioning, but their overabundance has been linked to unpleasant states of mind. In other words, you would not want to have nothing but alpha waves, but up to a point the more you have, probably, the better. Now that there are means of identifying these alpha waves, scientists have been able to observe their stimulation in a variety of activities. A number of the alternatives we have discussed in this book appear to produce alpha waves, including exercise, meditation, restful sleep and creative activity.

Clients who have received biofeedback training report slipping into meditation or trancelike states at those times when it is working. According to Dr. Brown, "Preliminary explorations using complex pattern feedback of both EKG and EEG, along with autonomic and EMG feedback, have disclosed that the actual experiences of altered awareness may be quite dramatic and profound."

The equipment used in such training generally translates brain waves into audible or visual signals that the client can use to monitor his or her ability to control emotional states and produce feelings of well-being. We tend to call this training rather than treatment because once a client has learned to link up what he or she feels with the machine's signals, he or she can produce these feelings at will without needing a machine to "feedback" the resultant alpha wave levels. After the assisted takeoff, the alpha ship can continue flying on its own.

Abstainers who have received biofeedback training have often reported less desire to use drugs. Well-motivated trainees have spoken of "powerful insight into their internal world of experience" that has helped solidify the value system involved in their recovery.

ACUPUNCTURE

Although acupuncture is not among the techniques that one could self-administer, the lessons we have learned from it can be applied to other treatment techniques that have come to us from outside the realm of Western medicine. In an earlier chapter we discussed the history of acupuncture's use in the treatment of narcotic withdrawal at the Haight Ashbury Free Medical Clinic. We pointed out that although it obviously worked, acceptance was long in coming for this Eastern treatment modality. Now that Western medicine understands at least one aspect of how it works, acupuncture has become an important tool in drug detoxification, treatment of chronic pain and control of drug hunger.

Acupuncture has been used for thousands of years in the Far East. In his book *Health and Healing: Understanding Conventional and Alternative Medicine*, Andrew Weil, M.D., points out, "Before the end of the Stone Age in what is now China, people may have used stone needles to treat illness and had identified specific points through which symptoms could be influenced." The techniques were perfected over the millennia and passed down in families. The theory underlying acupuncture is straightforward: The penetration and stimulation of the acupuncture needles at specific points on the body activate nerves that transmit impulses to the central nervous system and then to the diseased area. Because of the multiple interconnections of the nervous system, even the ear or the foot will have nerve endings directly related to most of the organs or muscles of the body. Until quite recently, however, Western medical schools treated acupuncture as a joke. If acupuncture was mentioned at all, it was only as an example of primitive superstition. The practice was compared to modern pain management with drugs to show how far "civilized" man has come in the treatment of disease.

As we discussed earlier, that was all changed with the discovery of opiate receptor sites and the role of acupuncture in stimulating the production of internal opiatelike substances. There are other ways in which these endorphins and enkephalons can be stimulated, including running and other forms of exercise, but these tend to be impractical during the acute withdrawal phase of treatment and may be inappropriate for dealing with the acute pain of early recovery, just as it would be difficult to prescribe "two miles a day, as needed" for dental postoperative pain.

The recovering narcotics user has a very low pain threshold, because the use of opiate and opioid drugs has led to a general shutdown of the body's own painkiller production centers, which take time to recover. The newly clean opiate abuser can be hypersensitive to pain.

An additional problem is that doctors cannot prescribe painkillers for addicts without risking a relapse into addiction. The codeine, or Demerol, or even Darvon that others may take to control pain are to the addict what a drink is to an alcoholic, and, with many addicts in or just beyond withdrawal, this is an important factor. If narcotic medication for acute pain in a recovering addict is needed, it should be given with extreme caution for short periods of time. A person who has used heroin or other narcotics has literally been feeling no pain for a long time. Often one of the most immediate results of withdrawal is pain. Teeth and other parts of the body that use pain to signal that something is wrong have been ignored, sometimes for years. These problems may require immediate medical attention and then pain control if the addict is to maintain any period of sobriety and abstention. Perhaps the most valuable function of acupuncture is its ability to control a wide range of pain without one's having to resort to psychoactive pain control medication.

Another important function of acupuncture for the recovering person, however, is its ability to affect drug hunger, not just for opiates but for a number of other substances as well. Success in this area has been noted for sedative and stimulant users. Acupuncture for the treatment of cocaine and cigarette addiction seems to have had notable success. Acupuncture has also been used for weight loss through appetite suppression. Although the action in opiate withdrawal and the treatment of chronic pain is becoming clear, we are still a long way from understanding everything about acupuncture, including why it can work with drugs other than opiates.

There are several different types of acupuncture procedures used for the treatment of opiate addiction. These range from an intensive short-term program wherein opiates are flushed from the brain receptor sites through the administration of naloxone to "staple-puncture," which involves the placing of surgical staples in the patient's ears for periods of up to six months. At the Haight Ashbury Free Medical Clinic, treatment is similar for a wide range of withdrawal and drug hunger problems.

In his report on our eighteen-month, federally funded research study on the efficacy of acupuncture treatment for opiate withdrawal, John Newmeyer, Ph.D., points out that part of the treatment strategy is the creation of a healing ambience for the clientele. Three teas are available before treatment: Detox Brew, Nutra Tea, and Relaxo-Brew, all herbal mixtures that induce mild relaxation. Negative ion generators are installed in the treatment rooms, and prohibitions against smoking, as well as against anyone other than clients and treatment personnel being in the rooms, are strictly enforced. All prospective clients are screened and receive a medical examination by a Clinic staff physician before entering acupuncture treatment.

The treatment itself follows a second examination based on Chinese medical principles. This includes an examination of the abdomen and tongue and a pulse diagnosis. For withdrawal, treatment is provided on an "as needed" basis; otherwise treatment usually takes place once a day.

Each session lasts about half an hour. The client lies on his or her back on a moderately soft surface in a warm, quiet, softly-lit room. Sterilized steel needles are used. For about ninety percent of clients, the acupuncture points used are the "lung" and "God's door" points in the ears. In the classical Chinese practice, the needles are "manipulated" during a session. This means that they are moved up and down by the practitioner so as to maintain a constant level of stimulation. Today this is done by feeding a minute electric current through the needles, just high enough to cause a light prickling. For this purpose, the Clinic uses a "Style 71.3 Multi-Purpose Therapy Apparatus" manufactured in the People's Republic of China.

The half hour spent on the acupuncture table can be viewed as an exercise in relaxation therapy. The quiet surroundings, the soft light and the need to lie still for a long period act together to engender a period of serenity in often-turbulent lives. In this regard, acupuncture is similar to biofeedback therapy, which also focuses one's attention on achieving a serene state.

Like running, yoga and meditation, acupuncture has a "kindling" period. It may take several sessions before the analgesic effects of treatment really make themselves felt. Coupled with the lack of a "chemical rush," this can make acupuncture less than appealing to many long-term opiate abusers. This may change as the technique becomes more accepted by a population that is used to standard Western procedures, especially in that it can work to raise the pain threshold of recovering addicts. However, it can be most effective in controlling drug hunger and combating stress and chronic or acute pain on an interim basis for the abstainer who is not ready for the more strenuous alternate activities but who doesn't wish to resort to chemicals in dealing with these problems.

RESTRICTED ENVIRONMENTAL STIMULATION THERAPY

Restricted Environmental Stimulation Therapy, usually called by its acronym, REST, also known as sensory isolation or sensory deprivation, SD, involves placing an individual in an environment of severely reduced stimulation. The two most frequently used methods of applying this therapy are lying on a bed in a dark, soundproof room or floating in buoyant liquid at skin temperature in a light-free, soundproof chamber. The flotation method was developed by John Lilly. While many users report a subjective sense of profound relaxation for sessions lasting one hour or less, physiological measures of clients in isolation for three or more hours indicate increased arousal and sympathetic nervous system activity. In repeated sessions, however, decreases in blood pressure have been noted during the relaxed sessions among clients with a tendency toward high blood pressure. At an optimal two hours or less, there appears to be a decrease in adrenal-axis hormones, while several researchers have reported decreased plasma norepinephrine in subjects given deep muscle relaxation training.

Anyone who has seen the movie *Altered States* has seen a flotation REST unit in action. However, there are no instances of anyone reverting into a missing link while immersed in one, although highly altered states of consciousness have been reported. Most units are like enclosed bathtubs that are large enough to hold a whole person in a horizontal position. The unit is filled with a saturated solution, usually of Epsom salts, that is dense enough to keep the subject from sinking. This solution is maintained at the subject's skin temperature. No light or sound is allowed into the chamber, and so all sensory input is cut to an absolute minimum.

In general, REST seems to have some effect in areas such as anxiety and stress that often figure in drug hunger and relapse problems, although the overall effects are so far inconclusive. There are anecdotal cases in which highly stressful problems have been solved during REST sessions, but there is no clear indication that this method is any more useful than general counseling or other methods would have been. In general, REST is thought to free one's consciousness from attention to the external senses and allow a greater concentration on internal goings-on. A case has been made among certain practitioners for increased ability to control heartbeat and respiration as a consequence of REST experience. Lilly made many anecdotal reports of altered states of consciousness, but these may have resulted from a combination of sensory deprivation and psychedelic drug ingestion.

Little has been written about the use of REST in the treatment of substance abuse and addiction. One study from Thomas H. Fine, director of the REST and Self Regulation Institute at the Medical College of Ohio, discusses the use of flotation REST in the treatment of chronic cigarette smoking. Twelve subjects entered and completed the program. All subjects had been smoking for at least two years. Their treatment involved three REST sessions. The first session was one hour long and was to introduce the subjects to the flotation experience. The second session was two hours long, with one hour of silence and one hour in which antismoking messages were played into the tank. The third session was four hours long, with the same messages played in the last two hours. These sessions were at least two but not more than five days apart. All subjects were told that they could terminate any REST session at any time. The results based on one-week and six-month follow-ups indicated a significant drop in smoking the first week, but little long-term effect that could be directly attributed to the REST sessions.

The indication is that REST may be helpful as an adjunct to other therapy but, using current methodology, is not a long-term effective treatment on its own. Conversations with Tom Fine, who has a long history in the substance-abuse treatment field and was a pioneer in the development of REST, show a lot of optimism. He feels that REST has great potential for good and that, with the further development of effective procedures, it will in time be an important adjunct to substance abuse and addiction therapy as well as an aid to recovery.

HYPNOTISM

Although no specific hardware is used in its practice, hypnotism is an approach to recovery and abstinence that involves regular sessions with a trained practitioner. Like acupuncture, but unlike biofeedback and sensory deprivation, hypnotism has been around a long time. Hypnotism is the induction of a trance state. Some refer to this as "twilight sleep." In this state, the subject is thought to be vulnerable to some degree of reprogramming in both the conscious and unconscious parts of the mind.

Hypnotism's use in general elicits a variety of public and scientific reactions. Some consider hypnotism to be a sound scientific practice, while others look on it as no more than sideshow charlatanism. Over the centuries it has supposedly been used to cure chronic pain and to give the practitioner total body-and-soul control over the client. Thrillers have featured plots in which people have committed murder or other illegal acts while under posthypnotic suggestion. Most practitioners point out, however, that it is impossible to force anyone into doing anything that goes against his or her basic moral fiber. There's no wonder that many myths, both positive and negative, have grown up around its use. In recent years it has even been used in attempts to prove reincarnation by regressing clients through past lives.

With its long history and wide use, it's surprising that only a handful of articles and research studies have involved the application of hypnotism to substance abuse and addiction. Most of what has been written involves the use of hypnotism in the treatment of alcoholism, but the gist of what has been learned seems equally appropriate to other forms of addiction. In fact, the reports suggest that further studies in such areas as compulsive gambling, rape and sexual abuse therapy and eating disorders could be profitable as well.

Although some treatment reports indicate that hypnotism can be helpful in the direct treatment of withdrawal, all agree that this is only true when the hypnotism is practiced as an adjunct to other therapy. Reviewers of the literature point out that there is a lack of sufficient research procedures to the studies to prove anything one way or the other, while those studies that do involve what are considered proper procedures indicate that the contribution of hypnotism to successful withdrawal and sobriety is negligible.

One approach that took a particular drubbing was that of using hypnotism to promote alcohol aversion. If, as we believe, the conviction among addicts that drugs are good lies at a very deep stratum, this criticism is well founded. What would most likely result would be hypnotic conditioning that runs counter to a deep-seated spiritual belief, and this could cause much extra stress for the subject. This puts us in mind of a friend who, in the 1950s, volunteered as a subject for a stage hypnotist. He told the hypnotist that he wanted to quit smoking and was given a posthypnotic suggestion that henceforth cigarettes would taste like bull feces. The suggestion apparently worked but did nothing for our friend's compulsion to smoke. For the next few days, every time he would reluctantly light up a cigarette, a look of horror and disgust would appear with the first puff and stay on his face through the whole cigarette. Eventually, he had to track down the hypnotist and fly several states away to have him remove the suggestion. "I had to," he said. "I was beginning to like the taste."

Much more success has been reported in the use of hypnotism to deal with postwithdrawal drug hunger. Again, however, practitioners point out that it should be used only as an adjunct to more comprehensive treatment.

One approach that forms the core of such treatment is that of teaching the subject autohypnotic relaxation. This is also called self-hypnosis and involves placing oneself into a light trance that is not unlike a state of meditation. Practitioners suggest that autohypnotic relaxation be practiced for fifteen to twenty minutes, twice a day, as a means of overcoming the anxiety often felt in the early stages of abstention, without the use of tranquilizers or other sedative-hypnotic drugs.

The deep-seated reliance on alcohol is considered worth working on, but from a positive approach rather than the negative drug-aversion techniques discussed above. It is argued by practitioners that alcohol, and by implication other drugs, serves many people as a means of disassociating from anxiety. The task for hypnosis, therefore, is to establish a new and viable defense mechanism through hypnotic suggestion that doesn't entail disassociation through the use of drugs.

While this approach, like others we have discussed, appears useful in the early stages of abstention, for the addict at least it does need to be backed up with a treatment or recovery program that aims to replace defense mechanisms through a variety of therapeutic approaches. It is also becoming well known that drug hunger isn't all a product of direct anxiety and can instead be triggered at various times, months and even years after one has entered recovery. Marc Schoen, Ph.D., refers to this as the "Conditioning Mode." Here we are directly involved with the third, or spiritual, head of the dragon. In his view, at this stage the urge to use comes from unresolved bonding. In the course of addiction, the drug has become intertwined with many things in the addict's life. Triggers may include stress but are by no means limited to it. When such bonding exists, these triggers can provoke drug hunger and bring about a relapse into use, even years into sobriety.

Some of these cues, or triggers, may be conscious, while others are unconscious. As with any ingrained and reinforced habit, these patterns of behavior can be hard to break. Human beings are highly resistant to change. Milton Erickson, who has done trance work with alcoholic clients, bypasses this resistance by using metaphors with his clients. For example, he will encourage the client to recall a time of strength and well-being and to try to reexperience the feelings of that time while in trance. These reexperienced feelings can then be connected to the triggers as an alternative to drug hunger and drug-seeking behavior. Schoen points out that if tension is the conditioned stimulus and relaxation the desired response, then these can be hooked together, eliminating alcohol or other drugs from the bonding process and creating a new cause/effect bonding that involves feelings of strength and well-being. This, he says, can be accomplished through positive posthypnotic suggestion.

A third phase cited by Schoen involves helping clients to continue a similar reprogramming on their own. This could be accomplished either during the light trance state of self-hypnosis or in a meditative state. In essence, instead of blocking urges that lead to drug hunger, the abstainer is encouraged, indeed given permission, to experience them. The task is then to work with the urges and the bonding system as it surfaces so as to link the urges to positive alternative responses, such as feelings of strength and well-being. The result can be that the abstainer gains control over these urges. Rather than being a conduit to relapse, they can become a means to growth and positive personal development.

There are many variables in the efficacy of hypnotism as a means to facilitate abstention and recovery. Individuals have varying degrees of susceptibility to hypnotic trance states that may or not be based on conscious or subconscious resistance. Hypnosis is not a treatment that can be forced. Either it works or it doesn't. For those who are good subjects, however, it does hold some promise as the beginning of a process.

RECENT DEVELOPMENTS IN STRESS REDUCTION

Stress reduction in general has become a cause célèbre in our culture, and a number of people and institutions are currently developing a variety of approaches that may be helpful to the abstainer. Some of these are direct products of Western technology, but others owe their existence more or less to new interpretations of the various Eastern disciplines that we discussed earlier in this chapter. Your authors do not have personal experience with any of these approaches, so we are presenting what information we have on them without comment on either their efficacy or their veracity.

Thalassotherapy

The name comes from the Greek word for sea, *thalassa*. The treatment seems to be a new twist on several approaches that we have already discussed, making use of several seawater relaxations as well as a variety of marine treatments. One technique is "hydro-relaxation," described as a passive tension and stress reliever. The client reclines in a hydromassage tank filled with heated seawater. Tiny air bubbles rise from the bottom, creating an air lather and acting as a cushion for the body. Japanese flute music plays in the background as a therapist helps the client relax through guided visual imagery. Another thalassotherapy technique is hydrotherapy feedback, in which the client floats in the hydromassage tub while a biofeedback therapist-monitor helps him or her achieve greater awareness and control of tension.

Chiropractor Pulse-Point

This practice uses the tenets of applied kinesiology, polarity and other chiropractic practices. Kinesiology holds that every organ is related to certain muscles, and in the pulse-point method the therapist lightly touches one hand to the painful area and the other to the corresponding body point. The therapist applies gentle pressure as the pulses from the two areas join in the same rhythm and then subside—a matter of five to twenty minutes. The complete session lasts thirty to forty-five minutes.

Ohashiatsu

This combination of shiatsu massage and Eastern psychology and meditation was originated by Wataru Ohashi. In shiatsu, also called acupressure, the fingers are pressed on certain points of the body called *tsubos* to ease aches, pains, tension and disease symptoms. Shiatsu has been available for some time from trained experts.

Hand-Warming

The Menninger Foundation has introduced this new therapy developed by Dr. Elmer E. Green, founder of the foundation's Biofeedback and Psychophysiology Center. It is used to relieve migraine headaches, high blood pressure and other stress-related circulatory problems by counteracting the body's "fight or flight" reaction to stress. Participants learn to relax the muscles in the walls of the hands so arteries expand, blood rushes in and the area is warmed. Leg-warming has also been introduced.

HOT AND COLD APPROACHES TO STRESS

Throughout history there have been a variety of aids developed for helping the human psyche decontaminate and reenergize itself. Any of these can play a role in furthering abstinence, recovery and general well-being. We have talked, for example, of the sensory-depriving REST tank, but there is also a lot to be said for uncovered sensuosity-enhancing immersions. The basic bathtub can be a most therapeutic instrument for cleaning and relaxing both the outer and inner self. The classical Greeks preferred cold, short baths in order to invigorate and stimulate the body. The Romans had three types of baths: a steam bath, or *caldarium*, to clean the skin; a warm bath, or *tepidarium*, to relax; and a cold bath, or *frigidarium*, to invigorate and stimulate. The French of Provence, versed in the science of phytotherapy, the study of herbs for healing, have developed a number of aromatic herbal bath oils to help restore physical and psychological well-being. They even have an invigorating and stimulating oil, but you don't have to use it in cold water.

Taking the waters, or soaking at exclusive spas, has long been a practice for the European upper crust, especially those who were recovering from chemical excesses. It took maritime Marin County, north of San Francisco, however, to raise soaking in a tub to a full social event.

However, water isn't always necessary for relaxing and reducing stress. Many Native American tribes had what they called "sweat lodges." These were well-insulated huts, often dug into the ground and with a framework covered with tightly woven thatch or animal skins. Rocks would be heated to red-hot in fires and then rolled into the hut, superheating the air. Water could be poured on the rocks, creating a steam-bath effect, or the dry heat could be maintained. These sweat sessions were considered very beneficial and were also seen as a social occasion for the men, who might pack into the sweat lodge like commuters on a Tokyo subway. These huts were usually constructed on the banks of a pond or stream so that when the users became fully heated they could make their way outside and dive into the cold water.

The modern-day equivalent of the sweat lodge has come to us not from the near-at-hand Native Americans but from Scandinavia. In Finland and other countries, this sweat hut is built out of wood and is called a sauna. The principle is the same, however. A heat source—a wood or coal stove or in some cases, hot rocks—superheats the air in a wooden box that usually has several benches at different elevations. The higher up one sits or lies, the hotter it gets. In Scandinavia, many people end their sauna sessions by running out and rolling in the snow. In the United States, a cold shower usually suffices.

All of these manipulations of hot and cold air and water have marked psychoactive effects and seem to be beneficial in fighting stress, depression and other dysphoric states while promoting relaxation and a sense of well-being.

Massage

Massage comes in a variety of forms, ranging from the soft and soporific back rub or foot rub to the demanding techniques of Rolfing. Many people have entered into massage therapy, and they can cause real damage if they don't know what they are doing. Guidelines here are similar to those we cited for yoga and exercise. In general, nothing that you do or have done to you should hurt. Pain indicates damage. You should check out credentials, and if something doesn't feel right, you should speak up or leave.

A variety of physical therapists, including chiropractors, say they have been instrumental in helping to prevent drug abuse relapse in their patients through the alleviation of chronic physical pain. Pain is indeed a major problem for the abstinent person, especially one who has been using his or her drug of choice to self-medicate that pain. Some of the physical therapies are quite controversial, and their use seems a matter of personal conviction.

Chemical Agents

A final area of hardware-assisted takeoff that we may mention here is that of actual chemical aids. Some of these we have already discussed, such as clonidine and the opiate antagonist naltrexone. There is also Antabuse, used to help some alcoholics stay away from drinking. Unlike naltrexone, which has no effect itself but works by blocking the opiate receptor sites, Antabuse makes the person who takes a drink sick by blocking the digestion of the alcohol.

A substance used in quitting smoking is a type of chewing gum that contains nicotine. This is not an alternative to a psychoactive substance but part of a timed withdrawal procedure similar in theory to methadone detoxification or the substitution and withdrawal techniques employed with sedative-hypnotic detoxification. The nicotine gum is available by prescription, but studies indicate that it should only be used in conjunction with counseling or other therapy if it is to be effective.

Some therapies, especially those involving hardware, tend to be subject to both well-meaning and larcenous quackery. The history of substance abuse treatment is laced with strange contraptions that were guaranteed to "cure" addiction or double your money back. Often these came with hearty endorsements from more or less famous people whose lives had been changed by the "miracle cure." One should always get more than one opinion and be wary of untested procedures. Often the simplest approaches work the best, and the less baggage you carry with you into abstinence and recovery, the better your chance for success.

AS THE DAYS GO ON

There are really a number of things in life that can serve as alternatives to alcohol and other drugs—activities that contribute to growth, to well-being and to being high in the finest sense of the term. Just as the use of drugs tends to build walls between us and ourselves, abstention can tear down those walls and reacquaint us with ourselves. With minds, bodies and spirits clear of drugs and their effects, we can come to appreciate the psychoactive qualities of many activities that we may have taken for granted. We can achieve the changes in states of consciousness possible through other means that may have been impossible for us while we were under the spell of drugs.

Creative activity, as we mentioned, is a prime producer of alpha waves. Painting a picture, drawing an image forth from stone or metal, even the act of writing and editing this book—all provide conduits for positive psychoactive experience once one is open to it and recognizes it for what it is. The primary act of human creativity, making and giving birth to another human being, can be a source of great pain or a passage to ecstasy. These and other gateways to rewarding psychoactive experience will be discussed in Chapter 6 in personal accounts by those who experienced them and through specific insight gathered in research and introspection by leaders in a variety of fields. The keys to these experiences are abstinence from destructive substances; and, through that abstinence, the development of self-knowledge; and, through the development of self-knowledge, sharing with others.

Such activities as yoga, meditation, exercise, creative sleeping and the hardware-assisted takeoffs are means of sensitizing us to ourselves. This doesn't happen overnight, but the effects are cumulative and increasingly powerful as they gain momentum. The self with whom we become reacquainted is likewise becoming powerful. It's no longer the compulsive being that was victim to every whim of fate and sought recourse and oblivion from its helplessness in chemical nostrums. As abstention and recovery strengthen your tripartite being moves from the realm of effects into the realm of causes. In a spiritual sense, God as you understand God may become a loving presence, a force that works through you instead of a wrathful deity working against you.

In progressing through abstention and recovery, however, we must keep in mind that no person is an island. The techniques that we have discussed for improving such things as self-knowledge, personal growth and well-being are just that. They are not the basis of recovery and are not meant to replace the long-term treatment and fellowship of both professional and peer support that we feel is necessary for successful recovery from addiction and for maintaining abstention. In other words, don't try to go it alone. With all the compassion and help in the world, with the range of twelve-step fellowships available, it makes no sense to tackle compulsion, loss of control and continued use on your own. That's the stuff of white knuckles. Even those of you who are not addicted but who are seeking abstention from what you perceive as a personal abuse problem or habit should seek the help and constructive companionship you need. Do as many of the alternatives as you can, but in the overall approach you take to abstinence and recovery, don't go it alone.

BRINGING IT ALL TOGETHER

At the center of our "how-to" information on abstention and recovery there is a pattern. The pattern is not of our making, nor did it originate with Alcoholics Anonymous or any of the self-help, twelve-step programs, nor is it a direct product of Eastern or Western science. We find hints of it in the origins of world religion and mythology, and much current psychology, both Eastern and Western, is based on it. It is elusive, its matter is intangible, and yet so many writers and thinkers have written about it that we can safely refer to it as intrinsic to most advanced human thought.

What we are speaking of is a pattern of growth that seems to apply to individual human beings, to humanity as a whole and, in all likelihood, to all of life. Recently, our colleague Charles L. Whitfield, M.D., wrote about the connection of this pattern to stress and to recovery from alcoholism and chemical dependency in his book *Stress Management and Spirituality during Recovery: A Transpersonal Approach*. Drawing on sources that range from ancient sages to current schools of psychology, he enunciates the pattern of growth as involving seven levels of consciousness. These are:

1. Survival
2. Passion
3. Mind
4. Acceptance
5. Understanding
6. Compassion
7. Unity of Consciousness

According to Whitfield, humanity has evolved through several of these levels. Human beings collectively functioned at the lowest, or survival, level from the time of the early humanoid beings, roughly three million years ago, until about 200,000 years ago. At this level, some degree of intellect separated early humans from most other living creatures, but they were primarily motivated by fear, and their solution to this fear was to "find food, shelter and to survive." About 200,000 years ago humanity began to develop other motivations besides fear; this was the age of magic. Ritual became important to successful hunting and gathering. As life became more organized, self-preservation was gradually superseded by self-gratification. Human evolution seems to have generally come into the next stage by about 2500 B.C., or 4,500 years ago. Earmarks of the dawning age of the mind included the development of spoken and written languages, making possible the communication and passing on of complex information. Many cultures in that era also shifted from hunter-gatherer to agricultural, lending even greater stability. Humanity could now operate out of thinking, reasoning, and communicating. Cities appeared, followed by more and more efficient means of communication and transportation. A thinking humanity developed technology and in time was crossing oceans in a few hours, building skyscrapers, communicating nearly instantly around the world and traveling to the moon. Yes, collectively we are still operating at the third level of consciousness.

We know that the other levels exist, not through collective human experience but through the individual lives of those few in each culture who have transcended, experienced, become and returned to the marketplace to tell the rest of us. These levels of consciousness and the means of achieving them have been related to us in a number of formats by those who have experienced them. These formats include the Twelve Steps of self-help, the Buddhist "eightfold path," the Ox panels, and much of what has been called mythic quest tales.

Myth is several things at once. For one, it's the "history" of prehistory, the stories that were passed down before events were written. But myth has a greater dimension than merely recording past events. Like poetry, it has the ability to take us directly to the soul, to the inner truths of life, if we can understand them. In his series of books *The Masks of God*, and in his *Hero With a Thousand Faces*, Joseph Campbell explores the unifying theme of "the quest." This theme runs through such diverse vehicles as the early Middle Eastern "Epic of Gilgamesh," Hopi and other American Indian tales, the Arthurian grail quest cycles, the Norse legends that led to Wagner's operas and even the exploits of Bilbo and Frodo Baggins on Tolkien's Middle Earth. These quests involve a series of actions in which the protagonists become separated from their familiar world and get a glimpse of something beyond. Often this is represented as a tangible something: a ring, a vessel used at the Last Supper, perhaps a beautiful and mysterious prince or princess or the footprint of an ox. The object of the quest usually has intrinsic magical qualities that promise to change the quester's life for the better. What happens, though, is that the quest itself irrevocably changes the quester. The journey is not a geographical one but leads through the higher levels of consciousness. The magic is not in the object but in the search itself.

If we consider the human baseline to be at level three, the mind, then the journey begins with an awakening to the existence of something beyond. The fourth level involves acceptance of the need for change in life. For the alcoholic or addict, this is the opening out into recovery and growth. This isn't an easy level for anyone. The comfortable abode of consciousness and the habits of a lifetime may be overturned. Whitfield refers to this as "acceptance through conflict."

As we pointed out earlier, these levels exist for individuals as well as for humanity as a whole. Most people involved in the abuse of alcohol or other drugs are somewhere within the first three levels. The fourth level of acceptance through conflict most often marks that point or recognition when one becomes aware that one indeed has a problem and must do something about it.

This level is often connected with the heart and can mark the transition from egocentric thinking and behavior to helping oneself through helping others. Many of the activities of self-help meetings involve the fourth level of consciousness.

Moving up from this pivotal level, we come to the fifth level, that of understanding. Whitfield also refers to this level as "natural knowing," "intuition in its broadest sense," and "knowing from the inside." At this point, one begins to let go of mind, or ego, and identify with a more universal consciousness. The fifth level corresponds to the third step in the Twelve Steps: "Made a decision to turn our will and our lives over to the care of God *as we understood Him.*" In a spiritual sense, one is part of that understanding, part of that greater consciousness—a cocreator, so to speak.

A danger that Whitfield points out here is that of the recovering person turning it *all* over to a Higher Power and forgetting his own role as a "cocreator." Although this may appear to happen in certain monastic orders, it should be remembered that although the lives of monks, and even those of wandering holy men, may appear to be lives of total surrender, they actually involve one's identification with and involvement in a Higher Power, not personal abdication of responsibility.

The sixth level is that of compassion, and it grows out of a love for life, all life. It involves seeing oneself in all things and all things in oneself. Being compassion, according to Whitfield, is different from being compassionate. It involves not helping as well as helping, letting others go their own way when they need to.

The seventh level is rarely achieved. What Whitfield calls "Unity Consciousness" involves total absorption into and unity with the Higher Power. He points out the paradox that in a spiritual sense this state already exists for everyone. What is involved here is recognition of that fact.

Even if the state of unity between the Higher Power and the individual consciousness has always existed, the prospect of fully realizing it, or even approaching it at any of the higher levels, can be discerned as threatening to the ego/mind. Ramakrishna described this process as the dissolving of the salt doll in the sea. The doll and the sea are of the same composition, and in a very real sense the doll becomes the sea. The ego/mind, however, identifies the doll form as its reality and looks on any such transpersonal transformation as a threat to its very existence. What the ego/mind fails to understand in its anxiety is that the fully realized individual at any of the higher levels of consciousness is also fully realized at all the other levels as well. A "whole" person is alive and functioning at all levels at the same time. This truth is reflected in the way recovering people approach the Twelve Steps. One does not abandon one step to go on to the next. Instead, each new step is an overlay on what is in progress in each preceding step. Spiritual growth involves establishing a firm foundation at each level before going on to the next and not abandoning ground that has been gained for ground that is sought.

This pattern is found in many forms and repeated again and again in the prosaic and the miraculous, the physical and the transcendent. The six changing lines of the *I Ching*, for example, can be seen as representing the levels of consciousness. Many cultures and their mystical orders subscribe to the existence of a human spiritual body that coexists with the physical body. The spiritual body includes seven *chakras*, or wheels of energy, that occupy points corresponding to the anus, the genitals, the solar plexus, the heart, the throat, the pineal gland and the top of the head. It is said that the development of each level of consciousness activates its corresponding *chakra*, from the bottom up. The turning on of all these centers activates a serpentine energy called *kundalini* that opens the fully realized individual to a full, conscious union with the Self, or Higher Power.

The gist of Dr. Whitfield's argument is that much of the stress generated by one's entering into recovery or becoming abstinent involves the transition between levels of consciousness. Stress, by itself, is neither good nor bad. It's a force in life to be dealt with it. If stress triggers anxiety and contributes a relapse into addiction or abuse, the outcome is harmful to us. On the other hand, if it can be channeled into spiritual growth and development, transitional stress can contribute greatly to our future well-being. The experience of hitting bottom in addiction is very similar to what many who have progressed far in spiritual development refer to as "the dark night of the soul." The crises and ensuing self-realization that may result from addiction can be the beginnings of deep changes for the good for those individuals who find their way; therefore both self-help through groups and personally employed alternatives are integral means to physical, mental and spiritual development.

Because this is a book on abstinence and recovery in all its aspects, we have barely introduced the topic of spirituality and how it can involve growth as an alternative to abuse. Many books have been written on the subject of spiritual development, and we recommend that anyone who has been intrigued by what we have to say pursue the subject through its complexities, letting your developing intuition be your guide toward a clearer understanding of the consciousness growth pattern. Many different spiritual disciplines have been developed over time, finding what Don Juan referred to as a "path with a heart," or the right discipline for oneself, is a matter of personal choice and experience.

CHOOSING HELP: ALTERNATIVE RESOURCES

In Eastern cultures, individuals usually belong to a philosophic group within a religion, much as we may be members of certain dioceses or congregations in our culture. This group usually reflects one's personal convictions. Often one is born into it, but certain individuals may shop around for the group and discipline that best fits their needs. The primary resource for health, personal growth and spiritual development, however, is a single human being, a master who is often called a *guru*.

There is a saying that you do not find your *guru*, your *guru* finds you. The literature of the East is filled with miraculous tales of how students and teachers have come together, and we will begin the next chapter with one of these, the story of Gudo and his illustrious student Mu-Nan. In general, the seeker finds a mentor in much the same ways as we find mentors and guides in the West. Sometimes this may mean a series of individuals; sometimes the *guru* is the voice of your own superior self.

Although it does occur, Western mentors rarely play the important role in our lives that Eastern *gurus* do. Most often they are teachers in school who help to guide our intellectual development, or seniors in business who help us develop our talents. If we are strongly religious, we may have a priest, rabbi or other spiritual advisor. It is not often that we become involved with one who guides us through all facets of our outer and inner lives. Usually what we seek is an individual or program that will provide either the counseling or support and training for a specific goal, and that is what we will consider here. What follows are some specific guidelines and resources that may be of help in facilitating your development through abstinence and recovery.

Whether you are seeking treatment, therapy or counseling or a *guru*, the basic guidelines are the same. Primarily, you want to find a group or individual that will help you toward your goals in ways that are compatible with your needs. To ascertain the appropriateness of the individual or program, you will need to do some checking. You can begin by checking out the background through someone you know and trust, or through an organization whose business it is to supervise or regulate the particular field involved. These could include:

1. Your family physician or clinic
2. State or local medical, psychiatric or counseling association
3. State or local substance abuse coordinator—usually a government official
4. National organizations pertaining to addiction and chemical dependency, such as the American Medical Society on Alcoholism and Other Drug Dependencies (AMSAODD), in New York City
5. Federal agencies, such as the National Institute on Drug Abuse (NIDA) and the National Institute on Alcohol Abuse and Alcoholism (NIAAA), both in Rockville, MD.
6. National organizations of health professionals, such as the American Medical Association and the American Psychiatric Association
7. Better business bureaus
8. Insurance providers associations
9. Consumer groups and agencies
10. State government agencies that regulate health providers and oversee their quality of care, such as state boards of medical quality assurance
11. Law enforcement agencies
12. Magazines and newsletters

As you can see, this is only a partial list, but it indicates some of the possibilities. We live in an imperfect world, and although there are many reputable individuals and programs, we are vulnerable to the machinations of those that range from the misguided to the out-and-out dangerous quacks, crooks and egomaniacs.

When actually confronting a potential helper, be cooperative and supply the needed information, but at the same time conduct your own interview. Don't be afraid to ask questions. Pose hypothetical situations and ask how these would be handled. Ask to see credentials and ask for references that you can contact. Inspect the facilities and, if at all possible, talk to both patients and staff members.

Be sure that, to the best of your knowledge, the individual or group has a solid grounding in the field and a clear understanding of the nature of addiction and chemical dependency. You don't want a psychiatrist, for example, who is going to prescribe Valium for the stress of abstinence, or, for that matter, a doctor who will refer you to a "country club" treatment program that may be ineffective and is beyond your means. Ask about the approach that they take to whatever they are doing, and ask what their own belief is. Do their goals for you coincide with what you're asking of yourself?

Some of this may be difficult, and you may want advice in seeking help. You have to be careful of those who play into your own denial system and tell you what you want to hear instead of what you need to hear. Discuss your options in detail with loved ones and professionals whom you trust. If physical activity is involved, see a doctor and make sure that you are up to it.

Finally, remember to watch for "a path with a heart." Your intuition can tell you a lot, and if something doesn't feel right, it probably isn't.

RESOURCES

The books and articles we have cited all appear in the Bibliography at the back of this book. We don't want to take up space repeating them here, but there are some exceptionally good reference sources for information on the alternatives we have discussed in this chapter, and we offer these as a beginning:

Ram Dass. *Journey of Awakening: A Meditator's Guidebook*. Bantam Books, New York, 1978. Contains a directory of groups that teach meditation and retreat facilities.

Peggy Taylor, Rex Weyler, and Rick Ingrasci. *Chop Wood Carry Water*. Jeremy P. Tarcher, Inc., Los Angeles, 1984. By the editors of *New Age Journal* (a good resource itself), this book provides lists of recommended reading and resources at the end of each chapter. Especially pertinent are those on intimate relationships, tuning the body, healing, inner guidance and perils of the path.

Harold J. Cornacchia. *Consumer Health.* The C.V. Mosby Company, Saint Louis, 1976. Lists consumer, business and professional organizations and contains many tips for selecting helpers, insurance considerations, etc.

Karl Polak. *The Solution: Emotional Illness—It's Causes and Treatment.* The Alternative Press, Hong Kong, 1986. A personal account of multicultural approaches to addiction, stress and mental illness.

Magazines, journals and newsletters that may be of help are as follow:

Alcohol and Drug Abuse Alert, edited by your authors, will be available from Alert Newsletters, 67 Peachtree Park Drive, NE, Atlanta, GA 30309 in 1987.

American Health, Fitness of Body and Mind, P.O. Box 10032, Des Moines, IA 50347.

East West Journal, P.O. Box 970, Farmingdale, NY 11737.

Vegetarian Times, 41 East 42nd St., Suite 921, New York, NY 10017.

Homeopathic Education Services, 2124 Kittredge St., Berkeley, CA 94704. Provides books, tapes and lists of practitioners and national organizations.

The New Consciousness Sourcebook, Box 1067, Berkeley, CA 94701.

New Age, 341 Western Ave., Brighton, MA 02135.

Growing and Sharing: Mastering Recovery | 6

In Chapter 5 we looked at some of the general alternatives, the activities that can help turn recovery and abstinence into an opportunity for great personal growth and achievement. In this chapter we turn to the more personal element and see what individuals have done. Some of these vignettes are from well-known people, while others are from those who live in contented obscurity. Some of the tips presented are from published studies, such as Gail Sheehy's excellent work on coping and prevailing, *Pathfinders*. Others are from students in Rick Seymour's pharmacology and introduction to substance abuse studies courses, recovering individuals learning to counsel others and share techniques that have worked in their own lives. Not all these vignettes are directly concerned with abstinence or recovery, but they all share techniques for promoting positive states of being—such things as contentment, self-assurance, and bliss—that we all hope for in our lives. They may not all be applicable to everyone. We present them here in the hope that some will strike a responsive chord in your life, so that whether you are a recovering addict, or cleaning up your chemical act, or looking for growth in general, these sharings may be of some help to you.

MU-NAN'S STORY

Once, when the Zen master Gudo was traveling to Edo, then as now the capital of Japan, he was caught by a rainstorm in a small village. At the house where he stopped to buy new sandals, he was invited to stay the night. In the household, though, he found much unhappiness. The woman of the house explained that her husband, though a good worker, was a gambler and a drunkard. He squandered the money he earned and then came home and abused her and the children. There was rarely enough to eat.

Gudo bought some wine and fish and waited in meditation for the husband to return home. Drunk, belligerent and hungry, the man came in after midnight and yelled to his wife for food and drink. In his state, he didn't notice that the hand that fed him and gave him wine was that of the Zen master. He ate, drank his fill and fell asleep on the spot. Gudo sat beside him in meditation throughout the night.

In the morning, the man awoke and demanded to know who the stranger was.

"I am Gudo of Kyoto," answered the Zen master, "and I am going on to Edo."

In those days, everyone knew the name of the Emperor's own teacher, and the husband was ashamed to have spoken harshly. His remorseful apologies broke against the master's equanimity. Gudo smiled.

"Everything in this life is impermanent," he explained. "Life is very brief. If you keep on gambling and drinking, you will have no time left to accomplish anything else, and you will cause your family to suffer, too."

With the Zen master's words the man awoke from the state he was in as though it had been a dream. He saw clearly what his life had become and what had to be done to change it.

"Let me carry your things for a little way," he said.

The two took the road toward Edo. Every few miles Gudo would stop and bid the man to return, but each time the man would ask to continue for a few more miles. Finally Gudo said, "Return now." The man shook his head.

"I am going to follow you all the rest of my life."

In Paul Reps's version of this story in *Zen Flesh. Zen Bones*, the one from which the dialogue is quoted, it turns out that the man became the successor to Gudo and founder of modern Zen teaching in Japan. He was called Mu-Nan, the man who never turned back.

The tale may come from medieval Japan, but its core meanings show clear antecedents to anyone who has followed the Twelve Steps and is familiar with their working. Gudo could not have talked to the man that night when he returned home in a state of drunkenness and rage. At dawn, with the coming of the light, Gudo's intervention had a good chance of success. In helping Mu-nan to kill his dragon, Gudo gained a successor—a new pair of sandals, to be sure. For Mu-nan, return would have been back to his former life. He had no choice but to go forward one step at a time. The path followed by Mu-nan and Gudo is much more than the road to Edo.

PATHFINDING

In writing her book *Pathfinders*, Gail Sheehy sifted through 60,000 extensive life-history questionnaires and interviewed in depth a number of the respondents. In part, she was searching for the secrets of well-being as evidenced by people who had persevered through the pain and trials of life, who had survived and surmounted a variety of life obstacles. Many of those she interviewed were willing to share the methods they had used to cope with both success and failure in life and to describe how they had dealt with the often adverse circumstances in their lives and had grown from the experience. Although addiction and alcoholism are not primary topics in *Pathfinders*, there is much of value in Sheehy's book for the individual seeking alternatives. We have selected a few points that seem particularly germane in what she generalized from her interviews.

In discussing reactions to change and transition, she compared people of high well-being to people of low well-being. She found that people of low well-being were usually threatened by rough passages and periods of uncertainty in their lives. These people tended to have four basic reactions to these situations:

Drink more, eat more, take drugs—indulge.
Pretend the problem does not exist.
Develop physical symptoms.
Escape into fantasy.

In general, these people appeared to be much more vulnerable to stress than their high well-being counterparts. In these four reactions we can see the classic echoes of addiction and denial. Each of these four reactions would tend to exacerbate whatever the problem might be.

On the other hand, people with a high well-being quotient—those whom Sheehy calls "pathfinders"—tend to use four coping devices to protect themselves whenever they risk change, or when change or uncertainty is forced upon them:

Work more.
Depend on friends.
See the humor in the situation.
Pray.

Just as we can see addiction, alcoholism or white knuckles in the first set of reactions, we can see recovery, twelve-step work and comfortable abstention and sobriety in the second. Sheehy points out that these coping mechanisms are usually not inborn but are developed during times of adversity. Resiliency seems to be the key. These people are not immune to failure. They may feel it as keenly as anyone else. But they develop the ability to rebound and, looking at things realistically, learn from their losses and failures. Life for them is a learning experience, just as it should be for the growing abstainer. If you don't have those qualities now, don't worry. Just try to practice them, and chances are good that they will develop. As another author, Richard Bach, said, anything you concentrate on tends to get bigger.

THE VALUE OF FRIENDSHIP

Later in her book Sheehy speaks of the value of friendship, kinship and support systems in dealing with specific problems, including suicide and alcoholism. She sees therapeutic group sessions as often being of limited value because they are more involved in expressing the problem than in transcending it. She ends this discussion, however, by offering a positive interpretation of friendship that seems singularly in keeping with the twelfth step.

> By fortifying us in the continuing need to seek new openings in our paths and to rebound from setbacks, friendships and kinship and support systems are important aids to the pathfinding process. But they also offer the incipient pathfinder the opportunity to become something more—an all-weather friend, a person who sees the strongest kinship ties all the way through, and a polestar or survivor guide. These are roles that the pathfinder becomes ideally suited to playing for others, thereby perpetuating the roundelay of full human friendship.

Sheehy's words on friendship provide a key to the success and functioning of twelve-step programs. Friendship is a dynamic relationship that involves both receiving and giving. One is neither all one nor all the other; the relationship keeps changing. The true friend to humanity is the one who returns to the marketplace in a helping stance, and here we see again an echo of the Ox panels. Returning to the marketplace is not the end. It's not the culmination of enlightenment but the beginning of a new step upward in one's personal development.

IN THE GARDEN

M. lives "somewhere between the suburbs and the country." Now well into recovery, she recommends a greening of the thumb approach. In gardening, it's often the quality rather than the quantity that's important, so if you live in an apartment and don't have a half acre or even a back yard at your disposal, don't reject her suggestion out of hand. Some of the best vegetables we ever tasted were grown on a fire escape.

Frequently heard in twelve-step meetings is the advice to "get out of oneself" and "live in the here and now." These are ideas essential to quality sobriety, but how is one to accomplish these on a daily basis? Any success that I have in these areas is fleeting and must be remembered, recaptured, repracticed and (oops!) relost, ad infinitum.

In addition to the AA program itself, I find "therapeutic hobbies" very helpful—that is, hobbies that do more than just pass the time but also help me get out of myself and live in the here and now.

The most effective for me is vegetable gardening. I have flowers and shrubs and tons of houseplants, but it's the veggies that are particularly good for the soul. On my worst days, when my mind is in overdrive and manufactured problems are about to bury me, I can find instant relief by going out and visiting the cukes, zukes, tomatoes, potatoes et al. They seem to say, "Hey! Life goes on beautifully whether you choose to pay attention or not. So why don't you wise up?" And I say, "Oh. Yeah. Okay."

There are some things I've learned (through trial and serious error) to enhance maximum therapeutic-ness. First, smaller is better! I've gotten into planting so much that the garden becomes a burden rather than a pleasure and encourages greedy, non-"here and now" thoughts like, "Gee, I'll have 520 pounds of onions three months from now." Also, I've gone for more and more low-maintenance-for-survival methods; that is, I can putter for hours if I want, but things won't croak if I miss a day or two.

Done right, the garden helps me achieve balance in many ways. I can practice a modicum of discipline without overdoing things. I become more focused on the process than on the result. This gives me a sort of surprised, grateful pleasure for every eggplant or pepper.

Perhaps most important, I think it is helping me learn to accept change peacefully. When it comes to the garden, I have no doubt, and indeed take comfort, that there is a season for all things. Even now, when all but the hardiest herbs are gone and ice covers the ground most mornings, I see the garden not as dead, but as just taking a well-deserved and much-needed snooze.

The trick is to expand this easy, comfortable faith in the Creator's schedule for veggies and apply it more regularly to my own existence. It's working!

ALL IN THE FAMILY

K. has looked beyond herself to bring recovery into the next generation. She shows that sins are not the only thing that one can pass on. In recovery, many good things can come to your children.

As a young mother in recovery, I literally raised my children with the Twelve Steps. This offered me a unique opportunity to practice "these principles in all my affairs" and allowed my children (now adults) to understand addictive disease from early in their lives. They were aware that there was a strong possibility that they would be more vulnerable to the disease than other children who did not have a family history of alcoholism. This turned out to be a very good thing. As a result of their knowledge, both children were able to recognize their own first early encounters with symptoms of the disease and go into abstention without experiencing long-term addiction. Both had what they now refer to as allergic reactions to drugs. One had a blackout at the age of fourteen and promptly joined a Twelve Step group on her own. Both were spared the pain and heartbreak of long-term addiction.

PLANNING

E. is now more than a decade into recovery and is doing very well, thank you. Her ability to plan in detail, set up as a means of maintaining sobriety, has helped her into a second career at this stage in her life.

I am a sixty-three-year-old woman who lives alone and was an active alcoholic for twelve years and went into recovery nine years ago. To this date, I haven't experienced a relapse. I credit my recovery with a strong commitment to the support that I have found in Alcoholics Anonymous and to a careful analysis of my own prior drinking style and personal needs in continuing to live a chemically free life.

The traditional cocktail hour was my most vulnerable time of the day, and I found that by planning my dinner during this hour I was able to eliminate my habitual early evening drinking. I also paid close attention to my diet and was careful to eat only nutritious and fresh foods. I dispensed with fast foods altogether and found that, in addition to improved feelings of good health, the extra time required in preparing my meals helped to occupy my mind and helped break the patterns that drinking had woven into my life.

Since entering recovery, I have never gone to bed without having a specific plan for the next day, no matter how trivial. When I wake up each morning, I know that at least one task requires my attention: weeding a patch of lawn, rearranging a closet, mending all the loose buttons in the house or going to the recycling center. I always have a plan for which I alone am responsible. Free time was my greatest enemy, and today I try to fill my life and have as little free time as possible.

A GOOD NIGHT'S SLEEP

Neither our informant nor his friend are in recovery. Both, however, have discovered a good means of restoring their energies and resisting stress.

Several years ago, an old and good friend came to visit. We were walking through Golden Gate Park and comparing notes on the twists and turns that our lives had taken. In our mid-forties, we had both experienced times of great stress. Furthermore, as young people in the psychedelic sixties, we had both turned to alcohol and drugs for recreation and support. We had developed dependencies on marijuana and tobacco and problems with alcohol along the way, and we had each stopped using any overtly psychoactive substance other than coffee.

I knew that my friend had gone through some difficult times with work and family, but he looked fit and was in good spirits. The troubles didn't appear to have borne him down. How did you cope, I asked.

"Mainly by getting a good night's sleep," he told me. "When things get overwhelming, I just shut down. If there are aspects I need to deal with, I do that, but as soon as I can I shut it all off and get a good night's sleep. You know, the worst thing that stress can do is worry you into a state of exhaustion. Your immune system goes to mush while you lie awake night after night stewing about all your problems. They'll still be there in the morning. You don't have to carry them everywhere you go."

I asked him if such repression isn't damaging in the long run, as the psychologists say.

"This isn't repression," he answered. "In repression, you're putting a lid on things, hiding them in your subconscious. What I do is just let go of it all. You know, it's like when you're out in a sailboat and things start going wrong. The wind is too strong, the boat is heeling too much for you to handle. What do you do? You let go of everything. The boat rights itself and comes into the wind until you're ready to deal with it again."

Having spent my share of nights tossing and turning, unable to shut off the machine, I saw all this as good advice. The opportunity to try it out came sooner than expected. A few months later, while my wife was away on an extended business trip and I was dealing with complex problems at the office and with personal finances, my mother had a stroke. As the only child of my sole surviving parent, I found myself being blown about in a sea of decisions and activities. My mother, an independent type, lived alone and had looked after her own affairs since my father's death many years earlier. There were papers to find, accounts to deal with, powers of attorney, insurance and making what could be life-or-death decisions in maintaining of her precarious hold on life. There were also the phone calls, not the least being from well-meaning friends and relatives, many of them wanting daily, even hourly reports on Mom's condition and on how the whole situation was progressing.

I remembered my friend's advice and reasoned that although my days and evenings were tightly packed for the time being, only an emergency call from the hospital would come in the middle of the night. To ensure this, I kept a list of the more insistent friends and relatives by the phone and called each of them. Within a few days, I had streamlined this by setting up a chain system—I called Aunt Maud, she called Cousin Jill, who in turn called Uncle Sam, etc. As I checked off the last name I could feel that I had done everything that I could for that particular day. My final act was to make a list of what absolutely needed to be done the following day, and as I wrote down each item I thought to myself, "I can forget about that one for now."

Once in bed, I used a mantra meditation to settle my mind and scatter any thoughts of the future after suggesting to myself that I would have a good night's sleep and wake up ready to resume the tasks at hand. A call from the hospital might come, but I wouldn't lie awake listening for it. Along with everything else, that was in the suspense file. In the eye of the storm, I was getting a good night's sleep.

DRAWING THE LINE

L. is a health professional who discovered that a major step he had to take was clearly defining just what he meant by abstinence.

Very few things in this world are clear-cut, presenting obvious points for drawing the line between good and bad, permissible and impermissible. This is a problem that many people entering recovery or contemplating "cleaning up their act" encounter. Where do you draw the line? At first this may seem easy. You eliminate the drugs that are giving you trouble. Then someone points out that other psychoactive substances may produce an alternative addiction or trigger a relapse into your drug of choice.

"Very well, then," you may say, "I'll eliminate all psychoactive substances."

That may be a noble approach, but can one actually do it? Many people in early recovery tend to rely heavily on coffee and cigarettes to get them through social interactions, even working their programs. Others may be in need of psychoactive medication, such as barbiturates for nondrug-related seizure activity. Psychoactive substances are very hard to avoid in our civilization. Caffeine appears in many nonalcoholic beverages and over-the-counter medications, while sugar, a stimulant, is found in many surprising places, such as salad dressing and spaghetti sauce. Nitrites are used as a primary preservative in meats and other processed foods. In a larger sense, virtually everything that we eat or drink has some effect on our central nervous system. If you doubt this, compare the way you feel after eating a steak—sedated—with the way you feel after eating spinach or a half-dozen oysters.

As a recovering health professional who has worked in the field of biochemistry, I have been acutely aware of the plethora of substances in our lives that do affect our brain chemistry. At the same time, being of a philosophic turn, I have been aware of my own need to define just what "abstention" means to me. I wanted to avoid danger to myself and felt that this meant avoiding anything that could increase my vulnerability to relapse or compromise my recovery. Obviously, I could not avoid all central-nervous-system-effective substances.

The conclusion that I reached for my own life is based on intent. I realized that although I could not block all potentially psychoactive substances from my life, I could avoid using anything for the purpose of getting high or changing my consciousness. I could not avoid getting high or changing consciousness, as these states are intrinsic to life itself. A consciousness that is unchanging is clinically dead. In using such alternatives to alcohol and other drugs as working the Twelve Steps, running, yoga, meditation and a healthy diet, I was in fact getting high and changing my consciousness. But I was doing it endogenously rather than exogenously, from within rather than by using external drugs. Therefore, my personal line is drawn at the abstention from using any substance for its psychoactive effect on my central nervous system. It's a line that I can live with.

WALKING THROUGH

It's said that those who forget the past are doomed to repeat it. In this case, a recovering individual's active memory of the dark side helps strengthen the recovery.

It has been my experience as a recovering alcoholic and addict that what I have named a "Walk Through" is the way I kept myself sober, early in sobriety and now. What I do is to take the first drink or line in my mind when the drug hunger hits and walk it through to the point in my using where I was either out of control, paranoid or completely disgusted with myself. A reminder of "the way I was" has a powerful effect on me. I don't ever want to be that way again. So far, by working my program and always, when drug hunger hits, reminding myself of how it was, I've managed to stay sober for nearly two years.

OF TIME AND RECOVERY

B. is a recovering addict who found a new relation to time and duration when he got out of the fast lane.

Time may be relative, as Einstein said. All I know is that when you're an addict, time is really out of it. You may spend hours on the nod, just doing nothing. Then terminal impatience can set in if you have to wait thirty seconds for an elevator or you get put on hold. You just can't deal with it.

On stimulants, you get the feeling that life is a sprint race. You have to come up on it fast because it ends so quickly. Most of the addicts that I've known couldn't handle time at all. If they thought about it, they had a sense that they didn't have long. Years could race by, but, let me tell you, if you were out of drug and your connection was late—that was *forever!*

In recovery, I've learned how to use time instead of letting it use me. Life isn't a sprint at all, it's a long-distance race where you have to learn to pace yourself. That's not to say I think I'm going to last forever. I'm feeling good, but not that good. It's more like I can allow myself to take the time to do what I want to do, but I don't want to waste what I've got. There's a saying—I don't know if it's Chinese, American Indian or Asian Indian—but it says: "Live your life as though you are going to live forever. Appreciate your life as though each moment may be the last." That says it.

EATING RIGHT, RIGHT?

D. dropped out of an urban high school and became a Haight Ashbury addict in the mid-sixties. After years of fast food and shooting galleries, he discovered that there's more to life than a needle and fries. Today he works at an organic truck farm northeast of San Francisco and lives his philosophy of food.

I've become a health food nut, and I love it. Back when I was geezing, it was nothing but deep fry. You know what I mean. The closest I ever got to a balanced meal was a slice of deluxe pizza. Usually it was french fries, onion rings. If I'd made a good deal and had extra coin, my ideal of culinary heaven was surf'n'turf—you know, a slab of steak and a lobster tail—yeah, and a bottle of champagne. Usually that was too much for me. Too rich. I'd leave the restaurant and upchuck.

When the roof finally caved in and I went for treatment, my counselor said that I was seriously malnourished. I couldn't argue with her. I was a sick man. The doc at the clinic did what he called a full workup on me and said he was amazed that I had a functioning liver and no ulcers. As it was, the drugs and booze had kept me from feeling a lot of pain from the problems I did have.

Along with my daily meds, the pharmacy gave me multiple vitamins. The pharmacist—he looked like one of Santa's elves—ho-ho-ho'd at me that they would help straighten out my deficiencies but were no replacement for what I really needed. Vegetables? You mean like that sour canned spinach they used to give us in grade school? No, thanks. Whole-grain bread? Hey! I knew all you clinic do-gooders were a bunch of misplaced hippies, but don't get ridiculous on me.

Then my counselor explained that the kind of food I had been eating created a lot of the same stresses that the drugs did, the things that had brought me into treatment. If I was serious about starting over, if I really wanted to get into abstinence and recovery, I had to do a lot more than just stop using drugs and alcohol. She explained that malnourishment wasn't just not eating enough, it was eating all the wrong things. I had to give myself not only enough food, but the right kinds of food. That meant staying away from junk food. I was too sick to argue, so I just said okay.

I had detoxified before, usually when my dealer got popped, but nobody had ever messed with my habits. This lady put me on a diet like I was her kid or something. She even brought me stuff from an organic garden where they don't use chemicals. I bit into an apple and actually tasted it. I mean I tasted it. It was like a long-ago childhood memory. And then I ate a tomato!

She explained that the wrong foods would give me feelings of depression that would remind me of the speed downside and get me wanting to use again. Getting enough sleep is important, too, and she got me into regular exercise. I didn't do it all at once but started easing into things toward the end of withdrawal. It all helped, but the food trip is what really turned me on. You know, the right stuff is not only the right stuff, it tastes good, too. I got interested and learned about carbohydrates, and amino acids, and natural vitamins. All that stuff, along with the exercise and sleeping right and all, does the same things, but I end up feeling good and feeling good about myself besides. It's not instant gratification like a shot of meth or heroin or a greasy bag of french fries, but it gets to you in time—and it stays with you.

So now I've been clean for almost three years. I'm working a program and into the steps and, like I said, I'm a health food nut. I've even got a steady job. I'm working for an organic truck farm, living out in the country and growing things. You ought to taste my tomatoes!

ABSTENTION AND THE CREATIVE PROCESS

C., a writer who is in recovery—not a recovering writer—has looked at the literary attitudes that may lead creative people to emulate others who have been successful in spite of chemical dependency problems. He points out some dangerous misconceptions and ways in which we may avoid them.

Volumes have been written about the creative process, and as is the case with most things about ourselves on which volumes have been written, we still know very little for sure about it. Theories abound as to what creativity is and where it comes from. A currently popular one is that the right hemisphere of the brain is the seat of nonverbal creativity, spirituality and intuition, while the left hemisphere is a linear switchboard for all the practical connections in our lives. Many books are now on the market that tell us how to exercise our right-brain capacities. Personally, I subscribe to the much more scientific theory of creativity that inspiration comes to us from a group of lovely maidens who must be coaxed from their home on Mount Olympus to our sides by a mixture of flattery, adulation and elbow grease.

Some scientists have postulated a strong link between addiction and what they refer to as "an overactive right-brain function." We are not sure just what that means. Maybe what they're saying is that the left brain gets jealous of too much creativity, so it goes out and gets drunk to compensate. There is a popular conception that highly creative people are more susceptible than others to abuse and addiction, but that could be a myth. A more dangerous myth is that great creativity *requires* a drug or alcohol problem. If anything, the likes of Ernest Hemingway, F. Scott Fitzgerald, Charles Baudelaire, Brendan Behan, and Dylan Thomas probably succeeded in spite of their drug proclivities rather than because of them. Who knows what these giants might have done with a clear sensorium?

The myth of "priming the pump" has led many an aspiring artist into the misconception that in order to succeed he or she must first learn to drink like Thomas, carouse like Behan, drag him- or herself "through the negro streets at dawn looking for an angry fix" with Allen Ginsberg and drop acid with Ken Kesey. Lord knows, I was one of them. I remember one of my lit teachers, bless her soul, saying regretfully that Words-worth's one problem was that he was "too normal." It took me years to realize that Wordsworth was also a great poet and that there were many other great artists who lived long and productive lives without the need or desire to streak across the empyrean like a roman candle burning at both ends.

My own heroes were Hemingway and Baudelaire, the one a macho American, sparing of words and heavy-handed on the bottle, the other a complex Frenchman who celebrated the dark mind of Poe and sampled all the psychoactives of his era. Creativity was a limited, hidden treasure, primed by psychoactive excesses. Because it was limited, I saved every-thing I wrote. Because of the excesses, everything I wrote came out in muddled fragments. I had great dreams of creating immortal prose and poetry and could spin novels into the mirror behind any bar in town. As time passed the pump got harder and harder to prime. And what came out?

On the night that I consciously entered into recovery, I dreamed that I was climbing a great staircase. A young man with slicked-back hair and a mustache was trying to convince me to go back with him. He was rugged-ly built but seemed somehow pinched and pallorous. His look of dis-appointment made me feel sorry to leave him there on the stairs and con-tinue on, but continue on I did. It was several weeks before I realized that the man on the stair was the young Ernest Hemingway.

In the years since that day, I have come to know that creativity is not some hidden pool of fossil fuel, but rather a force that fills the entire universe. Everyone, even the artist, is a conduit for that force, and the more you use it, the more it's there to use.

My list of published works is ever growing, and I see no sign of running out. I may not be famous yet, but you might recognize the name on my American Express gold card. I see the money and recognition as gifts from my sobriety and recovery, but they are not the main thing that keeps me writing. What keeps me at it is that it feels good. Now that I'm no longer loading up on alcohol and other drugs in order to get high, I'm aware of all the things that get us high on a daily basis. An important one for me is sitting down and letting the words come. It's much more than just a feel-ing of accomplishment, it's an actual rush, a feeling of ecstasy just as strong as any I ever felt on marijuana, cocaine or alcohol. And it's not just me.

I've talked this over with others who feel the same thing, and we agree that creative acts have a force similar to biofeedback, meditation, yoga or other exercise in activating all the internal stuff that sets off endorphins and alpha brain waves. When we were loaded all the time, we didn't get that. Now we do. It's as simple as that.

THE ULTIMATE CREATIVITY

A non-recovering but abstinent mother tells us what the ultimate in personal creativity meant to her and her way of life.

I'm not a recovering addict or alcoholic, but I have been abstinent from drugs, including alcohol, nicotine and, as much as possible, sugar and caffeine for about ten years. As a member of the counterculture in the sixties and early seventies, I not only used all of these, sometimes to excess, but also experimented with LSD, mescaline, mushrooms, amphetamines and cocaine. Although I did take Valium on occasion, I managed to avoid the narcotics and barbiturates.

On my twenty-fifth birthday I got the best present a woman could ever have. I learned that I was pregnant. My husband and I had been hoping for a child and had read about "natural childbirth." We found a hospital in our city that had recently started a natural-birth clinic, using their own adaptation of the Lamaze system. We signed up and began doing Lamaze training.

Lamaze isn't "painless" in the sense of eliminating pain or making us insensible to it the way drugs like morphine or ether do. Like many forms of exercise and concentration, it helps to rechannel what you feel and to change your interpretation of it. The way the doctor explained it, even when you're knocked out, or when the brain's pain centers are blocked, the pain is still there. You just don't experience it consciously. But the pain is still there, and you're experiencing it at a subconscious level. Furthermore, your baby can experience both your subconscious reaction to the pain *and* the bad effects of the drugs used to block it.

What Lamaze and similar forms of natural childbirth do is help you redefine what it is you're feeling. Instead of interpreting the powerful changes taking place during labor and birth as pain, you interpret them as powerful changes. You learn through prenatal training and exercise to understand them and work with them. Childbirth indeed involves a lot of physical effort and stress, but when you think about it, so does any form of strenuous physical activity, and you don't hear of runners or weightlifters taking painkillers in order to compete, do you?

Organized physical activity, the kind that you train for, produces its own internal compensators for the stress that the activity brings on. By now, we all know about runners and endorphins. Well, natural childbirth does the same thing. The regulated breathing and exercises involved in prenatal training not only strengthen the pelvic and other muscles involved in birth itself, but also prepare for the production of our natural internal compensators. The breathing is very similar to exercises found in hatha and tantric yoga. When the time comes, natural childbirth can be a very high experience.

The doctor gave me two good reasons to avoid psychoactive substances during my pregnancy. First, he said, the prenatal exercises are aimed at finely turning your mind and body for the peak experience of giving birth. Drugs or "foods" that affect your higher consciousness are going to interfere with that process, slow it down, maybe even make it ineffective. If you're talking to someone on the telephone, you don't play the radio or TV full blast at the same time. Second, you are engaged in the ultimate creativity. You're making a human being, and you want to make that person as perfect as you can. The raw materials in that creative process are everything that you take into your own body. Everything.

That was enough for me. My husband, a beautiful and understanding person, pointed out that even if he continued to use tobacco or marijuana it would be in the air I was breathing. We both stopped using anything that could possibly hurt our baby. After our daughter was born, we continued an abstinent life-style while I was nursing. As time passed we both realized that we felt really good, better than either of us could remember feeling in our adult lives. There were stresses and problems, but we were able to cope with them and grow through them. The childbirth training led to an interest in meditation and yoga.

All that was ten years ago. Today we both run on a regular basis, and our daughter and her little brother run with us. We have continued to meditate and do yoga regularly. We serve wine or beer to our friends but stick to juices and mineral water ourselves. Most of the food we cook is fresh and from scratch, so we can avoid most of the sugar and other such things found in processed foods.

I'm in my mid-thirties, my husband is forty, and we both look and feel younger than we did ten years ago. Sometimes I look at harried people chain-smoking on the street, or others who are obviously still using too much alcohol or other drugs, and I think, God, they don't know what they're missing.

HOW HELPING YOU HELPS ME

A Haight Ashbury Free Medical Clinic director who is a devotee of Satya Sai Baba explains how living a life of service to others can be one of the greatest services one can do for oneself.

"It is better to give than to receive." "Cast your bread upon the waters." Our language and culture are filled with statements to the effect that somehow the act of giving, the act of helping others, actually does more for us than it does for them. Like a familiar sign, these truths have been before our eyes for so long that we usually don't see them or think of them beyond possibly registering somewhere in our midconsciousness that we've encountered some more of the "pious nonsense."

Although many of us do it in our own way, the act of giving, in and of itself, doesn't fit in with our current cultural self-image of hard-nosed pragmatism. We seem to think that there has to be something in it for us on a direct material kickback level. "Sure I give to the Cancer Society. I can write it off my income tax." "If we support research on addiction, maybe Congress will ease up on our product restrictions."

What many of us fail to realize is that giving—of one's property, one's time, one's self—ranks very high among the therapeutic actions we can take for our own development. The anonymous groups recognize this and have built giving and sharing into their Twelve Steps. For them, salvation and recovery lies through sharing their own experiences with addiction and helping other addicts. Service and giving can be looked at from a much broader base, however.

In India, Satya Sai Baba has enunciated a philosophy that places giving and sharing at the center of spiritual development. Unlike many of the Eastern "gurus" known in the West, he asks his followers for nothing. Instead, he instructs them to help others directly and has been responsible for establishing hospitals, schools and other centers for the good of humanity. The core of his doctrine is simply that all creation and everything in it, including us, is God. If one is to love God, one must love all creation, all people. In doing so, one is cured by Love of all pettiness, hatred and grief. Grace J. McMartin, in her book *A Recapitulation of Satya Sai Baba's Divine Teachings*, quotes Satya Sai Baba on this:

"Man is born in society; he is bred in society; he is shaped well or ill by the subtle influence of society. He, in his turn, as a member of society influences the people who contact him. His life is turned or twisted by the standards, modes, and behavior patterns of the society into which he is born through the effects of his accumulated actions."

In society, love should be the prime motivator. Even though Satya Sai Baba pictures a universe in which the best thing you can do is be of service to others, he cautions that that should not become a motivation for doing good. He urges his followers to "forget the harm that anyone has done to you, and forget the good that you have done to others."

Eastern philosophies recognize a number of both subtle and overt reciprocities wherein the interactions we engage in affect our lives. Many of these fall within what some call karma. Karma is often seen as a particularly difficult concept for Western people to grasp, something tied in with a belief in reincarnation and divine string-pulling. And yet karma can be looked on as simply the cause-and-effect relationship of human interaction. It's the Eastern version of such well-known Western concepts as "As ye sow, so shall you reap," "What goes around comes around," or, as we say in California, "If you plant zucchini in the spring, you'll most likely be eating zucchini in the fall."

There is a lot of joy in service, and it is the kind of pleasure that lasts. Working at the Haight Ashbury Free Medical Clinic, where over half the treatment staff is composed of volunteers, we have had an opportunity to observe a great variety of people acting from altruistic motives. We've asked many of these volunteers why they do it, and the most frequent answers that we get are that it's a pleasure to help others and that the volunteers feel better about themselves when they are helping. There are material reciprocities involved. For example, medical and counseling volunteers gain invaluable experience for their own careers by treating the wide variety of cases that are seen at the Clinic, and they pick up a great deal of prestige from working with a program that has worldwide recognition for its treatment expertise. However, such considerations rarely seem to enter into the decision by volunteers to offer their services.

The paid staff at the Clinic, for that matter, is composed of pioneers and professionals in their fields who could be taking home large salaries from private hospitals and treatment centers instead of struggling for 1960s brown-rice wages under the collective belief that "quality health care is a right, not a privilege, and should be free for all who need it at the point of delivery." We joke about being stuck in the barrel, but it is nice to look in the mirror in the morning.

Maybe Satya Sai Baba is right. Maybe the most basic of joys is that generated by helping others. Maybe the solution to the "human condition" or the "existential problem" is simply extending a hand to your fellow human beings.

THE NATURE OF "REALITY"

Another staff person at the Clinic discusses what's real and gives us the benefit of his insight into centering beyond the storm.

Is it any wonder that many people turn to alcohol and other drugs? Those who do are often accused of "escaping from reality," but let's examine the popular view of what these people are accused of escaping from. Generally, our culture sees so-called reality as a pretty grim place. Whether we are willing to admit it or not, the way we speak of "reality" reveals how we feel.

When we say, "Let's get down to earth," or "in the real world," we're usually about to speak of something singularly unpleasant. References to reality usually precede discussion of strife, limitation, division or dissension, but is that "reality" really real? The earth one can get down to is, in its natural state, a thing of beauty. It's made of mountains and oceans, flowers, trees, blue skies, interesting cities and fascinating creatures that include other people. The "grim" reality is mostly an overlay that clouds all this beauty but is, in and of itself, an illusion, the so-called Maya of Sanskrit-speaking mystics.

We are born, we live, eventually we die. In this process, we interact with one another and with the raw materials of the universe. Rudolph Holtzinger, a Viennese psychotherapist who studied with Sigmund Freud and worked for a while at the Haight Ashbury Free Medical Clinic, believed that each one of us is a point in space that acts as a three-dimensional hologram. Each of us projects his own image of reality on the raw material of the universe, and therefore each of us is at the center of the universe. Obviously, this subjective universe has many centers, and at the edges our own holograms mingle with, modify and are modified by everyone else's holograms.

Reality, then, is what we make of it by shaping whatever is out there through our own projections. It follows that one cannot escape from reality by abusing alcohol and other drugs, or by any other means. We ourselves are the cocreators and inhabitants of our reality. What we *can* do by abusing alcohol and other drugs, or by succumbing to anxiety and other negative reactions to our projections, is make an unholy mess of our reality.

If this infinite room that we inhabit has gotten into disorder, it is incumbent on each of us to rearrange both the internal and external furnishings to our own liking and comfort. One way of starting to do this is to take inventory, separating what is real and lasting from what is illusive and transitory. In recovery or abstinence therapy, this can be seen as a changing of cues. It is also a centering technique for meditation and can involve the use of mantras or a variety of sights, sounds and feelings.

One of my own centering cues involves something that happened a number of years ago. I was sitting by a window while a wasp's nest of tribulations buzzed in my head. Outside the window the sky was very blue, and I found myself staring at a wooden telephone pole. The pole had been bleached white by the sun and presented a strong, clean contrast to the blue sky. I found myself thinking how simple and strong it looked. Eventually that pole would come down, but that did not matter to me or to it. For now, it was "eternal," and compared to it the anxieties and problems that I was experiencing were no more than ripples in the wind that faded as the simple strength of what I was seeing cleared them from my mind. There have been magical moments since that time when I've managed to pause and look beyond my own homespun anxieties to something real on the far side of the hologram.

WOODS

Finally, in closing this chapter, we hear from R., a recovering health professional who reentered his practice through the Clinic after undergoing the impaired health professional's diversion and treatment program. During treatment he developed a healthy regimen of daily exercise that is still providing him with recovery-strengthening insights, as well as some inspiration for the rest of us.

Spring. Early light. A few years ago, I would have stumbled to the fridge, looking for a beer to keep me going until the neighborhood bar opened at seven. The bar was a class place—dark wood paneling, quiet, inviting, no questions asked. Today I pulled on shorts and a T-shirt, laced a pair of Nikes and drove over the hill to the place where I run on Saturdays.

Rick Seymour had asked me a few days ago to write something for him about my recovery, something I did to help make it happen. I thought about that while I was warming up by the trail. Running is one thing that I do. Then, a lot of people are running, and it seems to help. I usually start the day with a couple of miles. On Saturdays, like today, I run about seven miles, usually a switchback trail up one leg of a mountain to a hidden lake, around the lake, and back down to my car. I've read that all this gets the endorphins pumping. All I know is that it feels good, and it makes me feel like I'm accomplishing something.

The path starts near sea level, and two white herons, their legs tucked up and their long wings looking prehistoric, fly over and dip to a nearby creek. The way isn't steep, but it's all uphill, and soon I'm breathing deep and hard. Recovery is a lot like running—it can be hard, very hard at times, but it makes you feel good.

The sun is just hitting the mountaintop when I reach the lake and start around, still thinking about recovery, the way my life was and the way it is now. It isn't just running. It's more like taking another path, one that leads away from oblivion, and doing it very deliberately. On the far side of the lake there's a deep gorge that leads back into the mountain. The trees are close together and mossy, and it looks like a good place to get lost in.

As I run past this darkened wood I smell a dampness, and for a moment I'm smelling that classical bar smell of stale beer, disinfectant and God knows what all. Ahead the path dips back out to the lake where the sun is just making its presence felt, coaxing a light film of mist into the air. I think of an old man and a bit of poetry he wrote. It's not necessarily about recovery, but then recovery is about other things, too. Oblivion is a form of death, and commitment is a form of transformation. That's what it's about to me. Ahead the path turns back toward town, and I know that Robert Frost wrote my answer for me:

The woods are lovely, dark, and deep,
But I have promises to keep,
And miles to go before I sleep,
And miles to go before I sleep.

No, Thanks, I Just Threw One Away: Survival in a Drug-Oriented Society | 7

Many years ago, a popular newspaper columnist came up with what he considered the perfect answer when offered a cigarette or a drink that he didn't really need. "No, thanks, I just threw one away." "Unfortunately," as he related in his column, "I have not as yet been offered a drink or a cigarette that I didn't really need. Consequently, I have never had an opportunity to use the line."

Many studies have indicated that while it may be easy to maintain abstinence and sobriety during treatment and in isolation, when the general societal cues for drinking and other drug use are largely absent, the recovering person's vulnerability to relapse increases geometrically with his reentry into society. As the pressures of life and social interaction resume the risks increase.

Just as the Taoist or Zen Buddhist seeker we met in Chapter 5 must eventually return to the marketplace after achieving unity with the universe in isolation, the recovering drug user returns from treatment to a society that is oriented toward the use of alcohol and other drugs. Self-help programs and treatment agencies often recommend major changes in one's life-style in order to avoid recontagion. This makes a certain amount of sense, but in a land where a joint or a line of cocaine can show up even in the best of living rooms, and where the business and social wheels are often greased with cocktails or "wine and cheese," total avoidance of contact is unrealistic.

Some purists in the recovering community may hold out for total isolation. Alcoholics Anonymous, however, recognizes the great difficulty of this and has the following to say in its "Big Book," *Alcoholics Anonymous*:

> Assuming we are spiritually fit, we can do all sorts of things alcoholics are not supposed to do. People have said we must not go where liquor is served; we must not have it in our homes; we must shun friends who drink; we must avoid moving pictures which show drinking scenes; we must not go into bars; our friends must hide their bottles if we go to their houses; we mustn't think or be reminded about alcohol at all. Our experience shows that this is not necessarily so.
>
> We meet these conditions every day. An alcoholic who cannot meet them still has an alcoholic mind: there is something the matter with his spiritual status. His only chance for sobriety would be some place like the Greenland Ice Cap, and even there an Eskimo might turn up with a bottle of scotch and ruin everything! Ask any woman who has sent her husband to distant places on the theory he would escape the alcohol problem.
>
> In our belief any scheme of combating alcoholism which proposes to shield the sick man from temptation is doomed to failure. If the alcoholic tries to shield himself he may succeed for a time, but he usually winds up with a bigger explosion than ever. We have tried these methods. These attempts to do the impossible have always failed.
>
> So our rule is not to avoid a place where there is drinking, *if we have a legitimate reason for being there.*

Our aim in this chapter is to help both the recovering person and the individual who has stopped using all psychoactive substances survive in social and business situations where alcohol or other drugs are being consumed. We also want people who care about someone in recovery to understand and respect the power of these social situations and to be aware of the real signs of an impending relapse. These are described in Chapter 8. We recognize that in such situations the cues that can precipitate drug hunger abound. You can see it, smell it, see others enjoying it and be offered it by well-meaning friends.

There are several ways *not* to react to these situations. One is to become a self-willed social cripple. Hiding in the corner and feeling sorry for yourself is a sign that you are trying to "white-knuckle" your way through. The "Big Book" has good advice for these situations:

> Why sit with a long face in places where there is drinking, sighing about the good old days. If it is a happy occasion, try to increase the pleasure of those there; if a business occasion, go and attend to your business enthusiastically. If you are with a person who wants to eat in a bar, by all means go along. Let your friends know they are not to change their habits on your account. At a proper time and place explain to all your friends why alcohol [or any other drug] disagrees with you. If you do this thoroughly, few people will ask you to drink. While you were drinking, you were withdrawing from life little by little. Now you are getting back into the social life of this world. Don't start to withdraw again just because your friends drink liquor.

Another sign of the white-knuckler can be constant proselytizing, urging all others around you to become abstainers whether they appear to have problems or not, whether they welcome your efforts or not. Most often, this is a sign that your sobriety is precarious and that you feel you must act out a strong hostility to use. As a secure person who is well centered and making use of viable alternatives to use, you don't have to be Carry Nation and carry an ax in order to protect your sobriety. The Big Book says of this, "We are careful never to show intolerance or hatred of drinking as an institution. Experience shows that such an attitude is not helpful to anyone."

Preaching abstinence and lecturing others on the "evils" of drugs can also be overenthusiasm on the part of individuals newly entered into sobriety. New converts of any kind are, after all, famous for their total immersion in a new-found belief. Many religious groups have found to their dismay that the new recruits from the ranks of "sinners" and "infidels" tend to go overboard when they become "protectors of the faith." Tolerance is, after all, a learned ability acquired through constant practice.

Reaction and proselytizing by an abstinent person in a social situation rarely constitute an honest attempt to "share the light," however. Most often this results from such negative emotions as pent-up anger and jealousy: "How dare you have fun while I'm being miserable!" The acting-out that results from these negative emotions can take a variety of forms. One white-knuckler we knew would pick fights with his wife over imagined insults if she had a cocktail with guests, and then he would stomp out of the house. Another, furious that his wife and in-laws had had wine with dinner at a family outing and were acting cheerful, almost wrecked the family car with all in it and then accused them of being drunk and distracting his driving. No self-respecting white-knuckler would ever admit that the problem is that, to his perception, everyone else is drinking, or smoking dope, or snorting, and he is not. He will brazen it through, even if that means being a total pain in the tail to everyone around him.

DEVELOPING FLEXIBILITY

One thing that Gail Sheehy points out in her book *Pathfinders* is that those folks with a high well-being quotient tend to grow more spontaneous as they get older. The low well-being folks tend to start out pretty rigid and get more so as time passes. These tendencies are reflected in the substance-abuse field, where it is noticed that addicts and others who have problems with drugs seem to be inflexible and unspontaneous in their thinking and actions. A holdover of inflexible thinking and behavior may contribute to the stress and white-knuckling experienced by many abstainers. The following insight was reported by one of our recovering clients and may have some bearing on this:

> The other evening I was riding home from work with my wife, and we were discussing finances. Although both of us are employed and have some additional income from consulting, the recent purchase of a house and improvements thereto have cut deeply into our cash flow. On top of that, my wife was granted a sabbatical, which means several months overseas, a trip for which I plan to take leave to accompany her. Such an undertaking means, however, that finances will be even tighter for a while.
>
> I ventured that we would have to cut expenses to a minimum in the half year before the trip, including all eating out. Now, we live in an area with many fine restaurants, and we love to try them. We usually go out to dinner once a week, eating at a new place each time. My wife thought about that for a while and then suggested that instead of dinners out we do periodic lunches instead. "It costs a lot less, and we'll both have the time."
>
> I thought that an excellent idea and agreed. Then it occurred to me that a few years ago my reaction would have been very different. As a practicing addict and alcoholic, and even in the early stages of abstention, my attitudes tended to be very rigid. Then I would have said something like, "If we can't have dinner in a good restaurant every Friday night, then there's no point to going out at all." Any attempt at compromise would have been greeted by scorn on my part. The world for me was black and white. There was only one right way to go about

things, and everything else was wrong. The only times that I ever broke out of that brittle shell were when I was drinking or using drugs.

While that was sinking in, it occurred to me that such linear, all-or-nothing thinking also colored my drinking. When I drank, I saw no point in going halfway. The purpose of all drugs was to get you "loaded." I couldn't drink without pushing it to the limit. My approach to everything in life was all-or-nothing.

I really don't know when my attitude began to change. Don't think I was even aware of it until the conversation about dinners and lunches. It may have had to do with finally drying out. Although I knew that I had problems, I didn't enter treatment or any recovery programs. What I did do was make use of various stress-management techniques. I had started running, doing aerobic exercise and sitting in meditation as general health measures while I was still actively using, but they didn't really start meaning something until after I stopped using.

You know, they say that yoga, exercise and some of those other things work to make your body more flexible, and now I believe it. The Zen teachers say that meditation will lead one to greater spontaneity, too. I think that it's working with me. Oh, I still go on the rampage about things sometimes, but I'm also more willing to compromise and look at alternative solutions to problems, solutions that don't lock me into impossibly ascetic behavior.

DEALING WITH RIGIDITY

Rigidity is one of the greatest dangers to recovery. The white-knuckler is either frozen or is reacting to protect his frozen state. There are many stories about sticks and tall buildings that are rigid and so break easily and those that are supple and bend with the wind. The only real protection for brittle sticks, sticks that have no give to them, is to bind themselves together to the exclusion of all else. In history and politics, this is the basis of fascism. Rods that would be broken on their own are bound together with fastenings, or *fasces*, and become a larger, rigid mass that excludes everything not of its own nature. The trouble with both political and social fascism is that in time the fasces become unraveled, and then the brittle sticks snap one by one—or a force greater than their combined stiffness breaks them all at once.

Rigidity in abstinence often snaps in a social-use situation, as the abstainer succumbs to drug hunger and the urgings of well-meaning friends to have "just one for old times' sake." Relapses rarely occur on the premise of "now I'm going to go out and get loaded." Often people have no idea just what hit them. Gradually, over time, the cues have caught them unawares, and without thinking they slip into the old habit. Or perhaps, thinking hard that it would be insane to take a drink or whatever, they do just that.

Drugs may cause stress, but the rigidity of white-knuckle sobriety can cause just as much stress, and stress causes accidents. There are times when trying too hard to avoid something seems to cause that very thing to happen. During World War II, there was a captain who hit the same channel marker three times while trying to get his newly commissioned destroyer out of the harbor. The first time was a pure accident. After repairs, he hit it the second time while telling another officer about what had happened. By the third time he left harbor, the marker had become an obsession. The captain panicked when his stress caused a momentary lapse in concentration, and he ordered the destroyer into full reverse. It hit a carrier, veered to port and scraped a cruiser, then veered far starboard and hit, yes, the marker for the third time. It's like a self-fulfilling prophecy.

POSITIVE SOCIAL ALTERNATIVES

Perhaps the best defense is in the advice given by Alcoholics Anonymous. First be sure that you have a legitimate reason for being where you are. Then relax and enjoy yourself. Awareness of the situation and your potential vulnerability to it doesn't have to engender stress-producing rigidity.

We know a couple who exemplify a positive approach to abstinence. Both have been in recovery most of their adult lives. Neither one experienced a personal drug or alcohol problem, but both of them had parents who died of complications from alcoholism. Recognizing that they, too, might be vulnerable to addiction, they independently chose a path of abstinence.

A handsome and happy couple, both from show business backgrounds, the two enjoy partying very much and entertain a great deal. Most of their friends drink, and the parties the couple give are "wet." Unlike the typical stand-up cocktail party, their gatherings always involve singing, dancing, and a lot of cohesiveness. She dances like a professional. He plays a mean ukulele, knows hundreds of songs by heart, including many he wrote himself, and has no end of tales from early days in vaudeville. We have never heard anyone accuse these folks of being boring because they don't drink. For that matter, their abstinence is rarely noticed.

The couple described above may be an extreme example, but they do personify our conviction that most negative social consequences of abstinence are in the eyes of the unhappy abstainer. The sense of being a social cripple is usually a subjective projection, and if it isn't, you are probably in the wrong place and have no legitimate reason for being there. If you are among people who can relate socially only by getting loaded, your sobriety will make them uncomfortable, and their inebriation will probably do the same for you. If all the others where you are turn out to be intent on getting drunk or stoned, and you find that you cannot communicate with them, then leave. You say you came to the party with Jack, who's over there running across the table with a lampshade on his head? Call a cab! You don't want that idiot driving you home anyway, do you?

In most social gatherings, if you are not busy feeling sorry for yourself, you'll discover that (1) nobody else is feeling sorry for you either, and (2) unless you're ramming your sobriety down everyone's throat, nobody else deeply cares if you are indulging in intoxicants or not.

Fortunately, in our culture abstention is becoming less and less of a stigma. There was, in truth, a time when, if someone in the crowd turned down several consecutive drinks, the whispers started. "I didn't know Joe had a *problem*." But in the current health-conscious decade, many people are deciding that the cocktail or glass of wine or beer is not mandatory at all social occasions.

If you are recovering from addiction or are on your own program of abstinence, the best course with family and good friends is to tell them that at a proper time. Then the subject is moot, and there is no issue. It should not be necessary to go into your life story with less intimate acquaintances. After all, your business is your business. But don't let us paint too rosy a picture. There are pitfalls, and we need to be aware of them in order to avoid them.

We have all encountered neanderthal hosts and hostesses who consider it their earthly duty to see that all guests partake heavily of their bounty. These are the ones who become mortally insulted if you turn down anything they offer. Such occasions may be candidates for "No, thanks, I just threw one away." At times, you may actually have to throw one away. Often these people dispense food at the table with the same heavy hand. They are deaf to refusals, but unlike your mother, who can invoke starving children in other countries, they cannot, *cannot* make you eat or drink what they've insensitively piled on your plate or poured into your glass.

In most cases, a simple and polite "No, thank you," will suffice when you're offered such things as cigarettes, joints, lines, pipes or syringes. With alcohol, there are usually viable alternatives. The household bar usually comes equipped with such nonalcoholic mixers as seltzer, tonic water, tomato juice and orange juice that you can ask for. Today there are many mineral waters and natural sodas available for those who want to avoid such drugs as sugar and caffeine as well as alcohol, and for those of us who consider most of the commercial soft drinks to be pure swill.

A most welcome development is the advent of "varietal" grape juices and other nonalcoholic drinks that have been developed for "adult tastes." Several companies are also experimenting with dealcoholized wines. In that these dealcoholized wines do contain some—in most cases less than one percent—residual alcohol, many in the recovering community feel that they may provide too much of a cue for the recovering alcoholic. However, these seem like a good idea for the nonrecovering nondrinker or the person who simply doesn't want to indulge.

At the end of this chapter we'll list and critique some of the varietal grape juices, dealcoholized wines and beers that are currently on the market.

Another social drug about which public and commercial consciousness is, fortunately, rising is caffeine, long as ubiquitous a stimulant in our society as alcohol has been a depressant. There are numerous herbal and noncaffeine teas on the market. Even chocolate has its caffeineless substitutes, such as carob. Coffee also has its share of substitutes. Most of these are roasted grain beverages that contain little or no caffeine. These leave a lot to be desired for those folks who are looking for "real coffee flavor," but they are good, robust and healthy hot beverages in their own right.

Until recently, anyone searching for coffee without the caffeine had one choice, Sanka. All that has changed. In the more urban parts of the United States one can now find excellent decaffeinated coffee, both ground and in the whole bean. There is some question as to the healthiness of the various processes used to decaffeinate these beans, but we have been using water-processed beans. They are more expensive than the chemically processed beans, but it may be worth it to your health in the long run. In areas where there are retail coffee shops, and increasingly on supermarket shelves, one can find several varieties of decaffeinated, including dark French, Ethiopian and Italian roasts. In better restaurants, an order of decaf will bring a steaming cup of fresh-brewed coffee instead of hot water and an orange foil packet, and in cafe's one can often find decaffeinated espresso and cappuccino. We have heard that the decaffeinated movement is spreading overseas as well. In our research, we have not yet tried ordering "café decafé" at the Deux Magots in Paris, but we will do so as soon as possible. (The authors are happy to verify just prior to publication that "decafiné" is available at Deux Magots and throughout France. In Italy and Switzerland, it's called "Cafe Hag.")

CROSSCULTURAL SURVIVAL:
AVOIDING INTERNATIONAL INCIDENTS
WHILE TRAVELING

International travel is something that we all enjoy but that, as abstinent people we may view with some trepidation. Can you turn down an *ouzo* in Athens without becoming skewered souvlaki on the spot? How does one gracefully decline a glass of vintage Bordeaux in the south of France? Trying to explain one's abstinence can be difficult, especially if you don't speak more than a few words of the language and your host doesn't speak yours.

In the course of writing this chapter, we posed the question, "In your culture, how does one politely refuse an alcoholic beverage at a gathering or in someone's home?" to several English as a Second Language classes. These classes were composed of students from all corners of the world, but their answers were surprisingly similar. Most said that one should simply say "No, thank you," or ask for fruit juice or water instead. We learned, however, that there are exceptions, and it helps to be up on local custom. For example, the French can usually avoid any discussion or ill will when offered a drink by patting their side, rolling their eyes heavenward and softly muttering, "*Ma foie.*" A rough translation is something like, "I have no doubt that your wine is ambrosia fit for the gods, but my poor liver won't stand it." Several students from Near Eastern countries pointed out that alcohol is taboo in their culture but added that under some circumstances one might have difficulty refusing the hashish candy or a toke on the communal water pipe.

Fortunately, in Europe and other parts of the world, Americans are gaining a reputation as either puritans or crazy health nuts. Our experience has been that even in areas and within subcultures where indulging in psychoactive substances is considered mandatory, a polite decline will be answered by a puzzled smile, a nod or shake of the head and a comprehending, "Ah, yes—American." In most homes there is some alternative available.

In Greece, for example, the legend of Pyramus and Thisbe, in which the gods reward good hosts and hostesses with bottomless milk jugs while turning all others into fish, is gospel. A household is more than shamed if you don't accept something. There, homemade lemonade, fresh milk or one of a variety of native herbal teas provide most pleasant escapes from the wrath of Zeus. In the Near East, mint tea is a social vehicle. Fruit juices are generally available, but remember that in most of Europe "cider" is an alcoholic beverage.

In cafe's—by and large the European equivalent of bars—there is absolutely no stigma attached to not drinking either alcohol or coffee, and a number of alternatives are available. These include the delightful Italian sodas and nonsweet, often bitter aperitif drinks as well as a variety of fruit juices. Many Europeans drink mineral water with their meals. They may drink wine, too, but mineral water is nearly always available in restaurants. In Italy there are tasty varieties of raisin juices, while the making of grape juices in Germany and Austria has risen to a fine art.

When traveling overseas, the best way to avoid feeling like a social cripple is to avoid acting like one. Friendliness, curiosity and a genuine interest in your surroundings and in those who inhabit them will mean a lot more than whether or not you raise a stein or a wine glass. Hosts and hostesses appreciate any knowledge you may have of their language and customs, so any homework you can do ahead will come in handy. Mostly, be ready to meet people at least halfway, and your trip through abstinence, and the world, should prove to be a most enjoyable one.

AND NOW THE GRAPE JUICE LIST, MONSIEUR

A most welcome development in recent years has been the proliferation of refreshments that serve as viable alternatives to alcoholic beverages. The "water wagon" of yore has expanded from the choice between soda water, mixers without the prime ingredient or heavily sugared and caffeinated soft drinks designed for prepubescent tastes to now include a widening range of mineral waters, nonalcoholic beers, dealcoholized wines and varietal grape juices.

The following list of these is offered not only for the abstainer looking for something that can be sipped in mixed company and the individual who just wants to lighten up on occasion but also for the host and hostess who have begun to realize that not everyone wants to lubricate every social occasion with alcohol. A move away from alcohol has been evident at many recent gatherings your authors have attended, in the course of which the grape juices and other nonalcoholic drinks were eagerly imbibed while the "real" wine and beer were mostly left alone.

Something of an oenophile before starting this book, Rick Seymour has compiled the following list of nonalcoholic alternatives. He has sampled many of the beverages listed here and describes those he found particularly noteworthy. These are by no means all that there are available, and more are coming onto a growing market all the time. However, this sampling gives an idea of what is available and where it can be obtained by individuals, wholesalers and retailers. You might ask your local store to stock some.

VARIETAL GRAPE JUICES

These are fresh, nonfermented grape juices that have never contained alcohol. As is the case with varietal wines, they are made from one predominant type of grape that is listed on the label and that gives the juice its distinctive flavor and other qualities. Many labels even list the vintage or year in which the grapes were picked. Their varietal quality, their lack of overt sweetness and the "finish" given to the products distinguish them from both the commercial grape juices that can be found in the juice sections of most grocery stores and the pure juices available at health food stores.

Buena Vista Johannisberg Riesling: Sonoma County Grape Juice. Produced and bottled by Buena Vista Winery, Carneros, Sonoma, California 95476. 750 ml. bottle @ $4.99. Comments: One of the oldest wineries in California has taken this first step into varietal production, and it is one of the best on the market. Vintage is listed. Bottle closely resembles their wine bottles with an etching of the winery and the founding Haraszthy family crest. Juice itself is clear and of good quality, showing the typical spiciness of the J. Riesling grape.

Felton Empire Johannisberg Riesling, Gamay Beaujolais, White Zinfandel, etc. Felton Empire Vineyards, Felton, California. 750 ml. Price varies. Comments: A winery that has branched out into several varietal juices. Production and distribution seem erratic so far, but the presentations hold their own without being particularly distinguished.

R. W. Knudsen Ruby Cabernet, Chenin Blanc, French Colombard, Chardonnay, Gewurztraminer, White Zinfandel, etc. R. W. Knudsen and Sons, Inc., Chico, California 95926. 750 ml. Price $2.29 and up depending on variety. Comments: Knudsen has been a long-term producer of fruit juices and "natural," i.e. additive-free, soft drinks and is now branching into an increasing variety of quality grape juices. The offerings reflect the specific grape involved and are good. The chardonnay and gewurtz may need more development, as they seem cloudy and lacking in finish. We hope they continue these, especially the cardonnay, which is the first of this varietal to be available on the juice market.

Lehr's Red, White Grape Juice. A. F. Richter & Co., Hamburg, West Germany. 750 ml. $2.99. Comments: These representatives of the extensive German grape juice production have been available for some time at health food stores and some supermarkets around the country. While not varietals, they have good flavor and are a step above American mass-produced grape juices.

Meiers Catawba White, Sparkling and Sparkling Pink. John C. Meier Co., Silverton, Ohio. 750 ml. Price varies. Comments: Meiers uses the highly herbaceous catawba grape to produce a truly unique still white grape juice well worth trying wherever it's available. Unfortunately, much of the uniqueness is lost in the two "sparkling" presentations.

Navarro Pinot Noir and Gewurtztraminer. Navarro Vineyards, Philo, California. 750 ml. $4.50. Comments: Two high quality grape juices from a first-rate "boutique" winery in western Anderson Valley. The gewurtz is the better of the two, but the pinot gets points for attempting a major red. Both are well worth trying.

Orlando Maison White Grape Juice. G. Gramp & Sons PTY. LTD., Rowland Flat, South Australia 5350. Imported by Kolarovitch Wines Imports, Yontville, California 94599. 750 ml. Price not known. Comments: Australian grape juice seems to be following their wines onto the world market—and a good thing, mates!

Pineyhill Vineyards Cabernet Sauvignon, Napa Gamay, Beaujolais Blanc, Gewurtztraminer, and Johannisburg Riesling. Pineyhill Vineyards, Calistoga, California 94515. 750 ml. $3.15 to $4.50 depending on variety. Comments: Specializing in grape juice, this vineyard in the famed Napa Valley has made a go of two premium red wine-grape juices. Without fermentation, the cabernet and gamay grapes are usually too sweet to be palatable, but Pineyhill has somehow managed to give these juices a dryness and flavor comparable to the wines that they produce. The cabernet has a distinctive green pepper taste often found in the region, the Napa gamay is the closest I've seen a grape juice come to having the fullness of a red, the beaujolais blanc is actually a blush juice and none of the presentations is lacking in flavor or finish.

White-Cooper Vineyards Anderson Valley Colombard-Semillon Grape Juice. White-Cooper Vineyards, Boonville, California 95415. 750 ml. $4.50. Comments: This may be the most elegant grape juice on the market. The label is distinctive-gray and white with a scallop shell in a simple design. The juice itself is light gold with an excellent finish and dry crispness that showcases the colombard and semillon grape flavor.

VARIETAL GRAPE JUICE COOLERS

Not to be outdone by the wine industry's recent development of bottled "coolers," one company is now producing varietal grape juice coolers. Doubtless more will follow.

Vinet Zinfandel, Gewurztraminer and Riesling. M.T.H., Inc., Sonoma, California 95476. Split bottles. $2.99 a four-pack. Comments: These grape juices are premixed with "pure Sonoma Mountain spring water" and lightly carbonated. They have more flavor than other carbonated grape juices. Good juice and *light* carbonation seem to be the keys.

DEALCOHOLIZED WINES

These products are actually wines that have undergone fermentation and then had most of the alcohol removed. Most of them are advertised as 99.51 percent alcohol-free. This makes them a good choice for someone who generally wants to lighten up on alcohol intake or the nonaddicted abstainer from intoxication—at .49 percent it would take an awful lot to get the least bit high. The recovering community, however, has raised a legitimate concern that even a less-than-one percent alcohol content is still an alcohol content and could at the very least erode the resolve of a recovering individual to avoid *all* psychoactive substances. For some people, this fuzzing of the line could be the first step toward a relapse.

Unlike varietal juices or wines, most de-alcoholized wine is a mixture of different grape juices into a generic product.

Ariel Free (White). Ariel Vineyards, San Jose, California 95126. 750 ml. $3.99. Comments: A mixture of Johannisberg Riesling, Chenin Blanc, Gewurztraminer and Muscat Canelli.

Castella Roselle and Spumante (Sparkling). Billabong Wines, Griffith, Australia. Comments: Both have a distinctive flavor reminiscent of Greek retsina wines—pleasant and refreshing if you like the taste of pine trees.

Giovane Sparkling White. Sanley Spa, Castel Bolognese, Italy. Imported by Hilton Commercial Group, Inc. Los Angeles, California. 750 ml. $5.94.

Hiney Brothers De-Alcoholized Wine and Natural Grape Juice (Red). Lamont Winery, Inc. 750 ml. $2.79.

St. Regis Vineyards California White, Rosé and Red. St. Regis Vineyards, San Francisco, California 94133. 750 ml. $2.99. Comments: Distributed by Joseph E. Seagram & Sons, Inc. these de-alcoholized wines have had national television advertising and are probably the most readily available nationwide.

Sante (White). Sante Vineyards, Lodi, California 95240. 750 ml. $3.99. Comments: Contains Chablis French Colombard, Chenin Blanc and other dry white wines.

NONALCOHOLIC BEERS

Birell. Swiss Gold, Tumwater, Washington 55165. Comments: Bills itself as being brewed from an imported Swiss recipe from Zurich.

Kaliber Light Malt Beverage. Arthur Guinness & Sons, Ireland.

Marke Clausthaler Herbfrishes Schankbier. Bindind Brauri A.G., Frankfurt/Main, W. Germany.

Patrizier Zero. Patrizier-Brau, Nurenburg, West Germany.

Texas Select. Richland Corporation, Dallas, Texas.

Wartek, Basel, Switzerland.

Can Anyone Go Home Again? Would Anyone Really Want To? | 8

There are two issues that we have not yet addressed that tend to bracket the subject of alternatives to alcohol and other drugs. On the one side is the issue of primary prevention. Primary prevention is concerned with helping people avoid addiction, alcoholism and other substance abuse by not getting involved in the abuse of drugs in the first place. On the other side is what some practitioners see and what many abusers hope is a viable alternative to lifelong abstention from psychoactive substances—that is, controlled use.

The concept of controlled use is about as controversial as a concept can get. First, let us point out that the current definition of addiction precludes the possibility of controlled use. By definition, an addict or alcoholic is a person who cannot control use. Use for the addict or alcoholic involves compulsion, *loss of control* and continued use in spite of adverse consequences. The sense within the recovering community is that after loss of control an addict or abuser is incapable of rebecoming a social drinker. Graphically put, "A cucumber can become a pickle, but once it's a pickle it can't go back to being a cucumber." Chuck Brissette, among others, has suggested that one way of cutting denial and proving to someone that he is indeed addicted is to say, "Okay. You think you can control your drinking? Go out and try it. If you can, more power to you. But if you can't, start thinking about treatment and recovery."

Not all abuse problems involve addiction, however. A pamphlet entitled "How to Know an Alcoholic," by Marty Mann, put out by the National Council on Alcoholism, Inc., points out that "social drinkers" may indulge in periodic heavy drinking, while members of two other categories, "heavy drinkers" and "occasional drunks," may be abusing alcohol but are not alcoholics. Ability to control drinking is cited as the key and the dividing line between these people and alcoholics.

There are many in the treatment field who agree that there are a number of people in our society who have substance-abuse and dependency problems but are not addicts. Some of these practitioners feel that the concentration in treatment on addiction and in recovery on lifelong abstention is keeping many of these people away from treatment that they may sorely need.

One of these is Jed Diamond, a licensed drug and alcohol abuse counselor and clinical social worker who has worked within both the professional and self-help spheres. Diamond is developing treatment and training techniques that he says are designed to provide "realistic" primary prevention of abuse for young people; help the chemically dependent and abusing but not addicted individual learn how to use moderately in a controlled fashion; and provide a spiritually grounded recovery program for those who are addicted to alcohol and other drugs. He agrees that "Alcoholics Anonymous and more recently Narcotics Anonymous and Cocaine Anonymous have proven that there is hope for people with serious addictions to alcohol and other drugs, and the self-help movement is the most effective treatment yet developed." However, he feels that misunderstandings and conflict between the "professional counselors" and "recovering" people in the self-help movement have, over the years, limited the effectiveness of the help that chemically dependent people have been getting. He adds, however, that "although there is a great deal of conflict in the field, there is also an air of rapport and cooperation. Often abstract theories of what works divide us, while honest sharing of what we do draws us together."

In 1983, I began my own program, the Center for Prospering Relationships, to place emphasis on preventing problems such as drug and alcohol abuse and to develop and refine the processes I had learned over the years to help those with chemical dependency problems. One of the most necessary aspects of growth for recovering and nonrecovering helpers is the development of spiritual awareness. As a professional I learned to discount spiritual experience because it was simplistic, irrational, and unscientific. In the self-help programs I learned that spirituality is not what you think. Dr. Bob, the cofounder of AA, spoke for me and many others when he said, "We're all after the same thing, and that's happiness. We want peace of mind. The trouble with us alcoholics was this: We demanded that the world give us happiness and peace of mind in just the particular way we wanted to get it. And we weren't successful. But when we take time to find out some of the spiritual laws, and familiarize ourselves with them, and put them into practice, then we do get happiness and peace of mind. . . ." There seem to be some rules that we have to follow, but happiness and peace of mind are always here, open and free to anyone.

Jed Diamond refers to his program as a comprehensive one for preventing problems associated with the use of alcohol, nicotine, caffeine, marijuana, cocaine, sugar, prescription medications and other mind-active drugs. It consists of five components:

1. A self-evaluating questionnaire, which helps a person understand his or her relationship with any mind-active drugs he or she uses.
2. An interview with an expert in drug-abuse prevention to help evaluate and interpret the results.
3. Exploration of options, including a six-session reeducation program, a three- to six-month stress reduction and health program, and referral for serious problems.
4. Implementation of appropriate plan with a follow-up evaluation every six months to monitor progress and ensure that potential problems are caught early on.
5. A program for professionals who work with people having drug or alcohol problems, including quarterly retreats to prevent burnout and a training program to teach skills and attitudes necessary to work effectively in the field year after year.

This program and others on this model take into consideration substances that we don't normally think of as drugs. In his questionnaire, Diamond includes coffee, nicotine, refined sugar, antihistamines, steroids, cough suppressants, cold remedies, nasal decongestants and appetite suppressants, and he asks twelve basic questions for each drug one uses that reflect on whether you are basically in good relationship to the drugs you are using. He emphasizes that his business is that of helping people avoid *abusing* drugs. He doesn't encourage drug use or discourage drug use. Instead, he helps people consider the negative and the positive aspects of using a particular drug, so that a clear decision can be made about what needs to be done.

CONSIDERATIONS ON CONTROLLED USE

Besides the fact that by definition alcoholics and addicts are seen as incapable of controlled use, there are several other factors that need to be taken into consideration in any discussion of controlled use. The first of these is that the nonmedical or recreational use of many drugs is illegal at international, national, state and local levels. Given their status, even the controlled user of many substances is risking fines or imprisonment. It would be foolish to consider, much less advocate, the controlled use of any illegal substance.

Other substances may be legal but are either so compelling in their nature or so patently toxic that even what may seem like controlled use is so detrimental to the user as to be impractical. An example that in our opinion fits both of these categories is tobacco. Although a massive industry is involved in the manufacture of cigarettes, cigars, chewing tobacco and other nicotine-containing products, all these products have been identified by the Federal Department of Health as causing dire results with frequent use. Further, their compelling nature tends to make use frequent. Andrew Weil, M.D., has said that machine-made cigarettes are probably the most addicting thing on earth, and many agree with that opinion. It is the rare person who can smoke on an occasional basis. All indications are that such substances as nicotine, though legal, should be avoided altogether.

There are other psychoactive substances, such as caffeine, sugar, nitrites and salt, that are virtually impossible to avoid in our culture. The best advice we can offer here is to be aware of the myriad forms these drugs can take and avoid them to the best of your ability and inclination. Learn to read labels on processed foods and commercial beverages, remembering that ingredients in the largest quantities are listed first. It's amazing the number of foods in which the first ingredient is salt or sugar. On the other hand, an increasing number of prepared foods are emphasizing natural ingredients. Some of the biggest producers of canned soups, for example, may not advertise it, but they are very good in this regard. Of course, the best way to avoid unwanted food additives is to fix meals from scratch with fresh ingredients whenever possible.

As we have said elsewhere, there is an increasing variety of sugar-free and caffeine-free products on the market. The artificial sweeteners may have their own problems, and in this department we tend to favor the nonsugar, nonrefined, natural sweeteners, such as fruit sweeteners, honey and maple syrup. Fruit juice-based soft drinks seem plenty sweet to us with nothing added. So far, water-processed coffee beans and the various grain beverages seem the best alternatives to regular coffee. Japanese green tea and the many herbal teas seem viable options over the darker, higher-caffeine-content standard tea.

All things considered, when we talk about controlled "recreational" use of psychoactives, we are talking primarily about alcohol. In truth, a goodly percentage of those who drink alcohol do so in a controlled manner most of the time. We repeat for emphasis, however, that the best course for anyone who has ever had problems with alcohol or any other psychoactive drug is total abstinence.

It may be possible for some individuals who have been "problem drinkers" to reprogram themselves, but this is a most difficult task and fraught with pitfalls. The dividing line seems to lie between drinking as a social exercise and drinking for the intoxicating effects of the alcohol. Most alcoholics and problem drinkers consider intoxication to be the *only* reason anyone would want to drink. They are conceptually incapable of understanding why anyone would want just one drink, and the possibility of anyone not finishing a drink is incomprehensible to them. David Smith characterizes the alcoholic as the person who rushes up to a bar advertising *ALL YOU CAN DRINK*—$1.00 and shouts, "Quick! Give me two dollars' worth!" For the alcoholic, one drink is too many, and one hundred are not enough. If any part of this description fits you, please take our advice and don't—DO NOT—consider controlled use as an option.

In the next subsection we'll be talking about the dynamics of relapse. The lure of being able to drink socially again, or to go back to an occasional snort of cocaine or, for that matter, to smoke an occasional joint or cigarette, is one of the prime factors in falling back into loss of control. As Thomas Wolfe said and every literature buff has repeated ever since, "You can't go home again." We say, well, maybe under certain circumstances you can—but do you really want to?

Think about it. Your addiction or abuse has been a gift, an obstacle in life that brings growth when it's surmounted. Recovery and abstinence are even greater gifts. Doors in your life have opened, and you probably feel better about yourself than you ever have before. You've even learned to navigate in a world where many are still caught up in habits and inhabiting levels of consciousness that you have transcended. You are flying while they're still tethered to the ground of temporary relief from suffering, often brought on by the substances they are trying to use for temporary relief. Do you really want to go home to that?

THE DYNAMICS OF RELAPSE

Contrary to what most people think, relapse into alcoholism, addiction or abuse doesn't start with the first drink, snort or hit. A study of 118 alcoholic patients conducted in 1973 by Terence T. Gorski and Alcoholism

Systems Associates revealed a behavior pattern involving the reactivation of denial, isolation, elevated stress and impaired judgment, all leading up to the taking of the first drink. The patients involved all met three basic criteria:

1. They had completed a twenty-one or twenty-eight day intermediate care treatment program.
2. They had been discharged with the conscious intention of remaining permanently sober.
3. They had eventually returned to loss of control over their consumption.

The common symptoms of their eventual relapse were compiled into the following list and published in *Counseling for Relapse Prevention* by Terence T. Gorski and Merlene Miller:

1. *Apprehension About Well-Being.* The alcoholic reported an initial sense of fear and uncertainty. There was a lack of confidence in the ability to stay sober. This apprehension was often extremely short-lived.
2. *Denial.* The patient reactivated his denial system in order to cope with apprehension and resultant anxiety and stress. The denial systems reactivated in this stage of relapse tend to correspond with the systems utilized to deny the presence of alcoholism during the initial phase of treatment. Most patients were aware of this denial with hindsight but reported they were unaware of the denial process while experiencing it.
3. *Adamant Commitment to Sobriety.* The patient convinced himself he would "never drink again." This self-persuasion was sometimes overt and blatant, but most often it constituted a very private decision. Many patients reported fear or apprehension of sharing that conviction with their therapist or with members of AA. Once a patient convinced himself he "would never drink again," the urgency of pursuing a daily program of recovery diminished.
4. *Compulsive Attempts to Impose Sobriety on Others.* This attempt to impose sobriety or individual standards for recovery on others was seldom overt. It generally manifested itself in private judgments about the drinking of friends and spouses and the quality of the sobriety programs of fellow recovering alcoholics. When dealing with issues of sobriety, the patient began to focus more on what other persons were doing than on what he was doing.
5. *Defensiveness.* The patient reported a noticeable increase in his defensiveness when talking about his problems or recovery program.
6. *Compulsive Behavior.* Behavior patterns became rigid and repetitive. The alcoholic tended to control conversational involvement either

through monopoly or silence. The tendency toward overwork and compulsive involvement in activities began to appear. Nonstructured involvement with people was avoided.

7. *Impulsive Behavior.* Patterns of compulsive behaviors began to be interrupted by impulsive reactions. In many cases the impulse was an overreaction to acute episodes of stress. There were also reports of impulsive activities being the culmination of a chronic stress situation. Many times these overreactions to stress formed the basis of decisions that affected major life areas and commitments to ongoing treatment.

8. *Tendencies Toward Loneliness.* Patterns of isolation and avoidance increased. There were generally valid reasons and excuses for this isolation. Patients reported short episodes of intense loneliness at increasing intervals. These episodes were generally dealt with by reactivating compulsive or impulsive behavior patterns rather than by pursuing responsible involvement with other persons.

9. *Tunnel Vision.* Patients tended to view their life in isolated fragments. They would focus exclusively on one area, preoccupy themselves with it, and avoid looking at other areas. Sometimes preoccupation was with the positive aspects, thus creating a delusion of security and well-being. Others preoccupied themselves with the negative aspects, thus assuming a victim position that confirmed their belief they were helpless and being treated unfairly.

10. *Minor Depression.* Symptoms of depression began to appear and persist. Listlessness, flat acceptance and oversleeping became common.

11. *Loss of Constructive Planning.* The patient's skills at life planning began to diminish. Attention to detail subsided. Wishful thinking began to replace realistic planning.

12. *Plans Begin to Fail.* Due to lack of attention to detail or the pursuit of unrealistic objectives, the plans began to fail.

13. *Idle Daydreaming and Wishful Thinking.* The ability to concentrate diminished, and concentration was replaced with fantasy. The "If Only Syndrome" became more common in conversation. The fantasies were generally of escape or of "being rescued from it all" by some unlikely set of circumstances.

14. *Feelings That Nothing Can Be Solved.* A failure pattern in sobriety was developed. In some cases the failure was real in terms of objective realities; in other cases it was imagined and based upon intangibles. The generalized perception of "I've tried my best, and it isn't working out" began to develop.

15. *Immature Wish to be Happy.* Conversational content and thought patterns became vague and generalized. The desire to "be happy" or to "have things work out" became more common without the

patient ever defining his role or responsibility in being happy or making things work out.

16. *Periods of Confusion.* The episodes of confusion increased in frequency, duration and severity of behavioral impairment.

17. *Irritation with Friends.* Social involvements including friends and intimate relationships, as well as treatment relationships formed with therapists and AA members, became strained and conflictual. The conflictual nature increased as confrontation of the alcoholic's progressively degenerating behavior increased.

18. *Easily Angered.* Episodes of anger, frustration, resentment and irritability increased. Overreaction became more frequent. Often the patient's fear of his extreme overreaction to the point of violence seriously increased the level of stress and anxiety.

19. *Irregular Eating Habits.* The patient began either overeating or undereating. The regular structure of meals was disrupted. Well-balanced means were often replaced by less nourishing "junk foods."

20. *Listlessness.* Extended periods of inability to initiate action developed. These were marked by inability to concentrate, anxiety and severe feelings of apprehension. Patients often reported this as a feeling of being trapped or of having no way out.

21. *Irregular Sleeping Habits.* Episodes of insomnia were reported. Nights of restlessness and fitful sleeping were reported. Episodes of sleeping marathons of twelve to twenty hours were reported at intervals varying between six and fifteen days. These sleeping marathons apparently resulted from exhaustion.

22. *Progressive Loss of Daily Structure.* Daily routines became haphazard. Regular hours of retiring and rising disappeared. The inability to sleep resulted in oversleeping. Meal structures disappeared. Complaints of inability to keep appointments became more common, and social planning decreased. Patients reported feeling rushed and overburdened at times and then faced large blocks of idle time in which they didn't know what to do. An inability to follow through on plans and decisions was also reported. The patients reported that they knew what they should do but were unable to overcome strong feelings of tension, frustration, fear or anxiety that prevented them from following through.

23. *Periods of Deep Depression.* Depression became more severe, more frequent, more disruptive and longer in duration. These periods generally occurred during nonstructured time and were amplified by fatigue and hunger. During these periods the patient tended toward isolation and reacted to human contact with irritability and anger, at the same time complaining that nobody cared.

24. *Irregular Attendance at Treatment Meetings.* Attendance at AA became sporadic. Therapy appointments were scheduled and then missed.

Attendance at treatment groups and home AA meetings became sporadic. Rationalization patterns developed to justify this. The effectiveness of AA and treatment was discounted. Treatment lost a priority ranking in the patient's value system.

25. *Development of an "I Don't Care" Attitude.* The patient generally reported that this "I don't care" stance masked a feeling of helplessness and extremely poor self-image.

26. *Open Rejection of Help.* The patient cut himself off from viable sources of help. This was sometimes accomplished dramatically through fits of anger or open discounts. Other times it was done through quiet withdrawal.

27. *Dissatisfaction with Life.* The patient began to think "things are so bad now I might as well get drunk, because they can't get any worse." Rationalizations, tunnel vision and wishful thinking began to give way to the harsh reality of how totally unmanageable life had become in the course of this period of abstinence.

28. *Feelings of Powerlessness and Helplessness.* This was marked by an inability to initiate action. Thought processes were scattered, judgment was distorted, concentration and abstract thinking abilities were impaired.

29. *Self-Pity.* The patient became indulgent in self-pity. This is often called the PLOM (Poor Little Old Me) Syndrome. This self-pity was often used as an attention-getting device at AA and with family members.

30. *Thoughts of Social Drinking.* The patient realized that drinking could normalize many of the feelings and emotions he was experiencing. The hope that perhaps he could again drink in a controlled fashion began to emerge. Sometimes the idea was challenged and put out of conscious thought; other times it was entertained. Again, with hindsight the patient realized he had few other alternatives but drinking. He felt he was facing a choice between insanity, suicide or a return to drinking.

31. *Conscious Lying.* Denial and rationalization became such extreme processes that even the alcoholic began to recognize the lies and deceptions. In spite of this recognition, he felt unable to interrupt the pattern.

32. *Complete Loss of Self-confidence.* The patient felt he couldn't get out of this trap no matter how hard he tried. He became overwhelmed by his inability to think clearly or initiate action.

33. *Unreasonable Resentments.* The patient felt severe anger with the world in general and with his inability to function. This anger was sometimes generalized, at other times focused at particular scapegoats, at other times turned against himself.

34. *Discontinued All Treatment.* Attendance at AA stopped completely. Patients who were taking Antabuse reported episodes of forgetting

to take it or manipulations to avoid taking it regularly. When a helping personal relationship was part of the treatment, strain and eventual termination of that relationship resulted. Patients dropped out
of professional treatment in spite of a realization that they were acting irrationally and needed help.

35. *Overwhelming Loneliness, Frustration, Anger and Tension.* The patient
reported feeling totally overwhelmed and feeling there were no
available options except returning to drinking, suicide or insanity.
The fear of insanity was intense. There were also intense feelings of
helplessness and desperation. Often drinking was an impulsive
behavior with little or no conscious preplanning.

36. *Started Controlled Drinking.* The efforts at control took two general
patterns: the effort to control quantities while drinking on a regular
basis, and the effort to engage in one short-term and low-
consequence binge.

37. *Loss of Control.* The ability to control was lost, sometimes very quickly, sometimes after varying patterns of "controlled drinking." The
patient, however, quickly returned to alcoholic drinking, which was
marked by symptoms as severe as or more severe than those present
during his or her last episode of active alcoholism.

DEALING WITH RELAPSE

It should be obvious from the above progression of symptoms that a
relapse into alcoholism or addiction is a process rather than an event.
Most individuals in recovery experience some sort of slippage, especially
early on. For these, a lapse can be a learning experience in the development of recovery. A few experience repeated relapses whenever they
attempt recovery, and in the past these have been the individuals who
experience the progressive nature of the disease and eventually die from
it.

While recovery in and of itself involves an evolution of consciousness,
the relapse process is a devolution, a falling backward. Although recovery
and relapse can follow rapidly on one another, with the individual shifting back and forth between the two, they don't occur simultaneously. As
Bob Dylan said, everybody not busy being born *is* busy dying.

There is an age-old myth that the frequent relapsers were hopeless
cases. These "hopeless cases" often became victims of a "revolving-door
policy" and were shunted from treatment provider to treatment provider
up until their final slide toward death. In reality, the treatment and
recovery communities are learning how to handle the relapse dynamic.
As we learn more about the dynamic of relapse, the potential for
successful intervention increases. An increasing number of patients who

would have died from the disease through repeated acute relapses even a few years ago are now successfully recovering. Intervention can take place at any point in the chain of symptoms described by Gorski and his associates. The important factor is recognition of these symptoms for what they are.

What we often see here is our old adversary white-knuckle sobriety in its many guises and evolutions. The victims of frequent relapse are suffering from severe forms of addiction that must be taken into account if successful recovery is to be achieved. One thing that has helped a great deal is the increasing realization that alcoholism and other forms of addiction are deeply rooted tripartite disease manifestations that call for long-term support. These are diseases that need to be fought on a number of fronts, including the adoption of such alternatives to use and aids to recovery as we have discussed in this book.

It behooves friends, loved ones, treatment personnel and fellow voyagers in recovery to be aware of the relapse dynamic and its signs and symptoms. Those who are close to a recovering person can be a vital help to the person who is encountering problems and is in danger of relapse. These signs and symptoms should be seen for what they are—part of the long-term disease of addiction. They should not occasion emotional outbursts or judgmental recriminations from those who detect them. On the other hand, they should not be passed over or ignored. The recovering person needs to be helped at these times, and whoever is working with him or her needs to be aware of the situation. Pass this information to those who can use it to help the recovering person know the danger and work with it.

White-knuckle sobriety can give rise to many emotional problems, as can any aspect of recovery. The best way to deal with them is to be aware of them and ready to treat them as part of a long-term disease.

The desire for controlled use by individuals in the midst of a relapse dynamic is usually not seen as a positive step but as one of several undesirable means of coping with what are perceived as insurmountable life problems. Awareness of the dynamics of relapse shows that the victim's recovery has ceased working for him and that he is looking for a way out. The third dragon head has remanifested itself and is broadcasting its message that drugs provide short-term relief. The situation resembles that in Gail Sheehy's discussion of high and low well-being responses to the stress of life problems. If controlled use were possible for an abuser, the secret would be a full revamping of that abuser's attitude so that the drug was not "needed."

This leads to something of a paradox. If you no longer need a substance that is probably not good for you in the first place, why would you want to go back to using it? Even if the risk was low, the reward would be even lower. The only fortunate thing about your abuse of alcohol, or whatever, is that in dealing with that abuse and overcoming it you have become a better person. In India, there is a special name, *ananda*, that signifies someone who has overcome or mastered a major life problem. *Mayananda*, for example, means one who has overcome illusion. All who are in the process of successful recovery or abstention are ananda: alcohol*ananda*, nicotine*ananda*, marijuan*ananda*, etc. Why would anyone want to trade this accomplishment for the dubious "freedom" of using something you've put so much effort into transcending? Maybe you can go home again, but who, when you think about it, would truly want to?

PRIMARY PREVENTION

Imagine that there is a bridge over a river. During a storm, the center span of the bridge has collapsed. Cars continue to drive onto the bridge, and when they reach the middle they fall through into the river. Now a rescue effort has been mounted. Volunteers dive into the river downstream, haul the survivors out of their cars and do their best to resuscitate these victims. There's a lot of traffic, so a tremendous effort is needed to reach all the cars that float by. That is treatment.

One of the rescuers suggests that someone climb up to the road on both sides of the river and put up signs warning drivers that the bridge is out. Perhaps some effort should also be put into working out a detour around the bridge. That's primary prevention.

Although it is usually thought of in conjunction with young people, primary prevention can take place at any age. It consists of any means that leads one to voluntarily avoid abuse of drugs or any other dangerous activity. Recognized prevention strategies include education, inducement, conditioning and preventional alternatives, to name a few. Sometimes prevention involves one individual and sometimes a group, such as a class in school or a whole society. Some prevention measures have involved the development of employment opportunities for poverty-level groups whose precarious socioeconomic position makes them particularly vulnerable to the "panacea" of drug abuse. Others involve creating teen centers or special projects that increase self-worth and provide drugfree activities.

Although virtually everyone thinks that primary drug- and alcohol-abuse prevention is necessary and a good idea, it is often a stepchild to treatment, an activity that is hard to implement and fund. This is not surprising in a society where physical results—body counts, if you will—mean so much. While treatment statistics, cure rates and arrest records are manipulated to support the "fact" that something is being accomplished in the "war against drugs," it is awfully hard to show how many young people are *not* using drugs as a result of primary prevention efforts. And yet there is general agreement that keeping young people from abusing alcohol and other drugs in the first place is our highest substance-abuse priority.

There are differing opinions on what constitutes effective substance-abuse prevention. The approaches based on these opinions have developed through recent decades, one or another gaining ascendency, depending often on the prevailing attitudes about drugs, politics, young people and a number of other factors.

What prevention existed prior to the 1960s often involved overblown claims as to the toxicity of illegal drugs. This was often called the "Reefer Madness" approach, after the movie of that name, which depicted the moral and physical disintegration of anyone who so much as sniffed a marijuana "reefer."

The reefer madness approach appears to succeed in situations where there is no actual knowledge of or experience with drugs in the population to which the prevention effort is directed. So long as illegal psychoactive drugs were confined to the ghetto and not a part of general middle-class experience, all the claims as to their dangers were tacitly accepted. In the late 1950s and early 1960s, however, this population began using marijuana. The emphasis in marijuana and other drug prevention had been on the immediate dire consequences of use. When these didn't materialize, the young people who were using marijuana concluded that they had been lied to, and if they had been lied to about that drug, they were probably being lied to about other drugs as well. (The cycle appears to be repeating itself in the growing use of "crack" and other forms of cocaine among young people. Stories about cocaine fatalities tend to be discounted when one is surrounded by users who don't appear to be suffering any immediate adverse effects. What is needed is a more thorough and meaningful prevention effort, one that the kids will accept as real to them.) There followed, as we know, a middle-class epidemic of barbiturate, amphetamine and heroin abuse. This lesson went unnoticed in enforcement prevention circles, and enforcement officers persisted in making presentations to high school classes where a majority of the kids were using marijuana on a regular basis, the gist of which were, "This is a bindle of heroin, this is methamphetamine, and this is a marijuana cigarette. They'll all kill you." We now know that all three are dangerous to us in different ways, but such oversimplification does everyone a disservice.

Current versions of "scare tactic" prevention involve a medical rather than moral approach. Often disputed research results are stated as incontrovertible evidence that this or that drug causes "permanent brain damage" or other irreversible disabilities. There is evidence that long-term effects of many things may be dangerous; these need to be researched as thoroughly as possible, and steps must be taken to inform the public of the risks involved in their use. We think this is very effective in decreasing the levels of tobacco smoking and becoming more effective in dealing with the toxicity and addiction potential of cocaine. But the effectiveness comes from thorough research and a realistic assessment of the problem. Overblown claims of permanent damage from even experimental use can backfire into another sixties-style loss of confidence in authority. An even more immediate result is the adverse effect of such claims on those who might seek treatment and successful programs of recovery but decide instead, "What's the use if, according to them, I'm already permanently disabled?"

In our opinion, a better approach is that of teaching the young a realistic assessment of drugs and their effects. Sound drug education, however, is not enough by itself, and it may even lead to unwarranted experimentation. It should be coupled with help in dealing with the problems that can lead to substance abuse. This includes learning to make sound value judgments, developing a positive self-image and learning to rely on one's inner resources rather than on chemicals in dealing with life's problems. This should be undertaken in kindergarten and continued all through schooling, with each level being taught in an understandable way.

Other resources are also very important in decreasing the perceived need for drugs. A successful drug prevention effort includes community involvement. Although there are situations in life that we can't do a whole lot about, including pervasive economic conditions, there are ways of helping our young people toward maturity and away from drug use other than threatening them with possible arrest and permanent brain damage. In the parlance of this computer era, we can make our communities youth-friendly.

Life as a whole may be a series of ongoing transitions, but during the period of puberty, or the teenage years, these become especially acute. Even in the middle class, young people are passing from the relative safety of childhood to the unknown universe of adult life at the same time that they are undergoing great physical changes that leave them emotionally vulnerable. In many cultures, these transitions are honored and recognized through rites of passage that provide ritualized transitions from childhood to adult status in the community. All too often in our own society, the young are left to their own devices in such important areas as job seeking, correct social behavior and all the things that involve just plain growing up.

Some communities are beginning to respond to these needs with such activities as adult mentorships, town meetings where young people can discuss their needs and concerns, and other means of access to the adult world. In one county that we know of, mentorships have been tied in with a program of vision quests, such as we described in Chapter 5, to provide both inner and outer development.

As important as the school and community are to primary prevention, the most important of all is the family. Until recently, the family has been largely ignored in substance abuse prevention efforts. In the last few years, recognition by parents of the seriousness of the situation has given birth to a national movement of concerned parents coming together over drug abuse issues.

This is as it should be. The home is where one's contact with the world begins and where one's survival training is initiated. Our multicultural studies have indicated that those cultures where the family is strongest and most nurturing are the most successful in dealing with substance abuse. Our own culture, with its advanced technology and extreme mobility, may not lend itself to reinforced extended family control, but that doesn't mean that our nuclear groupings cannot be strong and nurturing. Even in situations where there is only one parent, love and communication can be important factors.

A lot of prevention efforts are aimed at abstention, but in our world adults indulge in a certain amount of nonmedical drug use and the recreational use of alcohol and other substances. Given these circumstances, it is important that parents realistically assess their own use of psychoactive substances, and that they and their children be able to discuss drugs and drug use freely. Much has been said in therapeutic circles about the strong peer influences that affect young people. This may be true, but it is still the parents who provide the primary role models for their children from an early age. It is to us that our children look for a realistic view of adulthood, and it is therefore important for us to carefully examine our own behavior in relation to that of our children. Many parents who entered the parents' movement ready to tear up the schools and society at large for adversely influencing their children have come around to modifying their own drinking and other drug-using behavior, with positive results in the family. They have come to realize that—especially where mind-altering substances are concerned—the old "Do as I say, not as I do" doesn't wash.

In calibrating prevention efforts, it is of utmost importance to identify potential addiction as early as possible in its development. Scientists and researchers recognize this and are making strides in learning what may constitute early danger signs and other medical indicators. Society can do its part by providing realistic education about drugs and human growth and maturation, and by paying attention to young people and helping them into the adult world. Education, love, communication, support and the real values in your own life can minimize the dangers within your family.

RECOVERY AND PREVENTION

Prevention is especially important within the recovering community. As studies have shown, the children or even grandchildren of recovering parents are at much greater risk of addictive disease than their peers. Parents in general have a great responsibility in shaping their children's attitudes toward drugs, but a recovering parent has an even greater responsibility. The children of recovering parents need to be made aware of their special vulnerability and what their options are. The only people who can do this effectively are the recovering parents themselves. Recovering parents who don't know how to approach this subject with their children can find help in doing so, however. As there is counseling for intervention, counseling for the necessary family interaction around recovery is available as well. The most important point, though, is that of letting one's own life be a clear demonstration of the good that can come from sobriety and abstention.

The most important act, for yourself and your children, is making abstention and recovery a positive, life-enhancing activity rather than one of gloom and deprivation. If you are growing in recovery, interacting with support and making use of positive alternatives, you are on the right track. Much of what we have offered in this book can be shared with the whole family. One does not need to have been addicted to drugs or anything else in order to benefit from such things as exercise, a healthy diet and a maturing state of mind. Shared growth in the recovering family, making everyone part of the life-enhancing evolution, makes prevention what it ought to be—not prevention at all, but mutual growth in positive directions without the use of alcohol or other drugs.

THE "EFFECT" OF RECOVERY

Just as alcoholism, addiction and abuse spread their negative effects far beyond the specific addict or abuser, so the positive results of recovery can ripple out from the recovering individual. While this change may be consciously initiated through exercising the Twelve Steps of AA and the self-help movement, it is often a subtle process that progresses from the being of the recovering individual and influences all those who have contact with that individual.

In the East, there is thought to be radiant stuff called *prana* that exists throughout the universe but is especially concentrated in and emanantes from "realized" individuals. It is believed that the halos depicted in many religions may be representations of this *prana*. Many saintlike holy men and women are surrounded by followers who sit silently by the hour absorbing their *prana*. Some have described it as being like a spiritual sunbath.

Successfully recovering people and others who are in the process of life enhancement seem well endowed with *prana*. We have seen this in gatherings like the annual Plaza House conference for recovering health professionals. Their words and deeds are aimed outward, into the human marketplace. Their radiance is evident when we meet them and when we see the results of their activity.

We have seen in them that the end product of recovery or abstinence is not merely a transcendence of the need to use drugs, but a growth of humanity in its largest sense. It does not involve becoming an advocate of prohibition, but being an exemplar of what positive means of personal development can accomplish. The end product of abstinence and recovery is not an end at all. It is a looking up from bondage at the infinity of all that can be and the voicing of an assent to infinity's invitation.

We hope that the alternatives and insights we have offered within this book breathe life into your desire to be part of that YES, and that this book provides a springboard for your own study, inquiry and personal development. If that happens, our own wish is fulfilled.

POSTSCRIPT

It's still too early for happy endings, and maybe in the "process" of recovery we can't really talk about ending, but here is an update on Anita and Al.

Anita graduated from high school with honors and a grade average that got her into the university of her choice. Away from home for the first time in her life, she relied on new friends in an AA chapter made up mostly of other students and some faculty members from her university. She continued counseling as well. After graduating with a B.A. in psychology, she moved to the West Coast and enrolled in a graduate program for Marriage, Family, and Children Counseling, MFCC. In that program, she took Rick Seymour's course in the Physiology and Pharmacology of Substance Abuse. She drew on her personal experience as a recovering individual to provide insights in discussion that were a help to the class, and she has taken up both meditation and Hatha Yoga. We think that Anita will make an excellent counselor as she continues her own recovery, one day at a time.

Al completed his residential treatment after dropping out and relapsing once. Apparently he walked away from the treatment facility, hitched a ride into Los Angeles and lost himself for more than a week. He doesn't talk about that time but refers to the experience as really hitting bottom. "It nailed the lid on my addiction," he says, "but beyond that, don't ask."

Home again, he encountered problems with his wife and friends that led him into both family counseling and outpatient treatment in the East

Bay. He and his wife separated for a year, and he lived at a recovery house for professional people. During that time they continued in counseling together and worked at rebuilding their relationship. Madeline continued her regular Al-Anon meetings, and through the recovery house Al both attended Cocaine Anonymous meetings and joined a weekly cocaine support group. During that year Al graduated from biofeedback to meditation and took up running on a regular basis. Since that time, he's gotten involved in a lot of alternative activities, including a partnership in the ultimate creativity: Madeline is expecting their first child about the time this book comes out. Al resumed his stocks and bonds business after a great deal of soul searching and is still thinking of changing professions if it doesn't work out. He's taken up painting as a hobby and isn't bad at it. At the cocaine support group, he likes working with the young professionals who are new to the group. As one of the "old timers," he has a lot to tell them about recovery.

Bibliography and Recommended Reading

Alcoholics Anonymous. *Alcoholics Anonymous: The Story of How Many Thousands of Men and Women Have Recovered from Alcoholism. Third Edition.* Alcoholics Anonymous World Services, Inc., New York, 1976.

Ayers, William A., C.D.C., Mary Jo Starsiak, M.S., R.N., Phil Sokolay, M.S. The Bogus Drug: Three Methyl and Alpha Methyl Fentanyl Sold As "China White." *Journal of Psychoactive Drugs*, Vol. 13, No. 1:91-93, January/March, 1981.

Badgely, Ronald C., D.C. East Meets West: Biofeedback Therapy. *International Journal of Holistic Health & Medicine*, Vol. 1, No. 1, September-October, 1982.

Beck, Jerome E., and Dale V. Gordon. Psilocybian Mushrooms. *PharmChem Newsletter*, Vol. 2, No. 1:1-4, January/February, 1982.

Becker, Charles E., M.C., Robert L. Roe, M.D., Robert A. Scott, M.D. *Alcohol as a Drug: A Curriculum on Pharmacology, Neurology, and Toxicology.* Medcom Press, New York, 1974.

Bhagavan Sri Satya Sai Baba. *Bhagavatha Vahini.* Sri Sataya Sai Publication and Education Foundation, Brindavan, Whitefield, Bangalore, 1970.

Blum, Kenneth, Ph.D. *Handbook of Abusable Drugs.* Garner Press, Inc., New York, 1984.

242

Bowen, J. Scott, M.D., G. B. Davis, T. E. Kearny, and J. Bardin. Diffuse Vascular Spasm Associated with 4-bromo-2,5-Dimethoxyamphetamine Ingestion. *Journal of the American Medical Association*, Vol. 249, No. 11:1477-9, March, 1983.

Brown, Barbara B., Ph.D. *New Mind, New Body Bio-Feedback: New Directions for the Mind*. University of California Press, Berkeley, 1974.

Buck, William. *Mahabharata*. New American Library, New York, 1973.

Campbell, Joseph. *The Masks of God: Primitive Mythology*. The Viking Press, New York, 1959.

Chilton, W. Scott, Jeremy Bigwood, and Rober E. Jensen. Psilocin, Bufotenine and Serotonin: Historical and Biosynthetic Observations. *Journal of Psychoactive Drugs*, Vol. 11, No. 1-2:61-69, January/June, 1979.

Cohen, Sidney, M.D. Inhalants and Solvents. In *Youth Drug Abuse: Problems, Issues and Treatment*. G.M. Beschner and A.S. Friedman, eds. Lexington Books, Lexington, Mass., 1979.

———. *The Substance Abuse Problems*. The Haworth Press, New York, 1981.

Cohen, Sidney, M.D. and Donald M. Gallant, M.D. Diagnosis of Drug and Alcohol Abuse. In *Medical Monograph Series*, Charles Buchwald, Ph.D., Daniel Katz, James F. Callahan, M.A., eds. Career Teacher Center, State University of New York, Downstate Medical Center, Vol. 1, No. 6, October, 1981.

Cornacchia, Harold J., Ed.D. *Consumer Health*. The C. V. Mosby Company, St. Louis, 1976.

Cornacchia, Harold J., Ed.D., David J. Bentel, D. Crim, David E. Smith, M.D. *Drugs in the Classroom: A Conceptual Model for School Programs*. The C. V. Mosby Company, St. Louis, 1973.

Dass, Ram. *Be Here Now*. Lama Foundation, San Cristobal, 1971.

———. *Journey of Awakening: A Meditator's Guidebook*. Bantam Books, New York, 1978.

Dass, Ram and Stephen Levine. *Grist for the Mill*. Bantam Books, New York, 1979.

Delliou, D. Bromo DMA. New Hallucinogenic Drug. *Medical Journal of Australia*, Vol. 1, No. 2:38, 1980.

Diamond, Jed, L.C.S.W. *Advice From the Front Line. A Practical Guide for Helping Chemically Dependent People*. Unpublished manuscript.

Dye, Christina. The Name Game—Street Drugs—New, Exotic, Bizarre. *Street Pharmacologist*, Vol. 6, Nos. 11-12:38-39, November-December, 1983.

Ehrlich, Paul and Maureen McGeehan. Cocaine Recovery Support Groups and the Language of Recovery. *Journal of Psychoactive Drugs*, Vol. 17, No. 1:11-17, January/March, 1985.

Evans-Wentz, W. Y. *Tibetan Book of the Dead*. 3rd ed. Oxford University Press, New York, 1957.

———. *Tibetan Yoga and Secret Doctrines*. 2nd ed. Oxford University Press, New York, 1958.

Farb, Peter, and George Armelagos. *Consuming Passions: The Anthropology of Eating*. Houghton-Mifflin, Boston, 1980.

Fine, Thomas H. and John W. Turner, Jr. *Proceedings of the First International Conference on Rest and Self-Regulation*. Iris Publications, Toledo, 1985.

Fields, Rick, Peggy Taylor, Rex Weyler and Rick Ingrasci. *Chop Wood Carry Water: A Guide to Finding Spiritual Fulfillment in Everyday Life*. Jeremy P. Tarcher, Inc., Los Angeles, 1984.

Fremantle, Francesca and Trungpa, Chogyam. *The Tibetan Book of the Dead*. Shambhala, Berkeley, 1975.

Friedlander, Ira. *Wisdom Stories for the Planet Earth*. Harper & Row, New York, 1973.

Gabrynowicz, Jan. Hypnosis in a Treatment Programme for Alcoholism. *Medical Journal of Australia*, April 30, 1977:653-55.

Gay, George R. You've Come a Long Way, Baby! Coke Time for the New American Lady of the Eighties. *Journal of Psychoactive Drugs*, Vol. 13, No. 4:297-318, October/December, 1981.

Ginzburg, Harold, M.D. *Naltrexone: Its Clinical Utility*. National Institute on Drug Abuse Treatment Research Report OHHS. Publ. No. (ADM) 84-1358, Washington, D.C., 1984.

Gold, Mark, S., M.D. *800-COCAINE*. Bantam Books, Toronto, 1984.

Goldstein, Avram, M.D., S. Kaizer, R. Warren. Psychotropic Effects of Caffeine in Man. *Journal of Pharmacology. Experimental Theory*, Vol. 150, 1965.

Gorski, Terence T. *The Relapse Dynamic*. Alcohol Systems Associates, Hazel Crest, Illinois, 1982.

Gorski, Terence T. and Miller, Merlene. *Counseling for Relapse Prevention*. Herald House-Independent Press, Independence, MO, 1982.

————. *Staying Sober—A Guide for Relapse Prevention*. Herald House-Independent Press, Independence, MO, 1986.

Govinda, Lama Anagarika. *Foundations of Tibetan Mysticism*. Rider & Company, London, 1960.

————. *The Psychological Attitude of Early Buddhist Philosophy*. Rider & Company, London, 1961.

Grinspoon, Lester, M.D., and James B. Bakalar. *Cocaine: A Drug and Its Social Evolution*. Basic Books, Inc., New York, 1976.

————. *Psychedelic Drugs Reconsidered*. Basic Books, Inc., New York, 1979.

Heather, Nick and Ian Robertson. *Controlled Drinking*. Methuen & Co. Ltd., London, 1981.

Henderson, Gary, M.D. "China White": An Update on Identification and Testing. *The PharmChem Newsletter*, Vol. 11, No. 1:5-6, 1982.

Huxley, Aldous. *The Doors of Perception*. Harper & Row, Inc., New York, 1954.

Hylin, J. W., and D. P. Watson. Ergoline Alkaloids in Tropical Wood-roses. *Science*, Vol. 148:499-500, 1965.

Inaba, Darryl, Pharm. D. Popper Uh-Ohs or Uh-Oh Poppers! *Kryptonite Gazette*, Vol. 1, No. 3, September, 1974.

————. Snappers, Crackle-ers and Poppers. *Kryptonite Gazette*, Vol. 1, No. 2, August, 1974.

Institute of Medicine, National Academy of Science. *Marijuana and Health: A Report of a Study*. Arnold S. Relman, ed. National Academy Press, Washington, D.C., 1982.

Jellinek, E. M. *The Disease Concept of Alcoholism*. Hillhouse Press, New Haven, Conn., 1960.

Kapleau, Philip. *The Three Pillars of Zen: Teaching, Practice, and Enlightenment*. Harper & Row, New York, 1966.

Klaas, Joe. *The Twelve Steps to Happiness*. Hazelden Foundation, Center City, Minn., 1982.

Kleber, Herbert D., M.D. *Trexan (Naltrexone HCL): A Pharmacologic Adjunct for the Detoxified Opioid Addict*. E. I. DuPont de Nemours and Co., Inc., Wilmington, Del., 1984.

Kohn, George F. Toward a Model for Spirituality and Alcoholism. *Journal of Religion & Health*, Vol. 23, No. 3:250-59, Fall, 1984.

Kroeber, A. L. *Handbook of the Indians of California.* Dover Publications, Inc., New York, 1976.

LaBerge, Stephen, Ph.D. *Lucid Dreaming: The Power of Being Awake & Aware in Your Dreams.* Ballantine Books, New York, 1985.

Land, Donald R., Ph.D. *Eat Right!* Hazelden Foundation, Center City, Minn., 1985.

Lieber, Charles S., M.D. To Drink (Moderately) or Not to Drink. *The New England Journal of Medicine,* Vol. 310 (13):846-48, March 29, 1984.

Ling, Walter, M.D., and Donald R. Wesson, M.D. Naltrexone and Its Use in Treatment of Opiate Dependent Physicians. *California Society for the Treatment of Alcoholism and Other Drug Dependencies NEWS,* October, 1980.

Manguerra, Anthony S., Pharm. D., and Debra Freeman, Pharm. D. Acute Poisoning from the Ingestion of Nicotiana Glauca. *Journal of Toxicology: Clinical Toxicology,* Vol. 19, No. 8, 1982-1983.

Marder, Leon, M.D. Set Up, Loads, Doors or Four Doors. *California Society for the Treatment of Alcoholism and Other Drug Dependencies NEWS.* October/November, 1981.

Marlatt, G. A. The Controlled-Drinking Controversy: A Commentary. *American Psychologist,* October, 1983.

Mascaró, Juan. *The Dhammapada: The Path of Perfection.* Penguin Books, Baltimore, 1973.

Maslow, Abraham H., Ph.D. *The Farther Reaches of Human Nature.* The Viking Press, New York, 1971.

McCoy, Alfred W., Cathleen B. Read, Leonard P. Adams II. *The Politics of Heroin in Southeast Asia.* Harper & Row, New York, 1973.

Mc Martin, Grace J. *A Recapitulation of Satya Sai Baba's Divine Teachings.* Avon Printing Works, Hyderabad, 1982.

Mecca, Andrew M., Dr. P.H. A Cultural Response to Alcohol and Drug Abuse in America. *Contemporary Drug Problems,* Spring, 1982.

———. *Prevention Action Plan for Alcohol-Related Problems.* California Health Research Foundation, San Rafael, 1985.

———. *Comprehensive Alcohol & Drug Abuse Prevention Strategies.* California Health Research Foundation, San Rafael, 1984.

Menser, G. *Hallucinogenic and Poisonous Mushroom Field Guide.* And/Or Press, Berkeley, 1977.

Michaux, Henri. *Miserable Miracle: Mescaline*. City Lights Books, San Francisco, 1963.

Milam, Dr. James R. and Katherine Ketcham. *Under the Influence: A Guide to the Myths and Realities of Alcoholism*. Bantam Books, Inc., New York, 1983.

Miller, Neal E., T. X. Barber, Leo V. DiCara, Joe Kamiya, David Shapiro and Johann Stoyva. *Biofeedback and Self-Control 1973*. Aldine Publishing Company, Chicago, 1974.

Morgan, John P., and Doreen V. Kagan, M.S., eds. *Society and Medication: Conflicting Signals for Prescribers and Patients*. Lexington, Mass., 1983.

————. Street Amphetamine Quality and the Controlled Substances Act of 1970. *Journal of Psychoactive Drugs*, Vol. 10, No. 4:303-17, October/December, 1978.

————. The Dusting of America: The Image of Phencyclidine (PCP) in the Popular Media. In PCP: Problems and Prevention, Selected Proceedings of the National PCP Conference 1979, D. E. Smith, D. R. Wesson, M. E. Buxton, R. B. Seymour, M. P. Bishop, S. Ross, E. L. Zerkin, eds. *Journal of Psychoactive Drugs*, Vol. 12, Nos. 3-4:11-20, July/December, 1980.

Mothner, Ira and Alan Weitz. *How to Get Off Drugs*. Rolling Stone Press/Simon and Schuster, New York, 1984.

Musto, David. *The American Disease: Origins of Narcotic Control*. Yale University Press, New Haven, 1973.

Naranjo, Claudio. *The Healing Journey: New Approach to Consciousness*. Pantheon, New York, 1974.

National Commission on Marijuana and Drug Abuse. *Drug Use in America: Problem in Perspective*; second report, USGPO, Washington, D.C., 1973.

Newmeyer, John A., Ph.D., Gregory L. Johnson, and Steven Klot. Acupuncture as a Detoxification Modality. *Journal of Psychoactive Drugs*, Vol. 16 (3):241-61, July/September, 1984.

Nickerson, Mark, John O. Parker, Thomas D. Lowry, and Edward W. Swenson. *Isobutyl Nitrite and Related Compounds*. Pharmex, Ltd., San Francisco, 1979.

O'Connell, Kathleen R. *End of the Line: Quitting Cocaine*. The Westminister Press, Philadelphia, 1985.

Polak, Karl. *The Solution*. The Alternative Press, Hong Kong, 1986.

Proust, Marcel. *Remembrance of Things Past.* Random House, New York, 1982.

Rahula, Walpola. *What the Buddha Taught.* Grove Press, Inc., New York, 1974.

Reps, Paul. *Zen Flesh, Zen Bones: A Collection of Zen and Pre-Zen Writings.* Anchor Books, Garden City, New York. (In true Zen fashion, the book is undated.)

Sacramento Wire. Killer Drunk-Driver in Trouble Again. *San Francisco Chronicle.* Friday, April 19, 1985.

Schoen, Marc, Ph.D. A Conceptual Framework and Treatment Strategy for the Alcoholic Urge to Drink Utilizing Hypnosis. *International Journal of the Addictions*, Vol. 10, No. 3:403-15, 1985.

Seymour, Richard B., M.A. *MDMA.* Haight-Ashbury Publications, San Francisco, 1986.

———. The Chemical Muse. *Street Pharmacologist*, Vol. 5, No. 6, June, 1982.

Seymour, Richard B., M.A., Jacquelyne G. Gorton, R.N., M.S.C.S., and David E. Smith, M.D. The Client with a Substance Abuse Problem. In *Practice and Management of Psychiatric Emergency Care*, J. G. Gorton and R. Partridge, eds. The C. V. Mosby Company, St. Louis, 1982.

Seymour, Richard B., M.A., and David E. Smith, M.D. Marijuana, Addictive Disease and Recovery. In *Drug Use in Society: Proceedings of Marijuana and Health Conference, November 1983*, Joanne C. Gampel, ed. Council on Marijuana and Health, Washington, D.C., 1984.

———. *The Physician's Guide to Psychoactive Drugs.* The Haworth Press, New York, 1986.

Shawcross, William E. Recreational Use of Ergoline Alkaloids from *Argyreia Nervosa. Journal of Psychoactive Drugs*, Vol. 15, No. 4:251-59, October/December, 1983.

Sheehy, Gail. *Pathfinders.* Bantam Books, New York, 1981.

Shulgin, Alexander T. MMDA. *Journal of Psychoactive Drugs*, Vol. 8, No. 4:331, October/December, 1976.

Smith, David E., M.D. A Clinical Approach to the Treatment of PCP Abuse. In *PCP (Phencyclidine): Historical and Current Perspectives*, E. F. Domino, ed. NPP Books, Ann Arbor, 1981.

————. A New Prescription Drug Abuse Combination: Glutethimide and Codeine. *California Society for the Treatment of Alcoholism and Other Drug Dependencies NEWS*, October/November, 1981.

————. Importance of Gradual Dosage Reduction Following Low-Dose Benzodiazepine Therapy. *California Society for the Treatment of Alcoholism and Other Drug Dependencies NEWS*, April, 1979.

————. Editor's Note. PCP: Problems and Prevention, Selected Proceedings of the National PCP Conference 1979, D. E. Smith, D. R. Wesson, M. E. Buxton, S. Ross, R. B. Seymour, M. P. Bishop, E. L. Zerkin, eds. *Journal of Psychoactive Drugs*, Vol. 12, Nos. 3-4:v-viii, July/December, 1980.

————. Prescription Drugs and the Alcoholic: The Benzodiazepine—Therapeutic and Dependence Considerations. *Proceedings of the Eisenhower Medical Center Conference on Alcoholism*. Eisenhower Medical Center, Winter:42-48, 1981.

————. Treatment Considerations with Cocaine Abusers. In *Cocaine: A Second Look*, by Robert C. Petersen, Sidney Cohen, F. R. Jeri, David E. Smith, and Lee I. Dogoloff. American Council on Marijuana and Other Psychoactive Drugs, Rockville, Maryland, 1983.

Smith, David, M.D., Mildred Apter-Marsh, Ph.D., John Buffum, Pharm. D., Charles Moser, Ph.D., Don Wesson, M.D. *Socio-Sexual Issues in the Using and Recovering Alcoholic*. The Haworth Press, Inc., New York, 1984.

Smith, David E., M.D., and George R. Gay, M.D. *It's So Good, Don't Even Try It Once: Heroin in Perspective*. Prentice-Hall, Inc., Englewood Cliffs, New Jersey, 1972.

Smith, David E., M.D., Harvey B. Milkman, and Stanley G. Sunderwirth. Addictive Disease: Concept and Controversy. In *The Addictions: Multidisciplinary Perspectives and Treatments*, Harvey B. Milkman and Howard J. Shaffer, eds. Lexington Books/D.C. Heath and Company, Lexington, Mass., 1985.

Smith, David E., M.D., and Richard B. Seymour, M.A. Clinical Prespectives on the Toxicity of Marijuana: 1967-1981. *Marijuana and Youth: Clinical Observations on Motivation and Learning*. National Institute on Drug Abuse, Rockville, 1982.

————. *The Coke Book*. Berkeley Books, New York, 1984.

————. Dream Becomes Nightmare: Adverse Reactions to LSD. In LSD in Retrospect, Sidney Cohen, M.D. and Stanley Krippner, Ph.D., eds. *Journal of Psychoactive Drugs*, Vol. 17, No. 4:297-303, October/December, 1985.

————. Nonmedical Prescription Drug Use. In *Topics in Clinical Pharmacology and Therapeutics*, Robert F. Maronde, M.D., ed. Springer-Verliag, New York, 1986.

————. The Prescription of Stimulants and Anorectics. *Frequently Prescribed and Abused Drugs*, Vol. 2, No. 1, July 1980.

Smith, David E., M.D., Richard B. Seymour, M.A., and John P. Morgan, M.D. *The Little Black Pill Book*. Bantam Books, New York, 1983.

Smith, David E., M.D., Donald R. Wesson, M.D., and Richard B. Seymour, M.A. The Abuse of Barbiturates and Other Sedative Hypnotics. In *Handbook on Drug Abuse*, Robert I. DuPont, M.D., Avram Goldstein, M.D., and John O'Donnell, Ph.D., eds. National Institute on Drug Abuse and White House Office on Drug Abuse Policy, Washington, D.C., 1979.

Smith, David E., M.D., and Donald R. Wesson, M.D. Cocaine. *Journal of Psychoactive Drugs*, Vol. 10, No. 4:351-60, October-December, 1978.

————. Substance Abuse in Industry: Identification, Intervention, Treatment and Prevention. In *Substance Abuse in the Workplace*, David E. Smith, M.D., Donald R. Wesson, M.D., E. Leif Zerkin, and Jeffrey H. Novey, eds. Haight Ashbury Publications, San Francisco, 1985.

————. *Treating the Cocaine Abuser*. Hazelden Foundation, Center City, Minn., 1985.

————. *Treatment of Adverse Reactions to Sedative-Hypnotics*. U. S. Government Printing Office, Washington, D.C., 1974.

————. *Uppers and Downers*. Prentice-Hall, Englewood Cliffs, 1973.

Smith, David E., M.D., Donald R. Wesson, M.D., Millicent E. Buxton, Richard B. Seymour, M.A., Thomas J. Ungerleider, M.D., John P. Morgan, M.D., Arnold J. Mandell, M.D. and Gail Jara. *Amphetamine Use, Misuse and Abuse: Proceedings of the National Amphetamine Conference, 1978*, G. K. Hall & Co., Boston, 1979.

Sri Chinmoy. *Commentary on the Bhagavad Gita*. Rudolph Steiner Publications, Blauvelt, 1982.

Stamets, Paul. *Psilocybe Mushrooms and Their Allies*. Homestead Book Company, Seattle, 1978.

Suzuki, Daisetz T. *Introduction to Zen Buddhism*. Grove Press, New York, 1964.

Taimni, I. K. *The Science of Yoga*. The Theosophical Publishing House, India, 1961.

Trungpa, Chogyam. *Meditation in Action*. Shambhala, Berkeley, 1969.

———. *The Myth of Freedom and the Way of Meditation*. Shambhala, Berkeley, 1976.

Turek, I. S., R. A. Soskin, A. A. Kurland. Methylenedioxyamphetamine (MDA) Subjective Effects. *Journal of Psychoactive Drugs*, Vol. 6, No. 1:7-14, January/March, 1974.

Unger, Kathleen Bell, M.D. Methadone in the Relief of Pain. *California Society for the Treatment of Alcoholism and Other Drug Dependencies NEWS*, April, 1984.

Wadden, Thomas A. and James H. Penrod. Hypnosis in the Treatment of Alcoholism: A Review and Appraisal. *The American Journal of Clinical Hypnosis*, Vol. 24, No. 1:41-47, July, 1981.

Wasson, R. Gordon. The Divine Mushroom of Immortality. In *Flesh of the Gods*, P. T. Furst, ed. Praeger, New York, 1972.

Weil, Andrew T., M.D. *Health and Healing: Understanding Conventional and Alternative Medicine*. Houghton Mifflin Company, Boston, 1983.

———. Nutmeg as a Psychoactive Drug. *Journal of Psychoactive Drugs*, Vol. 3, No. 2:72-80, Spring, 1971.

———. *The Marriage of the Sun and Moon: A Quest for Unity in Consciousness*. Houghton Mifflin Company, Boston, 1980.

———. *The Natural Mind: A New Way of Looking at Drugs and the Higher Consciousness*. Houghton Mifflin Company, Boston, 1972.

Weil, Andrew T., M.D. and Winifred Rosen. *Chocolate to Morphine: Understanding Mind-Active Drugs*. Houghton Mifflin Co., Boston, 1983.

Wesson, Donald R., M.D. Naltrexone Approved by MDA. *California Society for the Treatment of Alcoholism and Other Drug Dependencies NEWS*, Vol. 11, No. 4:8, December, 1984.

Wesson, Donald R., M.D., and David E. Smith, M.D. *Barbiturates: Their Use, Misuse and Abuse*. Human Sciences Press, New York, 1977.

———. Low Dose Benzodiazepine Withdrawal Syndrome: Receptor Site Mediated. *California Society for the Treatment of Alcoholism and Other Drug Dependencies NEWS*, Vo. 9, No. 1:1-5, January/February, 1982.

Whitfield, Charles L., M.D. *Stress Management and Spirituality during Recovery: A Transpersonal Approach*. In draft.

Wilford, Bonnie Baird. *Drug Abuse: A Guide for the Primary Care Physician.* American Medical Association, Chicago, 1981.

Wilhelm, Richard. *The I Ching or Book of Changes.* Pantheon Books, New York, 1970.

Wineck, C. L. A Death Due to 4-Bromo-2.5-Dimethoxyamphetamine. *Clinical Toxicology,* Vol. 283, 1970.

Wood, Ernest. *Great Systems of Yoga.* The Citadel Press, New York, 1968.

Zinberg, Norman E. *Alternate States of Consciousness.* The Free Press, New York, 1977.

———. *Drug, Set, and Setting: The Basis for Controlled Intoxicant Use.* Yale University Press, New Haven, Conn., 1984.

INDEX